Viking Tales of Old Iceland 2

Original Texts, Translations, and Word Lists

Translated by
Matthew Leigh Embleton

Viking Tales of Old Iceland 2

The Tale of Helgi Thórisson (*Old Norse*) 3
The Tale of Helgi Thórisson (*Old Icelandic*) 31
The Tale of Auðun of the West Fjords (*Old Norse*) 61
The Tale of Auðun of the West Fjords (*Old Icelandic*) 91
The Tale of Thorstein Staff-Struck (*Old Norse*) 124
The Tale of Thorstein Staff-Struck (*Old Icelandic*) 166

Cover: Old Norse text over an outline of Iceland. Author's design.

The original Old Norse and Old Icelandic texts are in the public domain.
These translations ©2022 Matthew Leigh Embleton
©2025 Matthew Leigh Embleton (This Edition)

Acknowledgments

I have long been fascinated by languages and history, and I am very grateful to the special people in my life who have supported and encouraged me in my work. Thank you for believing in me. You know who you are.

Introduction

Old Norse is a North Germanic language spoken by inhabitants of Scandinavia from about the 7th to the 15th centuries. Old Icelandic is a variety of Old West Norse that emerged during the Norse settlement of Iceland in the second half of the 9th century. The rich tradition of Icelandic story telling survived by oral tradition over several centuries before being written down in the 13th Century. The Tales of Icelanders are known as Íslendingaþættir. The word 'þáttr' (plural: 'þættir') translates as a strand of rope or a yarn, comparable to the word 'yarn' in English sometimes used to refer to a story.

The texts are presented in Old Norse and Old Icelandic, in their original form, with a literal word-for-word line-by-line translation, and a Modern English translation, all side-by-side. In this way, it is possible to see and feel how the worked and how it has evolved. This book is designed to be of use and interest to anyone with a passion for the Old Norse or Old Icelandic language, Norse history, or languages and history in general.

The Tale of Helgi Thórisson (*Old Norse*)

Old Norse	Literal	English
1	**1**	**1**
Þórir hét maðr, er bjó í Nóregi á bæ þeim, er á Rauðabergi heitir.	Thorir (name) was-named a-man, who settled in Norway (place) in a-farm that, was so Raudaberg (place) named.	There was a man named Thorir who lived in Norway on a farm that was named Raudaberg.
Þessi bær er skammt frá Víkinni.	This farm was short-distance from The-bay.	The farm was a short distance away from the bay.
Þórir átti tvá syni.	Thorir (name) had two sons.	Thorir had two sons.
Hét annarr Helgi, enn Þorsteinn annarr; báðir váru þeir þrifligir menn, ok var þó Helgi framar um íþróttir.	Was-named one Helgi (name), was Thorstein (name) another; both were they thriving men, and was though Helgi (name) above in sports.	One was named Helgi, the other was named Thorstein; they were both thriving men, though Helgi surpassed in sports.
Faðir þeira var hersir at nafnbót.	Father theirs was a-local-chief of rank.	Their father was a local chief of high rank.
Hann var í vináttu vit Óláf konung.	He was in friendship with Olaf (name) the-king.	He was friends with King Olaf.
Þat var á einu sumri, at þeir bræðr höfðu kaupferð norðr til Finnmerkr ok höfðu smjör ok flesk til kaups vit Finna.	It was in one summer, that the brothers had trading-voyage north to Finnmark (place) and had butter and bacon to trade with Sámi (name).	It was one summer, that the brothers had a trading voyage north to Finnmark, and they had butter and bacon to trade with the Sámi people.
Fengu þeir góða kaupferð ok heldu aptr at áliðnu sumri ok kómu um dag vit nes þat, er hét Vímund.	Got they good trade and busy returned in late summer and came about a-day to headland that, was named Vimund (name).	They had a good and busy trade and returned late in the summer and came about one day to a headland that was named Vimund.
Þar var allgóðr skógr.	There were all-good forests.	There were all-good woods.
Gengu þeir á land upp ok fengu nokkurt mösurtré.	Went they to land up and got some maple-tree.	They went up to the land and got some maple trees.
Verðr Helga lengra gengit í skóginn enn öðrum mönnum.	Became Helgi (name) longer going in the-forest than other people.	Helgi went further into the woods than the other people.

The Tale of Helgi Thórisson (Old Norse)

Old Norse	Literal	English
Síðan kastar yfir myrkri miklu, svá at hann hittir ekki til skipsins á þeim aptni; tekr nú ok skjótt at dimma af nótt.	Then cast over darkness great, so that he found not to ship and then after; took now and quickly to darkness of night.	Then a great darkness cast over, so that he could not find the ship; and then afterwards the darkness of night took quickly.
Þá sér Helgi, hvar tólf konur ríða ór skóginum.	Then saw Helgi (name), were twelve women riding through the-forest.	Then Helgi saw that there were twelve women riding through the forest.
Þær váru allar á rauðum hestum ok í rauðum reiðklæðum.	They were all on red horses and in red riding-clothes.	They were all on red horses and in red riding-clothes.
Þær stigu af baki.	They stepped from horseback.	They stepped down from their horses.
Allr reiðingr hestanna þá glóaði vit gull.	All riding horses then shone with gold.	All the horses they were riding shone with gold.
Ein bar þar af öllum um vænleik, ok allar aðrar þjóna henni, þessi inni sköruligu konu.	One surpassed there of all about beauty, and all others served her, this the bold-like woman.	One of them surpassed all the others in beauty, and all the others served this bold looking woman.
Hestar þeira gengu á gras.	Horses they went to graze.	The horses then went to graze.
Eptir þat settu þær niðr eitt fagrt tjald.	After that set they down one fair tent.	After that they set down a fair tent.
Var þat stafat með ýmsum litum ok víða gullskotit, ok öll höfuðin váru vit gull búin, er af upp gengu landtjaldinu, ok svá stöngin, er upp stóð, ok mikill gullknappr ofan á.	Was it staved with various colours and widely gold-laid, and all heads were with gold prepared, was of up going land-tent, and so the-pole, that up stood, and large golden-ball above it.	It was striped with various colours and widely laden with gold, and all the heads were prepared with gold, and so it was of this land tent, that all the poles that stood up had a large golden ball on top.
Ok er þær höfðu um búizt, reistu þær borð ok báru á margs konar krásir.	And when they had about prepared, raised they a-table and bore out many kinds-of food.	And when they had prepared all about, they raised a table and brought our many kinds of food.
Þá tóku þær handlaugar, vatnskarl ok munnlaugar, gervar af silfri, ok allt laugat í gulli.	Then took they hand-washing, basins and mouth-basins, fashioned of silver, and all bathed in gold.	They took to washing their hands, with basins and jugs, fashioned of silver, and all bathed in gold.

The Tale of Helgi Thórisson (Old Norse)

Old Norse	Literal	English
Helgi stóð nærri tjaldi þeira ok horfði á.	Helgi (name) stood near tent theirs and looked about.	Helgi stood near their tent and looked about.
Sú, er fyr þeim var, mælti:	So, was before them was, spoke:	The one who was in front of them spoke:
"Helgi, gakk hingat, ok þigg hér mat ok drykk með oss".	"Helgi (name), come here, and accept here food and drink with us".	"Helgi, come here, and accept food and drink with us".
Hann gerir svá.	He did so.	He did so.
Helgi sér, at þar er fríðr drykkr ok önnur fæðsla ok væn ker.	Helgi (name) saw, that there was beautiful drink and also feast and fair vessels.	Helgi saw that there were beautiful drinks and a feast with fair drinking vessels.
Þá váru borð ofan tekin ok hvílur búnar, ok váru þær miklu skrautligri enn annarra manna sængr.	Then were tables down taken and beds prepared, and were these much splendid than other peoples beds.	Then the tables were taken down and the beds were prepared, and these were much more splendid than other peoples' beds.
Sú kona spyrr Helga, er fyr þeim var, hvárt hann vilda heldr liggja einn saman eðr hjá henni.	So the-woman asked Helgi (name), that for them was, either he wished rather to-lay alone together or beside her.	The woman who was at the front asked Helgi if he wished to lay alone or beside her.
Helgi spyrr hana at nafni.	Helgi (name) asked her of name.	Helgi asked her name.
hon svarar:	she answered:	She answered:
"Ek heit Ingibjörg, dóttir Guðmundar af Glæsisvöllum".	"I am-named Ingibjorg (name), daughter Gudmund (name) of Glasir-Plains (place)".	"I am named Ingibjorg, daughter of Gudmund of Glasir Plains".
Helgi mælti:	Helgi (name) spoke:	Helgi spoke:
"Hjá þér vil ek liggja".	"Beside you wish I to-lay".	"I wish to lay beside you".
Ok svá gerðu þau þrjár nætr í samt.	And so did they three nights of together.	And so they did for three nights together.
Var þá bjart veðr; standa þau þá upp ok klæðast.	Was then bright weather; stood they then up and clothed.	When the weather was bright; they stood up and clothed.
Ingibjörg mælti þá:	Ingibjorg (name) spoke then:	Ingibjorg then spoke:

The Tale of Helgi Thórisson (Old Norse)

Old Norse	Literal	English
"Nú munum vit hér skilja.	"Now shall we here separate.	"Now we shall separate here.
Eru hér kistlar tveir, annarr er fullr af silfri, enn annarr af gulli, er ek vil gefa þér, ok seg engum manni, hvaðan þat kom".	There-are here chests two, one is full of silver, and another of gold, am I will to-give to-you, and say none person, from-where that came".	Here are two chests, one is full of silver, and another of gold, and I will give them to you, and you shall tell no person, where they came from".
Eptir þat ríða þær burt sama veg sem þangat, enn hann fór til skips síns.	After that rode they away the-same way as from-there, that he travelled to ships his.	After that they rode away the same way as they had come from, and he travelled to his ships.
Fagna þeir honum vel ok spyrja, hvar hann dvaldist, enn hann vill þar eigi frá segja.	Welcomed they him well and asked, where he dwelled, but he wished there not from to-say.	They welcomed him well and asked where he had stayed, but he did not wish to say.
Halda þeir þá suðr með landi ok koma heim til föður síns ok hafa aflat mikils fjár.	Held they then south along land and came home to father theirs and had surplus much wealth.	They held south along the land and came to their father's home and had much wealth.
Faðir Helga ok bróðir spyrja, hvaðan honum kom svá mikit fé sem hann hafði í kistlunum, enn hann vill þat ekki segja.	Father Helgi (name) and brother asked, from-where he came so much wealth as he had in chests, but he wished that not to-say.	Helgi's father and brother asked where he came by so much wealth as he had in his chests, but he did not wish to say.

2

Nú líðr svá fram til jóla.	Now passed so from until Yule.	Now it passed on to Yule.
Þat var eina nótt, at kemr á býsna veðr.	It was one night, that came an extreme weather.	And it was one night that there came extreme weather.
Þorsteinn mælti vit bróður sinn:	Thorstein (name) spoke with brother his:	Thorstein spoke with his brother:
"Vit skulum standa upp ok vita, hvat líðr um skip okkart".	"We should stand up and know, what passes about ship ours".	"We should get up and find out what is happening with our ship".
Þeir gera svá, ok var þat fast vel.	They did so, and was it fastened well.	They did so, and it was fastened well.

The Tale of Helgi Thórisson (Old Norse)

Old Norse	Literal	English
Helgi hafði látit gera drekahöfuð á skip þeira upp á stafnana ok búa vel fyr ofan sjó.	Helgi (name) had made done dragon's-head on ship theirs up in ship's-prow and prepared well for above the-sea.	Helgi had a dragon's head made for their ship's prow and it was decorated well above the sea level.
Fór þat fé þar til, er Ingibjörg gaf honum, dóttir Guðmundar konungs, enn sumt læsti hann í drekahálsinum.	Travelled the wealth there to, that Ingibjorg (name) gave him, daughter-of Gudmund (name) the-king, but some locked he in the-dragon's-neck.	The wealth that Ingibjorg, daughter of King Gudmund, gave him had travelled there but some of it was locked in the dragon's neck.
Þá heyra þeir brest mikinn.	Then heard they a-crash great.	Then they heard a great crash.
Þar ríða at þeim tveir menn ok höfðu Helga í burt með sér.	There riders at them two men and had Helgi (name) to away with them.	Then two men rode towards them and took Helgi away with them.
Veit Þorsteinn eigi, hvat af honum verðr.	Knew Thorstein (name) not, what of him became.	Thorstein did not know what became of him.
Fellr þá veðrit skjótt.	Fell then weather away.	The weather then fell away.
Þorsteinn kemr heim ok segir föður sínum þenna atburð, ok þykkir þetta mikil tíðendi.	Thorstein (name) came home and told father his these events, and thought that much news.	Thorstein came home and told his father of these events, and thought that this news was very much.
Ferr hann þegar á fund Óláfs konungs ok segir honum, hvar komit var, ok biðr hann nú verða vissan um, hvar er sonr hans er niðr kominn.	Travelled he straight-away to meet Olaf (name) the-king and said to-him, what came was, and asked him now to-become knowledge about, where was son his and son become.	He travelled straight away to meet King Olaf and told him what had happened, and asked him for knowledge about where his son was and what had become of him.
Konungr segist þat gera mundu, sem hann beiddi, enn kveðst þó óvíst hugr um segja, hverr nyt frændum hans mynda at honum verða.	The-King said that do would, that-which he asked, but said though uncertain thought about said, any use kinsman he should to him become.	The king said that he would do what he asked, but said that it was uncertain to say, if his kinsman would be of any use after what had happened to him.
Síðan fór Þórir heim, ok líðr svá þetta ár ok allt fram á jól annat ár, ok sitr konungr á Alreksstöðum um vetrinn.	After travelled Thorir (name) home, and passed so that year and all from to Yule another year, and sat the-king in Alreksstead (place) about winter.	Afterwards Thorir travelled home, and so passed that year to Yule, and the king sat in Alreksstead over the winter.

The Tale of Helgi Thórisson (Old Norse)

Old Norse	Literal	English
Þá kemr átti dagr jóla, ok um kveldit ganga þrír menn í höllina fyr Óláf konung, þá er hann sat yfir borðum.	Then came eighth day Yule, and about evening went three men in the-hall before Olaf (name) the-king, then as he sat over the-table.	Then came the eighth day of Yule, and at about evening three men entered the hall before King Olaf, as he sat across the tables.
Þeir kveðja hann vel.	They greeted him well.	They greeted him well.
Konungr heilsar þeim vel í móti.	The-King greeted them well in return.	The king greeted them well in return.
Er þar kominn Helgi, enn menn kenna ekki hina tvá.	Then there came Helgi (name), but people knew not the two.	Then there came Helgi, but people did not know who the other two were.
Konungr spurði þá at nafni, enn hvárrtveggi kveðst Grímr heita.	The-King asked then the names, and each said Grim (name) was-named.	The king asked their names, and each said their name was Grim.
"Erum vit sendir af Guðmundi á Glæsisvöllum hingat til yðar.	"We-are with sent of Gudmund (name) of Glasir-Plains (place) here to you.	"We have been sent by Gudmund of Glasir Plaines here to you.
Hann sendi yðr kveðju sína ok þar með tvau horn".	He sends you greetings his and there as-well two horns".	He sends you greetings and here as well two horns".
Konungr tók við, ok váru gullbúin.	The-King received with, and was gold-inlaid.	The king received them, and they were inlaid with gold.
Þetta váru allgóðir gripir.	They were all-gold treasures.	They were all good treasures.
Óláfr konungr átti tvau horn, er Hyrningar váru kallaðir, ok þó at þau væra harðla góð, þá váru þau þó betri, er Guðmundr sendi honum.	Olaf (name) the-king had two horns, were Hyrnings (name) were called, and though that they were greatly good, then were they though better, that Gudmund (name) sent him.	King Olaf had two horns, that were called Hyrnings, and though they were great, the ones that Gudmund had sent him were better.
"Þess beiddi Guðmundr konungr yðr, herra, at þér værið vinir hans, ok þótti mestu varða um yðra þykkju, meir enn allra annarra konunga".	"This bids Gudmund (name) the-king to-you, lord, that to-you become friend his, and thinks most warrant about yours things, more than all other kings".	"This Gudmund asks you, lord, that you become his friend, as he values you as more important than all other kings".
Konungr segir þá engu, enn lætr vísa þeim til sætis félögum.	The-King answered then not, but had directed them to seats company.	The king did not answer then, but directed them to the seats with company.

The Tale of Helgi Thórisson (Old Norse)

Old Norse	Literal	English
Konungr lætr fylla hornin Gríma af góðum drykk ok lætr byskup blessa ok lét færa þeim Grímum, at þeir drykki fyrst af.	The-King had filled the-horns Grim (name) of good drink and had bishop bless and had brought them Grims (name), that they drank first of.	The king had the Grim horns filled of good drink and had a bishop bless them and bring them to the Grims, so that they drank first.
Þá kvað konungr vísu þessa:	Then spoke the-king a-verse this:	Then the king spoke this verse:
"Gestir skulu hornum í gegn taka, meðan hvílast látum þenna þegn Guðmundar, ok af samnafna sínum drekki; svá skal Grímum gott öl gefast".	"The-guests shall horns to directly take, while rest have they thane Gudmund (name), and of same-name theirs drink; so shall Grims (name) good ale give".	The guests shall these horns directly take, while they have rest thane of Gudmund, of his namesake theirs drink; so shall the Grims give good ale".
Þá taka Grímar vit hornunum ok þykkjast nú vita, hvat byskup hefir yfir lesit drykkinum.	Then took Grims (name) with the-horns and realised now certainly, what the-bishop had over read drinks.	Then the Grims took the horns and realised now with certainty, what the bishop had read over these drinks.
Þeir segja þá:	They said then:	They then said:
"Eigi ferr nú fjarri því, sem Guðmundr, konungr várr, gat til.	"Not travel now far-away because, as Gudmund (name), the-king ours, could to.	"Now do not go far from what Gudmund, our king, could do.
Er þessi konungr prettóttr ok kann illa gott at launa, því at konungr várr gerði til hans sæmiliga.	Is this king deceitful and can evil good to repay, therefore the king aware be to him well-enough.	This king is deceitful and repays good with evil, therefore the king should be well enough aware.
Stöndum nú upp allir ok verðum í brottu heðan".	Stand now up all and have to away hence".	Let's get up and go right now".
Svá gera þeir.	So did they.	They did so.
Verðr þá hark mikit í stofunni.	Became then noise much in the-room.	Then there was much noise in the room.
Þeir slógu niðr drykkinum af hornunum ok slökktu login.	They threw down the-drinks of the-horns and put-out lights.	The threw down the drinks from the horns and put out the lights.
Þá heyrðu þeir bresti stóra.	Then heard they crash great.	Then they heard a great crash.

The Tale of Helgi Thórisson (Old Norse)

Old Norse	Literal	English
Konungr bað guði til gæta ok bað menn upp standa ok stöðva þetta hark.	The-King prayed God to guard and bid men up stand and stop this racket.	The king prayed to God to guard him and asked his men to stand up and stop this racket.
Síðan verða þeir Grímar úti ok Helgi með þeim.	Afterwards were they The-Grims (name) outside and Helgi (name) with them.	Afterwards the Grims were outside and Helgi was with them.
Váru þá ljós upp tendruð í konungs herbergi.	Were then lights up lit in the-king's room.	Then the lights were lit up in the king's room.
Sjá þeir þá drepna þrjá menn, enn þar liggja hornin Grímar á gólfinu hjá inum dauðum.	Saw they then killed three men, and there laid horns The-Grims' (name) by the-floor beside the dead.	They then saw that three men had been killed, and the Grims' horns were on the floor beside the dead.
"Þetta er undr mikit", sagði konungr, "ok væra betr, at slík yrði sjaldan.	"This is strange much", said the-king, "and should-be better, that such becomes seldom.	"This is very strange", said the king, "and it would be best if this becomes seldom.
Ok þat hef ek heyrt sagt af Guðmundi af Glæsisvöllum, at hann sé mjök fjölkunnigr ok illu megi helzt vit hann skipta, ok eru þeir menn illa komnir, er undir hans valdi eru, ef vér mættum nokkut at gera".	And that have I heard said of Gudmund (name) of Glasir-Plains (place), that he is a-great skilled-in-magic and evil may keep with him divide, and they-are the people evil comes, who under his control are, if we may anything to do".	And I have heard said of Gudmund of Glasir Plains, that he is greatly skilled in magic and his evil keeps dividing, and the people under his control are evil, even if anything may be done about it".
Konungr lét varðveita hornin Gríma ok af drekka, ok dugir þat vel.	The-king had preserved the-horns Grims' (name) and of drank, and enough it-was well.	The king had the Grim horns preserved and drank from them, and all was well enough.
Þar er nú kallat Grímaskarð ofan at Alreksstöðum, er þeir hafa austan farit, ok er þat engra manna at fara þar síðan.	There is now called Grim-Pass (place) over at Alreksstead (place), where they had east travelled, and is that no people to travel there since.	There is a mountain pass called Grim Pass over at Alreksstead where they travelled east, and no people have travelled there since.

3

Nú líðr af vetrinn, ok kemr annarr átti dagr jóla, ok er konungr í kirkju ok hirð hans at hlýða messu.	Now passed of winter, and came another eighth day Yule, and was the-king in church and retainers his at attending mass.	Now it passed to winter, and another eighth day of Yule, and the king was in church with his retainers attending mass.

The Tale of Helgi Thórisson (Old Norse)

Old Norse	Literal	English
Þá koma þar þrír menn til kirkjudyra, ok er einn eptir, enn tveir fara í brott ok mæla þetta áðr:	Then came there three men to church-door, and was one after, but two travelled to away and spoke this before:	Then there came three men to the church door, one of they stayed behind, but two travelled away and said before they went:
"Hér færum vit þér Gretti, konungr, ok er ekki víst, nær þú færir af þér".	"Here travelled with to-you Gretti (name), king, and that not certain, when you bring out-of you-to".	"Here we bring to you Gretti, king, and it is not certain how you will be able to get rid of him".
Kenna menn þar Helga.	Knew people there Helgi (name).	People came to know that it was Helgi.
Síðan gengr konungr til borða, ok er menn tala vit Helga, verða menn þess varir, at hann er blindr.	Afterwards went the-king to the-table, and as people spoke with Helgi (name), became people this aware, that he was blind.	Afterwards the king went to the tables, and as people spoke with Helgi, the became aware, that he was blind.
Frétti konungr þá, hverju gegndi um hans hag eðr hvar hann hefði verit þessa stund alla.	Inquired the-king then, each reason about his circumstances and where he had been this time all.	The king then inquired about each of the reasons of his circumstances and where he had been all this time.
Hann segir þá konungi fyrst frá því, er hann fann konurnar í skóginum, þá frá því, er þeir Grímar gerðu veðrit at þeim bræðrum, er þeir vildu bjarga skipinu, ok síðan höfðu þeir Grímar hann með sér til Guðmundar á Glæsisvöllum ok færðu hann Ingibjörgu, dóttur Guðmundar.	He told then the-king first from accordingly, and he found women in the-forest, then from accordingly, that they The-Grims (name) made a-storm that they the-brothers, and they wished to-save the-ship, and afterwards had they The-Grims (name) him along himself to Gudmund (name) of Glasir-Plains (place) and travelled he Ingibjorg (name), daughter-of Gudmund (name).	He told the king accordingly from the beginning, how he found the women in the forest, that the Grims who were brothers had made a storm come upon the brothers, and how they wishes to save their ship, and afterwards how they took him to Gudmund of Glasir Plains and delivered him to Ingibjorg, daughter of Gudmund.
Þá mælti konungr:	Then spoke the-king:	Then the king spoke:
"Hversu þótti þér þar at vera?"	"How-so thought you there to be?"	"How did you find it there?",
"Allgott", segir hann, "ok hverrgi hefir mér betra þótt".	"All-good", said he, "and nowhere have I better thought".	"All good", said he, "and nowhere have I thought better".
Þá spurði konungr at um siðu Guðmundar konungs ok at fjölmenni eðr athöfn.	Then asked the-king that about customs Gudmund (name) the-king and to followers or deeds.	Then the king asked about the customs of Gudmund and his followers and their deeds.

The Tale of Helgi Thórisson (Old Norse)

Old Norse	Literal	English
enn hann lét yfir öllu vel ok sagði, at hans var miklu fleiri enn hann fengi talit.	then he had over all well and said, that he was much more than he got counted.	Then he had said well about all, and that there was more than he could count to tell them.
Konungr mælti:	The-king spoke:	The king spoke:
"Hví fóru þér svá skjótliga í brott í fyrra vetr?"	"Why travelled you so shortly to away the first winter?"	"Why did you travel away so quickly the first winter?",
"Guðmundr konungr sendi þá til at svíkja yðr", segir hann, "en fyr bænir yðrar lét hann mik lausan, svá at þér mættið vita, hvat er af mér væra orðit.	"Gudmund (name) the-king sent them to of fool you", said he, "but for prayers yours had he me released, so that you may know, what was of me was become.	"King Gudmund sent them to fool you", he said, "but for your prayers he had me released, so that you may know what had become of me.
enn því fóru vér svá skjótt í brott næstunni, at þeir Grímar höfðu ekki náttúru til at drekka þann drykk, er þér létuð signa.	but because travelled we so shortly to away the-last-time, that they The-Grims (name) had not the-nature to of drink the drink, which you had signed.	But because we travelled so quickly away the last time, the Grims did not have the nature to drink the drink that you had signed.
Urðu þeir þessu reiðir, at þeir sá sik yfirstigna, ok því drápu þeir menn yðra, at svá sagði Guðmundr konungr fyrir, ef þeir fengi eigi mein yðr gert.	Became they this angry, that they saw themselves surpassed, and therefore killed they people yours, that so told Gudmund (name) the-king before, if they got not harm yours done.	They became angry that you had surpassed them, and therefore they killed your people, because King Gudmund told them to do so, if they could not do harm to you.
enn hann sýndi tign sína í því, at hann sendi yðr hornin, at þér mundið þá síðr eptir mér leita".	but he showed prestige his in because, that he sent you the-horns, that you remember then less afterwards me seeking".	But he showed his prestige in sending you the horns, so that you would remember less about seeking me".
Konungr spurði:	The-king asked:	The king asked:
"Hví fórtu nú í brott öðru sinni?"	"Why travelled now to away the-other with?"	"Why did you go away this time?",
Hann svarar:	He answered:	he answered:
"Ingibjörg olli því.	"Ingibjorg (name) caused therefore.	"Because of Ingibjorg.

The Tale of Helgi Thórisson (Old Norse)

Old Norse	Literal	English
hon þóttist ekki mega liggja hjá mér nema með meinlætum, ef hon kæmi vit mik beran, ok því fór ek mest í brott, enda vilda Guðmundr konungr eigi þreyta vit yðr, þegar hann vissi, at þér vilduð mik í brott hafa.	she thought not may lay beside me without with malignance, if she came with me bare, and because-of travelled I most to away, and wished Gudmund (name) the-king not tired with you, as-soon-as he knew, that you willed me to away at-sea.	She thought that she may no longer lay beside me without feeling uneasy whenever she came into contact with me bare, and for that reason most I travelled away, and King Gudmund did not wise to be tired of you, as soon as he knew that you willed me to go away to sea.
enn um tign ok risnu Guðmundar konungs má ek ekki í fám orðum segja ok um fjölmenni þat, er með honum er".	but about prestige and hospitality Gudmund (name) the-king may I only of few words to-say and about followers that, are with him are".	But about the prestige and hospitality of King Gudmund I have little words to say about it or the followers that are with him there".
Konungr spurði:	The-king asked:	The king asked:
"Hví ertu blindr?"	"Why are-you blind?"	"Why are you blind?"
Hann svarar:	He answered:	He answered:
"Ingibjörg Guðmundardóttir greip ór mér bæði augun, þá er vit skildum, ok sagði, at konur í Nóregi mundri mín skamma stund njóta".	"Ingibjorg (name) Daughter-of-Gudmund (name) gripped from me both eyes, then when we separated, and said, that women in Norway (place) would my short while enjoy".	"Ingibjorg, daughter of Gudmund, gripped both my eyes from me, and then when we separated, she said that women in Norway would enjoy my company for a short while".
Konungr sagði:	The-king said:	The king said:
"Makligr væra Guðmundr meingerða af mér fyr þau manndráp, er hann gerði, ef guði vilda þat vera láta".	"Properly would-be Gudmund (name) harmed of me for those murders, that he did, if God would that be allowed".	"Gudmund would be properly harmed by me for those murders that he did, if God would allow it".
Síðan var sent eptir Þóri, föður Helga, ok þakkaði hann honum vel, er sonr hans var aptr kominn ór trölla höndum.	Afterwards was sent after Thori (name), father Helga's (name), and thanked he him well, that son his was returned come from monsters hands.	Afterwards Helgi's father Thorri was sent for and he thanked him well that his son was returned from the hands of such monsters.
Ferr hann síðan heim, enn Helgi er eptir með konungi ok lifir til annarrar jafnlengdar.	Travelled he then home, but Helgi (name) was after with the-king and lived until another equal-length.	He then travelled home, but Helgi was thereafter with the king and lived another year.

The Tale of Helgi Thórisson (Old Norse)

Old Norse	Literal	English
enn konungr hefir hornin Gríma með sér, þá er hann fór síðasta sinn ór landi.	then the-king had the-horns Grims' (name) with him, then when he travelled last his out-of land.	Then the king had the Grim horns with him, when he travelled last out of the land.
enn þat segja menn, þá er Óláfr konungr hvarf af Orminum langa, at hyrfi ok hornin ok hafa engi maðr þau sét síðan.	is it said people, then that Olaf (name) the-king disappeared from Serpent long, that disappeared also the-horns and has no man them seen since.	It is said by people, that then King Olaf disappeared from The Long Serpent, and that the horns also disappeared and no man has seen them since.
Ok lýkr hér frá Grímum at segja.	And concludes here from The-Grims (name) to say.	And here concludes what may be said about the Grims.

Word List (Old Norse to English)

Word List (Old Norse to English)

Old Norse	English
A, a	
aðrar	others
af	from, of, out-of
aflat	surplus
alla	all
allar	all
allgóðir	all-gold
allgóðr	all-good
Allgott	all-good
allir	all
Allr	all
allra	all
allt	all
Alreksstöðum	Alreksstead (place)
annarr	another, one
annarra	other
annarrar	another
annat	another
aptni	after
aptr	returned
at	at, in, of, that, the, to
atburð	events
athöfn	deeds
augun	eyes
austan	east
Á, á	
á	about, an, and, by, in, it, of, on, out, so, to
áðr	before
áliðnu	late
ár	year
átti	eighth, had
B, b	
bað	bid, prayed
báðir	both
bæ	a-farm
bæði	both
bænir	prayers
bær	farm
baki	horseback
bar	surpassed
báru	bore
beiddi	asked, bids
beran	bare
betr	better
betra	better
betri	better
biðr	asked
bjarga	to-save
bjart	bright
bjó	settled
blessa	bless
blindr	blind
borð	a-table, tables
borða	the-table
borðum	the-table
bræðr	brothers
bræðrum	the-brothers
brest	a-crash
bresti	crash
bróðir	brother
bróður	brother
brott	away
brottu	away
búa	prepared
búin	prepared
búizt	prepared
búnar	prepared
burt	away
byskup	bishop, the-bishop
býsna	extreme
D, d	
dag	a-day
dagr	day
dauðum	dead
dimma	darkness
dóttir	daughter, daughter-of

15

Word List (Old Norse to English)

Old Norse	English
dóttur	daughter-of
drápu	killed
drekahálsinum	the-dragon's-neck
drekahöfuð	dragon's-head
drekka	drank, drink
drekki	drink
drepna	killed
drykk	drink
drykki	drank
drykkinum	drinks, the-drinks
drykkr	drink
dugir	enough
dvaldist	dwelled

E, e

Old Norse	English
eða	and, or
ef	if
eigi	not, only
Ein	one
eina	one
einn	alone, one
einu	one
eitt	one
Ek	I
ekki	not
en	and, but, is, than, that, then, was
enda	and
engi	no
engra	no
engu	not
engum	none
Eptir	after, afterwards
er	am, and, are, as, is, that, then, was, were, when, where, which, who
ertu	are-you
eru	are, there-are, they-are
Erum	we-are

F, f

Old Norse	English
Faðir	father
fæðsla	feast
færa	brought
færðu	travelled
færir	bring
færum	travelled
Fagna	welcomed
fagrt	fair
fám	few
fann	found
fara	travel, travelled
farit	travelled
fast	fastened
fé	wealth
Fellr	fell
félögum	company
fengi	got
Fengu	got
ferr	travel, travelled
Finna	Sámi (name)
Finnmerkr	Finnmark (place)
fjár	wealth
fjarri	far-away
fjölkunnigr	skilled-in-magic
fjölmenni	followers
fleiri	more
flesk	bacon
föður	father
fór	travelled
fórtu	travelled
fóru	travelled
frá	from
frændum	kinsman
fram	from, from
framar	above
Frétti	inquired
fríðr	beautiful
fullr	full
fund	meet
fylla	filled
fyrir	before, for
fyrra	first
fyrst	first

G, g

Word List (Old Norse to English)

Old Norse	English
gæta	guard
gaf	gave
gakk	come
ganga	went
gat	could
gefa	to-give
gefast	give
gegn	directly
gegndi	reason
gengit	going
gengr	went
gengu	going, went
gera	did, do, done
gerði	be, did
gerðu	did, made
gerir	did
gert	done
gervar	fashioned
Gestir	the-guests
Glæsisvöllum	Glasir-Plains (place)
glóaði	shone
góð	good
góða	good
góðum	good
gólfinu	the-floor
gott	good
gras	graze
greip	gripped
Gretti	Gretti (name)
Gríma	Grim (name), Grims' (name)
Grímar	Grims (name), the-Grims (name), the-Grims' (name)
Grímaskarð	Grim-Pass (place)
Grímr	Grim (name)
Grímum	Grims (name), the-Grims (name)
gripir	treasures
guð	God
Guðmundar	Gudmund (name)
Guðmundardóttir	daughter-of-Gudmund (name)
Guðmundi	Gudmund (name)
Guðmundr	Gudmund (name)
gull	gold
gullbúin	gold-inlaid
gulli	gold
gullknappr	golden-ball
gullskotit	gold-laid

H, h

Old Norse	English
hafa	at-sea, had
hafði	had
hafi	has
hag	circumstances
Halda	held
hana	her
handlaugar	hand-washing
Hann	he, him
hans	he, him, his
harðla	greatly
hark	noise, racket
heðan	hence
hef	have
hefði	had
hefir	had, have
heilsar	greeted
heim	home
heita	was-named
heiti	am-named
heitir	named
heldr	rather
heldu	busy
Helga	Helga's (name), Helgi (name)
Helgi	Helgi (name)
helzt	keep
henni	her
hér	here
herbergi	room
herra	lord
hersir	a-local-chief
hestanna	horses
Hestar	horses
hestum	horses
hét	named, was-named
heyra	heard
heyrðu	heard

Word List (Old Norse to English)

Old Norse	English
heyrt	heard
hina	the
hingat	here
hirð	retainers
hittir	found
hjá	beside
hlýða	attending
höfðu	had
höfuðin	heads
höllina	the-hall
höndum	hands
honum	he, him, to-him
horfði	looked
horn	horns
hornin	horns, the-horns
hornum	horns
hornunum	the-horns
hugr	thought
Hún	she
hvaðan	from-where
hvar	were, what, where
hvarf	disappeared
hvárrtveggi	each
hvárt	either
hvat	what
hver	any
hvergi	nowhere
hverju	each
Hversu	how-so
Hví	why
hvílast	rest
hvílur	beds
hyrfi	disappeared
Hyrningar	Hyrnings (name)

I, i

Old Norse	English
illa	evil
illu	evil
Ingibjörg	Ingibjorg (name)
Ingibjörgu	Ingibjorg (name)
inni	the
inum	the

Í, í

Old Norse	English
í	in, of, the, to
íþróttir	sports

J, j

Old Norse	English
jafnlengdar	equal-length
jól	Yule
jóla	Yule

K, k

Old Norse	English
kæmi	came
kallaðir	called
kallat	called
kann	can
kastar	cast
kaupferð	trade, trading-voyage
kaups	trade
kemr	came
kenna	knew
ker	vessels
kirkju	church
kirkjudyra	church-door
kistlar	chests
kistlunum	chests
klæðast	clothed
kom	came
koma	came
kominn	become, came, come
komit	came
komnir	comes
kómu	came
kona	the-woman
konar	kinds-of
konu	woman
konung	the-king
konunga	kings
konungi	the-king
konungr	king, the-King
konungs	the-king, the-king's
konur	women

Word List (Old Norse to English)

Old Norse	English
konurnar	women
krásir	food
kvað	spoke
kveðja	greeted
kveðju	greetings
kveðst	said
kveldit	evening

L, l

Old Norse	English
læsti	locked
lætr	had
land	land
landi	land
landtjaldinu	land-tent
langa	long
láta	allowed
látit	made
látum	have
laugat	bathed
launa	repay
lausan	released
leita	seeking
lengra	longer
lesit	read
lét	had
létuð	had
líðr	passed, passes
lifir	lived
liggja	laid, lay, to-lay
litum	colours
ljós	lights
login	lights
lýkr	concludes

M, m

Old Norse	English
má	may
maðr	a-man, man
mæla	spoke
mælti	spoke
mættið	may
mættum	may
Makligr	properly

Old Norse	English
manna	people, peoples
manndráp	murders
manni	person
margs	many
mat	food
með	along, as-well, with
meðan	while
mega	may
megi	may
mein	harm
meingerða	harmed
meinlætum	malignance
meir	more
menn	men, people
mér	I, me
messu	mass
mest	most
mestu	most
mik	me
mikil	much
mikill	large
mikils	much
mikinn	great
mikit	much
miklu	great, much
mín	my
mjök	a-great
mönnum	people
mösurtré	maple-tree
móti	return
mundi	should
mundið	remember
mundu	would
munnlaugar	mouth-basins
munum	shall
myrkri	darkness

N, n

Old Norse	English
nær	when
nærri	near
næstunni	the-last-time
nætr	nights
nafnbót	rank
nafni	name, names

Word List (Old Norse to English)

Old Norse	English
náttúru	the-nature
nema	without
nes	headland
niðr	down, son
njóta	enjoy
nokkurt	some
nokkut	anything
norðr	north
Noregi	Norway (place)
nótt	night
nú	now
nyt	use

O, o

Old Norse	English
ofan	above, down, over
ok	also, and
okkart	ours
olli	caused
orðit	become
orðum	words
Orminum	serpent
oss	us

Ó, ó

Old Norse	English
Óláf	Olaf (name)
Óláfr	Olaf (name)
Óláfs	Olaf (name)
ór	from, out-of, through
óvíst	uncertain

Ö, ö

Old Norse	English
öðru	the-other
öðrum	other
öl	ale
öll	all
öllu	all
öllum	all
önnur	also

P, p

Old Norse	English
prettóttr	deceitful

R, r

Old Norse	English
Rauðabergi	Raudaberg (place)
rauðum	red
reiðingr	riding
reiðir	angry
reiðklæðum	riding-clothes
reistu	raised
ríða	riders, riding, rode
risnu	hospitality

S, s

Old Norse	English
sá	saw
sæmiliga	well-enough
sængr	beds
sætis	seats
sagði	said, told
sagt	said
sama	the-same
saman	together
samnafna	same-name
samt	together
sat	sat
sé	is
seg	say
segir	said, told
segist	said
segja	said, say, to-say
sem	as, that-which
sendi	sends, sent
sendir	sent
sent	sent
sér	him, himself, saw, them
sét	seen
settu	set
Síðan	after, afterwards, since, then

Word List (Old Norse to English)

Old Norse	English
síðasta	last
síðr	less
siðu	customs
signa	signed
sik	themselves
silfri	silver
sína	his
sinn	his
sinni	with
síns	his, theirs
sínum	his, theirs
sitr	sat
Sjá	saw
sjaldan	seldom
sjó	the-sea
skal	shall
skamma	short
skammt	short-distance
skildum	separated
skilja	separate
skip	ship
skipinu	the-ship
skips	ships
skipsins	ship
skipta	divide
skjótliga	shortly
skjótt	away, quickly, shortly
skóginn	the-forest
skóginum	the-forest
skógr	forests
sköruligu	bold-like
skrautligri	splendid
skulu	shall
skulum	should
slík	such
slógu	threw
slökktu	put-out
smjör	butter
sonr	son
spurði	asked
spyrja	asked
spyrr	asked
stafat	staved
stafnana	ship's-prow
standa	stand, stood
stigu	stepped
stóð	stood
stöðva	stop
stofunni	the-room
Stöndum	stand
stöngin	the-pole
stóra	great
stund	time, while
Sú	so
suðr	south
sumri	summer
sumt	some
svá	so
svarar	answered
svíkja	fool
sýndi	showed
syni	sons

T, t

Old Norse	English
taka	take, took
tala	spoke
talit	counted
tekin	taken
tekr	took
tendruð	lit
tíðendi	news
tign	prestige
til	to, until
tjald	tent
tjaldi	tent
tók	received
tóku	took
tólf	twelve
trölla	monsters
tvá	two
tvau	two
tveir	two

Þ, þ

Old Norse	English
þá	them, then
þær	these, they
þakkaði	thanked

Word List (Old Norse to English)

Old Norse	English
þangat	from-there
þann	the
Þar	there
Þat	it, it-was, that, that, the
þau	them, they, those
þegar	as-soon-as, straight-away
þegn	thane
þeim	that, them, then, they
þeir	the, they
þeira	theirs, they
þenna	these, they
þér	to-you, you, you-to
Þess	this
þessa	this
Þessi	this
þessu	this
þetta	that, they, this
þigg	accept
þjóna	served
þó	though
Þóri	Thori (name)
Þórir	Thorir (name)
Þorsteinn	Thorstein (name)
þótt	thought
þótti	thinks, thought
þóttist	thought
þreyta	tired
þrifligir	thriving
þrír	three
þrjá	three
þrjár	three
þú	you
því	accordingly, because, because-of, therefore
þykkir	thought
þykkjast	realised
þykkju	things

U, u

um	about, in
undir	under
undr	strange
upp	up
Urðu	became

Ú, ú

úti	outside

V, v

væn	fair
vænleik	beauty
væri	should-be, was, were, would-be
værið	become
valdi	control
var	was, were
varða	warrant
varðveita	preserved
varir	aware
várr	aware, ours
váru	was, were
vatnskarl	basins
veðr	weather
veðrit	a-storm, weather
veg	way
Veit	knew
vel	well
vér	we
vera	be
verða	became, become, to-become, were
Verðr	became
verðum	have
verit	been
vetr	winter
vetrinn	winter
við	to, with
víða	widely
Víkinni	the-bay
vil	will, wish
vildi	wished, would
vildu	wished
vilduð	willed
vill	wished

Word List (Old Norse to English)

Old Norse	English
Vímund	Vimund (name)
vináttu	friendship
vinir	friend
vísa	directed
vissan	knowledge
vissi	knew
víst	certain
vísu	a-verse
vit	we, with
vita	certainly, know

Y, y

yðar	you
yðr	to-you, you, yours
yðra	yours
yðrar	yours
yfir	over
yfirstigna	surpassed
yrði	becomes

Ý, ý

ýmsum	various

Word List (English to Old Norse)

Word List (English to Old Norse)

English	Old Norse	English	Old Norse
		answered	svarar
		as-soon-as	þegar
		accept	þigg
		accordingly	því
		aware	varir, várr
		a-storm	veðrit
		a-verse	vísu

A, a

about	á, á
an	á
and	á, á, á, á, áðr, af
all	alla, allar, allgóðir, allgóðr, Allgott, allir, Allr, allra, allt
all-gold	allgóðir
all-good	allgóðr, Allgott
Alreksstead (place)	Alreksstöðum
another	annarr, annarrar, annat
after	aptni, at, at
at	at
a-farm	bæ
asked	beiddi, beiddi, beran, betr, betra
a-table	borð
a-crash	brest
away	brott, brottu, burt, byskup
a-day	dag
alone	einn
afterwards	eptir, er
am	er
are	er, er
as	er, er
are-you	ertu
above	framar, Frétti
at-sea	hafa
am-named	heiti
a-local-chief	hersir
attending	hlýða
any	hver
allowed	láta
a-man	maðr
along	með
as-well	með
a-great	mjök
anything	nokkut
also	ok, ok
ale	öl
angry	reiðir

B, b

by	á
before	áðr, af
bid	bað
both	báðir, bæ
bore	báru
bids	beiddi
bare	beran
better	betr, betra, betri
bright	bjart
bless	blessa
blind	blindr
brothers	bræðr
brother	bróðir, bróður
bishop	byskup
but	en
brought	færa
bring	færir
bacon	flesk
beautiful	fríðr
be	gerði, gerði
busy	heldu
beside	hjá
beds	hvílur, hyrfi
become	kominn, kominn, kominn, komit
bathed	laugat
bold-like	sköruligu
butter	smjör
because	því
because-of	því
became	Urðu, væn, vænleik
beauty	vænleik
basins	vatnskarl

Word List (English to Old Norse)

English	*Old Norse*
been	verit
becomes	yrði

C, c

crash	bresti
company	félögum
come	gakk, gat
could	gat
circumstances	hag
came	kæmi, kallaðir, kallat, kann, kastar, kemr, kenna
called	kallaðir, kallat
can	kann
cast	kastar
church	kirkju
church-door	kirkjudyra
chests	kistlar, kistlunum
clothed	klæðast
comes	komnir
colours	litum
concludes	lýkr
caused	olli
customs	siðu
counted	talit
control	valdi
certain	víst
certainly	vita

D, d

deeds	athöfn
day	dagr
dead	dauðum
darkness	dimma, dóttir
daughter	dóttir
daughter-of	dóttir, dóttur
dragon's-head	drekahöfuð
drank	drekka, drekka
drink	drekka, drekki, drepna, drykk
drinks	drykkinum
dwelled	dvaldist

English	*Old Norse*
directly	gegn
did	gera, gera, gera, gerði
do	gera
done	gera, gerði
daughter-of-Gudmund (name)	Guðmundardóttir
disappeared	hvarf, hvárrtveggi
down	niðr, njóta
deceitful	prettóttr
divide	skipta
directed	vísa

E, e

events	atburð
eighth	átti
eyes	augun
east	austan
extreme	býsna
enough	dugir
each	hvárrtveggi, hvárt
either	hvárt
evil	illa, illu
equal-length	jafnlengdar
evening	kveldit
enjoy	njóta

F, f

from	af, áliðnu, alla, allar, allgóðir
farm	bær
father	Faðir, fæðsla
feast	fæðsla
fair	fagrt, fám
few	fám
found	fann, fast
fastened	fast
fell	Fellr
Finnmark (place)	Finnmerkr
far-away	fjarri
followers	fjölmenni
full	fullr

25

Word List (English to Old Norse)

English	Old Norse	English	Old Norse
filled	fylla	had	átti, augun, austan, bað, báðir, bæ, bæði, bær, baki
for	fyrir		
first	fyrra, fyrst		
fashioned	gervar	horseback	baki
from-where	hvaðan	has	hafi
food	krásir, kveðja	held	Halda
forests	skógr	her	hana, handlaugar
fool	svíkja	hand-washing	handlaugar
from-there	þangat	he	Hann, hann, hans
friendship	vináttu	him	hann, hans, hans, hans
friend	vinir	his	hans, harðla, heðan, hef, hefði

G, g

got	fengi, Fengu
guard	gæta
gave	gaf
give	gefast
going	gengit, gengu
Glasir-Plains (place)	Glæsisvöllum
good	góð, góða, góðum, gott
graze	gras
gripped	greip
Gretti (name)	Gretti
Grim (name)	Gríma, Gríma
Grims' (name)	Gríma
Grims (name)	Grímar, Grímaskarð
Grim-Pass (place)	Grímaskarð
God	guð
Gudmund (name)	Guðmundar, Guðmundardóttir, Guðmundi
gold	gull, gullbúin
gold-inlaid	gullbúin
golden-ball	gullknappr
gold-laid	gullskotit
greatly	harðla
greeted	heilsar, heim
greetings	kveðju
great	mikinn, mikit, miklu

hence	heðan
have	hef, hefði, hefir, hefir
home	heim
Helga's (name)	Helga
Helgi (name)	Helga, Helgi
here	hér, herra
horses	hestanna, Hestar, hestum
heard	heyra, heyrðu, heyrt
heads	höfuðin
hands	höndum
horns	horn, hornin, hornum
how-so	Hversu
Hyrnings (name)	Hyrningar
harm	mein
harmed	meingerða
headland	nes
hospitality	risnu
himself	sér

H, h

I, i

in	á, á, áðr, af
it	á, áðr
if	ef
I	Ek, en
is	En, enda, Eptir
inquired	Frétti
Ingibjorg (name)	Ingibjörg, Ingibjörgu
it-was	þat

K, k

Word List (English to Old Norse)

English	Old Norse	English	Old Norse
killed	drápu, drekahöfuð	mass	messu
kinsman	frændum	most	mest, mestu
keep	helzt	much	mikil, mikill, mikils, mikinn
knew	kenna, kirkju, kirkjudyra	my	mín
kinds-of	konar	maple-tree	mösurtré
kings	konunga	mouth-basins	munnlaugar
king	konungr	monsters	trölla
knowledge	vissan		
know	vita		

L, l

N, n

late	áliðnu	not	eigi, eigi, Ein
lord	herra	no	engi, engra
looked	horfði	none	engum
locked	læsti	noise	hark
land	land, landi	named	heitir, heldr
land-tent	landtjaldinu	nowhere	hvergi
long	langa	near	nærri
longer	lengra	nights	nætr
lived	lifir	name	nafni
laid	liggja	names	nafni
lay	liggja	north	norðr
lights	ljós, login	Norway (place)	Noregi
large	mikill	night	nótt
last	síðasta	now	nú
less	síðr	news	tíðendi
lit	tendruð		

M, m

O, o

more	fleiri, flesk	of	á, á, á, á
meet	fund	on	á
made	gerðu, gerir	out	á
may	má, maðr, maðr, mættið, mættum	others	aðrar
		out-of	af, aflat
man	maðr	one	annarr, annarra, aptr, ár, at, at
murders	manndráp		
many	margs	other	annarra, aptr
malignance	meinlætum	or	eða
men	menn	only	eigi
me	mér, messu	over	ofan, okkart
		ours	okkart, Óláf
		Olaf (name)	Óláf, Óláfr, Óláfs
		outside	úti

Word List (English to Old Norse)

English	Old Norse
English	Old Norse

P, p

prayed	bað
prayers	bænir
prepared	búa, búin, búizt, búnar
passed	líðr
passes	líðr
properly	Makligr
people	manna, manna, manni
peoples	manna
person	manni
put-out	slökktu
prestige	tign
preserved	varðveita

Q, q

quickly	skjótt

R, r

returned	aptr
reason	gegndi
racket	hark
rather	heldr
room	herbergi
retainers	hirð
rest	hvílast
repay	launa
released	lausan
read	lesit
return	móti
remember	mundið
rank	nafnbót
Raudaberg (place)	Rauðabergi
red	rauðum
riding	reiðingr, reiðklæðum
riding-clothes	reiðklæðum
raised	reistu
riders	ríða
rode	ríða

English	Old Norse
realised	þykkjast
received	tók

S, s

so	á, á, aðrar
surplus	aflat
surpassed	bar, bjarga
settled	bjó
Sámi (name)	Finna
skilled-in-magic	fjölkunnigr
shone	glóaði
she	Hún
sports	íþróttir
spoke	kvað, kveðst, launa, lausan
said	kveðst, launa, lausan, leita, lesit, líðr
seeking	leita
should	mundi, mundið
shall	munum, nær, nærri
son	niðr, nokkurt
some	nokkurt, norðr
serpent	Orminum
saw	sá, sæmiliga, sætis
seats	sætis
same-name	samnafna
sat	sat, seg
say	seg, segir
sends	sendi
sent	sendi, sendir, sent
seen	sét
set	settu
since	síðan
signed	signa
silver	silfri
seldom	sjaldan
short	skamma
short-distance	skammt
separated	skildum
separate	skilja
ship	skip, skipinu
ships	skips
shortly	skjótliga, skjótt
splendid	skrautligri

Word List (English to Old Norse)

English	Old Norse
such	slík
staved	stafat
ship's-prow	stafnana
stand	standa, standa
stood	standa, stigu
stepped	stigu
stop	stöðva
south	suðr
summer	sumri
showed	sýndi
sons	syni
straight-away	þegar
served	þjóna
strange	undr
should-be	væri

T, t

English	Old Norse
to	á, aðrar, af, af, aflat
that	at, at, at, bað, bænir, bar, bjarga
the	at, at, bað, bænir, bar, bjarga, bjó, borð
to-save	bjarga
tables	borð
the-table	borða, borðum
the-brothers	bræðrum
the-bishop	byskup
the-dragon's-neck	drekahálsinum
the-drinks	drykkinum
than	en
then	En, en, engi, engra, engu
there-are	Eru
they-are	eru
travelled	færðu, færum, Fagna, fara, fara, farit, fé, ferr
travel	fara, fara
to-give	gefa
the-guests	Gestir
the-floor	gólfinu
the-Grims (name)	Grímar, Grímar
the-Grims' (name)	Grímar
treasures	gripir
the-hall	höllina
to-him	honum
the-horns	hornin, hornunum
thought	hugr, Hún, hvar, hvar, hvar
trade	kaupferð, kaupferð
trading-voyage	kaupferð
the-woman	kona
the-king	konung, konungi, Konungr, konungs
the-king's	konungs
to-lay	liggja
the-last-time	næstunni
the-nature	náttúru
the-other	öðru
through	ór
told	sagði, sagt
the-same	sama
together	saman, samnafna
to-say	segja
that-which	sem
them	sér, sét, settu, síðan
themselves	sik
theirs	síns, sínum, sitr
the-sea	sjó
the-ship	skipinu
the-forest	skóginn, skóginum
threw	slógu
the-room	stofunni
the-pole	stöngin
time	stund
take	taka
took	taka, tala, tekin
taken	tekin
these	þær, Þær
they	Þær, þakkaði, þann, Þar, þat, þat, þat
thanked	þakkaði
there	Þar
those	þau
thane	þegn
to-you	þér, þér
this	Þess, þessa, Þessi, þessu, þetta
though	þó
Thori (name)	Þóri
Thorir (name)	Þórir

Word List (English to Old Norse)

English	Old Norse
Thorstein (name)	Þorsteinn
thinks	þótti
tired	þreyta
thriving	þrifligir
three	þrír, þrjá, þrjár
therefore	því
things	þykkju
tent	tjald, tjaldi
twelve	tólf
two	tvá, tvau, tveir
to-become	verða
the-bay	Víkinni

U, u

use	nyt
us	oss
uncertain	óvíst
until	til
under	undir
up	upp

V, v

vessels	ker
Vimund (name)	Vímund
various	ýmsum

W, w

was	en, engi, engra, engu, engum
were	er, er, er, er, er, Eru
when	er, er
where	er, er
which	er
who	er
we-are	Erum
welcomed	Fagna
wealth	fé, ferr
went	ganga, gefa, gegndi
was-named	heita, heitir
what	hvar, hvar

English	Old Norse
why	Hví
woman	konu
women	konur, konurnar
with	með, meðan, menn, mönnum
while	meðan, menn
would	mundu, munum
without	nema
words	orðum
well-enough	sæmiliga
would-be	væri
warrant	varða
weather	veðr, veðrit
way	veg
well	vel
we	vér, verða
winter	vetr, vetrinn
widely	víða
will	vil
wish	vil
wished	vildi, vildi, vildu
willed	vilduð

Y, y

year	ár
Yule	jól, jóla
you	þér, þér, Þess, þessa
you-to	þér
yours	yðr, yðra, yðrar

The Tale of Helgi Thórisson (*Old Icelandic*)

Old Icelandic	Literal	English
1	**1**	**1**
Þórir hét maður, er bjó í Noregi á bæ þeim, er á Rauðabergi heitir.	Thorir (name) was-named a-man, who settled in Norway (place) in a-farm that, was so Raudaberg (place) named.	There was a man named Thorir who lived in Norway on a farm that was named Raudaberg.
Þessi bær er skammt frá Víkinni.	This farm was short-distance from The-bay.	The farm was a short distance away from the bay.
Þórir átti tvá syni.	Thorir (name) had two sons.	Thorir had two sons.
Hét annar Helgi, en Þorsteinn annar; báðir voru þeir þrifligir menn, og var þó Helgi framar um íþróttir.	Was-named one Helgi (name), was Thorstein (name) another; both were they thriving men, and was though Helgi (name) above in sports.	One was named Helgi, the other was named Thorstein; they were both thriving men, though Helgi surpassed in sports.
Faðir þeirra var hersir að nafnbót.	Father theirs was a-local-chief of rank.	Their father was a local chief of high rank.
Hann var í vináttu við Óláf konung.	He was in friendship with Olaf (name) the-king.	He was friends with King Olaf.
Það var á einu sumri, að þeir bræður höfðu kaupferð norður til Finnmerkr og höfðu smjör og flesk til kaups við Finna.	it was in one summer, that the brothers had trading-voyage north to Finnmark (place) and had butter and bacon to trade with Sámi (name).	It was one summer, that the brothers had a trading voyage north to Finnmark, and they had butter and bacon to trade with the Sámi people.
Fengu þeir góða kaupferð og heldu aptr að áliðnu sumri og kómu um dag við nes það, er hét Vímund.	Got they good trade and busy returned in late summer and came about a-day to headland that, was named Vimund (name).	They had a good and busy trade and returned late in the summer and came about one day to a headland that was named Vimund.
Það var allgóður skógr.	there were all-good forests.	There were all-good woods.
Gengu þeir á land upp og fengu nokkurt mösurtré.	Went they to land up and got some maple-tree.	They went up to the land and got some maple trees.
Verður Helga lengra gengið í skóginn en öðrum mönnum.	Became Helgi (name) longer going in the-forest than other people.	Helgi went further into the woods than the other people.

The Tale of Helgi Thórisson (Old Icelandic)

Old Icelandic	Literal	English
Síðan kastar yfir myrkri miklu, svo að hann hittir ei til skipsins á þeim aptni; tekur nú og skjótt að dimma af nótt.	Then cast over darkness great, so that he found not to ship and then after; took now and quickly to darkness of night.	Then a great darkness cast over, so that he could not find the ship; and then afterwards the darkness of night took quickly.
Þá sért Helgi, hvar tólf konur ríða úr skóginum.	Then saw Helgi (name), were twelve women riding through the-forest.	Then Helgi saw that there were twelve women riding through the forest.
Þær voru allar á rauðum hestum og í rauðum reiðklæðum.	They were all on red horses and in red riding-clothes.	They were all on red horses and in red riding-clothes.
Þær stigu af baki.	They stepped from horseback.	They stepped down from their horses.
Allr reiðingr hestanna þá glóaði við gull.	All riding horses then shone with gold.	All the horses they were riding shone with gold.
Ein bar það af öllum um vænleik, og allar aðrar þjóna henni, þessi inni sköruligu konu.	One surpassed there of all about beauty, and all others served her, this the bold-like woman.	One of them surpassed all the others in beauty, and all the others served this bold looking woman.
Hestar þeirra gengu á gras.	Horses they went to graze.	The horses then went to graze.
Eptir það settu þær niður eitt fagrt tjald.	After that set they down one fair tent.	After that they set down a fair tent.
Var það stafat með ýmsum litum og víða gullskotit, og öll höfuðin voru við gull búin, er af upp gengu landtjaldinu, og svo stöngin, er upp stóð, og mikill gullknappr ofan á.	Was it staved with various colours and widely gold-laid, and all heads were with gold prepared, was of up going land-tent, and so the-pole, that up stood, and large golden-ball above it.	It was striped with various colours and widely laden with gold, and all the heads were prepared with gold, and so it was of this land tent, that all the poles that stood up had a large golden ball on top.
og er þær höfðu um búizt, reistu þær borð og báru á margs konar krásir.	and when they had about prepared, raised they a-table and bore out many kinds-of food.	And when they had prepared all about, they raised a table and brought our many kinds of food.
Þá tóku þær handlaugar, vatnskarl og munnlaugar, gervar af silfri, og allt laugat í gulli.	Then took they hand-washing, basins and mouth-basins, fashioned of silver, and all bathed in gold.	They took to washing their hands, with basins and jugs, fashioned of silver, and all bathed in gold.

The Tale of Helgi Thórisson (Old Icelandic)

Old Icelandic	Literal	English
Helgi stóð nærri tjaldi þeirra og horfði á.	Helgi (name) stood near tent theirs and looked about.	Helgi stood near their tent and looked about.
Sú, er fyrir þeim var, mælti:	So, was before them was, spoke:	The one who was in front of them spoke:
"Helgi, gakk hingað, og þigg hér mat og drykk með oss".	"Helgi (name), come here, and accept here food and drink with us".	"Helgi, come here, and accept food and drink with us".
Hann gerir svo.	He did so.	He did so.
Helgi sért, að það er fríður drykkr og önnur fæðsla og væn ker.	Helgi (name) saw, that there was beautiful drink and also feast and fair vessels.	Helgi saw that there were beautiful drinks and a feast with fair drinking vessels.
Þá voru borð ofan tekin og hvílur búnar, og voru þær miklu skrautligri en annarra manna sængr.	Then were tables down taken and beds prepared, and were these much splendid than other peoples beds.	Then the tables were taken down and the beds were prepared, and these were much more splendid than other peoples' beds.
Sú kona spyr Helga, er fyrir þeim var, hvort hann vildi heldur liggja einn saman eða hjá henni.	So the-woman asked Helgi (name), that for them was, either he wished rather to-lay alone together or beside her.	The woman who was at the front asked Helgi if he wished to lay alone or beside her.
Helgi spyr hana að nafni.	Helgi (name) asked her of name.	Helgi asked her name.
Hún svaraði:	She answered:	She answered:
"eg heiti Ingibjörg, dóttir Guðmundar af Glæsisvöllum".	"I am-named Ingibjorg (name), daughter Gudmund (name) of Glasir-Plains (place)".	"I am named Ingibjorg, daughter of Gudmund of Glasir Plains".
Helgi mælti:	Helgi (name) spoke:	Helgi spoke:
"Hjá þér vil eg liggja".	"Beside you wish I to-lay".	"I wish to lay beside you".
og svo gerðu þau þrjár nætr í samt.	and so did they three nights of together.	And so they did for three nights together.
Var þá bjart veður; standa þau þá upp og klæðast.	Was then bright weather; stood they then up and clothed.	When the weather was bright; they stood up and clothed.
Ingibjörg mælti þá:	Ingibjorg (name) spoke then:	Ingibjorg then spoke:

The Tale of Helgi Thórisson (Old Icelandic)

Old Icelandic	Literal	English
"Nú munum við hér skilja.	"Now shall we here separate.	"Now we shall separate here.
Eru hér kistlar tveir, annar er fullr af silfri, en annar af gulli, er eg vil gefi þér, og seg engum manni, hvaðan það kom".	There-are here chests two, one is full of silver, and another of gold, am I will to-give to-you, and say none person, from-where that came".	Here are two chests, one is full of silver, and another of gold, and I will give them to you, and you shall tell no person, where they came from".
Eptir það ríða þær burt sama veg sem þangað, en hann fór til skips síns.	After that rode they away the-same way as from-there, that he travelled to ships his.	After that they rode away the same way as they had come from, and he travelled to his ships.
Fagna þeir honum velkominn og spyrja, hvar hann dvaldist, en hann vilt það eigi frá segja.	Welcomed they him well and asked, where he dwelled, but he wished there not from to-say.	They welcomed him well and asked where he had stayed, but he did not wish to say.
Halda þeir þá suður með landi og koma heim til föður síns og hafi aflat mikils fjár.	Held they then south along land and came home to father theirs and had surplus much wealth.	They held south along the land and came to their father's home and had much wealth.
Faðir Helga og bróðir spyrja, hvaðan honum kom svo mikið fé sem hann hafði í kistlunum, en hann vilt það ei segja.	Father Helgi (name) and brother asked, from-where he came so much wealth as he had in chests, but he wished that not to-say.	Helgi's father and brother asked where he came by so much wealth as he had in his chests, but he did not wish to say.

2

Nú líður svo fram til jóla.	Now passed so from until Yule.	Now it passed on to Yule.
Það var eina nótt, að kemur á býsna veður.	it was one night, that came an extreme weather.	And it was one night that there came extreme weather.
Þorsteinn mælti við bróður sinn:	Thorstein (name) spoke with brother his:	Thorstein spoke with his brother:
"við skulum standa upp og viti, hvað líður um skip okkart".	"we should stand up and know, what passes about ship ours".	"We should get up and find out what is happening with our ship".
Þeir gera svo, og var það fast velkominn.	They did so, and was it fastened well.	They did so, and it was fastened well.

The Tale of Helgi Thórisson (Old Icelandic)

Old Icelandic	Literal	English
Helgi hafði látit gera drekahöfuð á skip þeirra upp á stafnana og búa velkominn fyrir ofan sjó.	Helgi (name) had made done dragon's-head on ship theirs up in ship's-prow and prepared well for above the-sea.	Helgi had a dragon's head made for their ship's prow and it was decorated well above the sea level.
Fór það fé það til, er Ingibjörg gaf honum, dóttir Guðmundar konungs, en sumt læsti hann í drekahálsinum.	Travelled the wealth there to, that Ingibjorg (name) gave him, daughter-of Gudmund (name) the-king, but some locked he in the-dragon's-neck.	The wealth that Ingibjorg, daughter of King Gudmund, gave him had travelled there but some of it was locked in the dragon's neck.
Þá heyra þeir brest mikinn.	Then heard they a-crash great.	Then they heard a great crash.
það ríða að þeim tveir menn og höfðu Helga í burt með sért.	there riders at them two men and had Helgi (name) to away with them.	Then two men rode towards them and took Helgi away with them.
Veit Þorsteinn ei, hvað af honum verður.	Knew Thorstein (name) not, what of him became.	Thorstein did not know what became of him.
Fellr þá veðrit skjótt.	Fell then weather away.	The weather then fell away.
Þorsteinn kemur heim og svarar föður sínum þenna atburð, og þykir þetta mikil tíðendi.	Thorstein (name) came home and told father his these events, and thought that much news.	Thorstein came home and told his father of these events, and thought that this news was very much.
fer hann þegar á fund Óláfs konungs og svarar honum, hvar komið var, og biður hann nú verða vissan um, hvar er sonur hans er niður kominn.	travelled he straight-away to meet Olaf (name) the-king and said to-him, what came was, and asked him now to-become knowledge about, where was son his and son become.	He travelled straight away to meet King Olaf and told him what had happened, and asked him for knowledge about where his son was and what had become of him.
konungur segist það gera mundu, sem hann beiddi, en kveðst þó óvíst hugr um segja, hver nyt frændum hans mundi að honum verða.	the-King said that do would, that-which he asked, but said though uncertain thought about said, any use kinsman he should to him become.	The king said that he would do what he asked, but said that it was uncertain to say, if his kinsman would be of any use after what had happened to him.
Síðan fór Þórir heim, og líður svo þetta ár og allt fram á jól annat ár, og situr konungur á Alreksstöðum um veturinn.	After travelled Thorir (name) home, and passed so that year and all from to Yule another year, and sat the-king in Alreksstead (place) about winter.	Afterwards Thorir travelled home, and so passed that year to Yule, and the king sat in Alreksstead over the winter.

The Tale of Helgi Thórisson (Old Icelandic)

Old Icelandic	Literal	English
Þá kemur átti dagr jóla, og um kveldið ganga þrír menn í höllina fyrir Óláf konung, þá er hann sat yfir borðum.	Then came eighth day Yule, and about evening went three men in the-hall before Olaf (name) the-king, then as he sat over the-table.	Then came the eighth day of Yule, and at about evening three men entered the hall before King Olaf, as he sat across the tables.
Þeir kveðja hann velkominn.	They greeted him well.	They greeted him well.
konungur heilsar þeim velkominn í móti.	the-King greeted them well in return.	The king greeted them well in return.
Er það kominn Helgi, en menn kenna ei hina tvá.	Then there came Helgi (name), but people knew not the two.	Then there came Helgi, but people did not know who the other two were.
konungur spurði þá að nafni, en hvárrtveggi kveðst Grímr heita.	the-King asked then the names, and each said Grim (name) was-named.	The king asked their names, and each said their name was Grim.
"Erum við sendir af Guðmundi á Glæsisvöllum hingað til yðar.	"We-are with sent of Gudmund (name) of Glasir-Plains (place) here to you.	"We have been sent by Gudmund of Glasir Plaines here to you.
Hann sendi yður kveðju sína og það með tvö horn".	He sends you greetings his and there as-well two horns".	He sends you greetings and here as well two horns".
konungur tók við, og voru gullbúin.	the-King received with, and was gold-inlaid.	The king received them, and they were inlaid with gold.
Þetta voru allgóðir gripir.	They were all-gold treasures.	They were all good treasures.
Óláfr konungur átti tvö horn, er Hyrningar voru kallaðir, og þó að þau væri harðla góð, þá voru þau þó betri, er Guðmundr sendi honum.	Olaf (name) the-king had two horns, were Hyrnings (name) were called, and though that they were greatly good, then were they though better, that Gudmund (name) sent him.	King Olaf had two horns, that were called Hyrnings, and though they were great, the ones that Gudmund had sent him were better.
"Þess beiddi Guðmundr konungur yður, herra, að þér værið vinir hans, og þótti mestu varða um yðra þykkju, meir en allra annarra konunga".	"This bids Gudmund (name) the-king to-you, lord, that to-you become friend his, and thinks most warrant about yours things, more than all other kings".	"This Gudmund asks you, lord, that you become his friend, as he values you as more important than all other kings".
konungur svaraði þá öngu, en lætur vísa þeim til sætis félögum.	the-King answered then not, but had directed them to seats company.	The king did not answer then, but directed them to the seats with company.

The Tale of Helgi Thórisson (Old Icelandic)

Old Icelandic	Literal	English
konungur lætur fylla hornin Gríma af góðum drykk og lætur byskup blessa og lét færi þeim Grímum, að þeir drykki fyrst af.	the-King had filled the-horns Grim (name) of good drink and had bishop bless and had brought them Grims (name), that they drank first of.	The king had the Grim horns filled of good drink and had a bishop bless them and bring them to the Grims, so that they drank first.
Þá kvað konungur vísu þessa:	Then spoke the-king a-verse this:	Then the king spoke this verse:
"Gestir skulu hornum í gegn taka, meðan hvílast látum þenna þegn Guðmundar, og af samnafna sínum drekki; svo skal Grímum gott öl gefast".	"The-guests shall horns to directly take, while rest have they thane Gudmund (name), and of same-name theirs drink; so shall Grims (name) good ale give".	The guests shall these horns directly take, while they have rest thane of Gudmund, of his namesake theirs drink; so shall the Grims give good ale".
Þá taka Grímar við hornunum og þykjast nú viti, hvað byskup hefir yfir lesit drykkinum.	Then took Grims (name) with the-horns and realised now certainly, what the-bishop had over read drinks.	Then the Grims took the horns and realised now with certainty, what the bishop had read over these drinks.
Þeir segja þá:	They said then:	They then said:
"ei fer nú fjarri því, sem Guðmundr, konungur vor, gat til.	"not travel now far-away because, as Gudmund (name), the-king ours, could to.	"Now do not go far from what Gudmund, our king, could do.
Er þessi konungur prettóttr og kann illa gott að launa, því að konungur vor gerði til hans sæmiliga.	Is this king deceitful and can evil good to repay, therefore the king aware be to him well-enough.	This king is deceitful and repays good with evil, therefore the king should be well enough aware.
Stöndum nú upp allir og verðum í brottu héðan".	Stand now up all and have to away hence".	Let's get up and go right now".
svo gera þeir.	so did they.	They did so.
Verður þá hark mikið í stofunni.	Became then noise much in the-room.	Then there was much noise in the room.
Þeir slógu niður drykkinum af hornunum og slökktu login.	They threw down the-drinks of the-horns and put-out lights.	The threw down the drinks from the horns and put out the lights.
Þá heyrðu þeir bresti stóra.	Then heard they crash great.	Then they heard a great crash.

The Tale of Helgi Thórisson (Old Icelandic)

Old Icelandic	Literal	English
konungur bað guð til gæta og bað menn upp standa og stöðva þetta hark.	the-King prayed God to guard and bid men up stand and stop this racket.	The king prayed to God to guard him and asked his men to stand up and stop this racket.
Síðan verða þeir Grímar úti og Helgi með þeim.	Afterwards were they The-Grims (name) outside and Helgi (name) with them.	Afterwards the Grims were outside and Helgi was with them.
voru þá ljós upp tendruð í konungs herbergi.	were then lights up lit in the-king's room.	Then the lights were lit up in the king's room.
Sjá þeir þá drepna þrjá menn, en það liggja hornin Grímar á gólfinu hjá inum dauðum.	Saw they then killed three men, and there laid horns The-Grims' (name) by the-floor beside the dead.	They then saw that three men had been killed, and the Grims' horns were on the floor beside the dead.
"Þetta er undr mikið", sagði konungur, "og væri betur, að slík yrði sjaldan.	"This is strange much", said the-king, "and should-be better, that such becomes seldom.	"This is very strange", said the king, "and it would be best if this becomes seldom.
og það hef eg heyrt sagt af Guðmundi af Glæsisvöllum, að hann sé mjög fjölkunnigr og illu megi helst við hann skipta, og eru þeir menn illa komnir, er undir hans valdi eru, ef vér mættum nokkut að gera".	and that have I heard said of Gudmund (name) of Glasir-Plains (place), that he is a-great skilled-in-magic and evil may keep with him divide, and they-are the people evil comes, who under his control are, if we may anything to do".	And I have heard said of Gudmund of Glasir Plains, that he is greatly skilled in magic and his evil keeps dividing, and the people under his control are evil, even if anything may be done about it".
konungur lét varðveita hornin Gríma og af drekka, og dugir það velkominn.	the-king had preserved the-horns Grims' (name) and of drank, and enough it-was well.	The king had the Grim horns preserved and drank from them, and all was well enough.
það er nú kallat Grímaskarð ofan að Alreksstöðum, er þeir hafi austan farið, og er það engra manna að fara það síðan.	there is now called Grim-Pass (place) over at Alreksstead (place), where they had east travelled, and is that no people to travel there since.	There is a mountain pass called Grim Pass over at Alreksstead where they travelled east, and no people have travelled there since.

3

Nú líður af veturinn, og kemur annar átti dagr jóla, og er konungur í kirkju og hirð hans að hlýða messu.	Now passed of winter, and came another eighth day Yule, and was the-king in church and retainers his at attending mass.	Now it passed to winter, and another eighth day of Yule, and the king was in church with his retainers attending mass.

The Tale of Helgi Thórisson (Old Icelandic)

Old Icelandic	Literal	English
Þá koma það þrír menn til kirkjudyra, og er einn eptir, en tveir fara í brott og mæla þetta áður:	Then came there three men to church-door, and was one after, but two travelled to away and spoke this before:	Then there came three men to the church door, one of they stayed behind, but two travelled away and said before they went:
"Hér færum við þér Gretti, konungur, og er ei víst, nær þú færir af þér".	"Here travelled with to-you Gretti (name), king, and that not certain, when you bring out-of you-to".	"Here we bring to you Gretti, king, and it is not certain how you will be able to get rid of him".
Kenna menn það Helga.	Knew people there Helgi (name).	People came to know that it was Helgi.
Síðan gengur konungur til borða, og er menn tala við Helga, verða menn þess varir, að hann er blindr.	Afterwards went the-king to the-table, and as people spoke with Helgi (name), became people this aware, that he was blind.	Afterwards the king went to the tables, and as people spoke with Helgi, the became aware, that he was blind.
Frétti konungur þá, hverju gegndi um hans hag eða hvar hann hefðu verið þessa stund alla.	Inquired the-king then, each reason about his circumstances and where he had been this time all.	The king then inquired about each of the reasons of his circumstances and where he had been all this time.
Hann svarar þá konungi fyrst frá því, er hann fann konurnar í skóginum, þá frá því, er þeir Grímar gerðu veðrit að þeim bræðrum, er þeir vildu bjarga skipinu, og síðan höfðu þeir Grímar hann með sért til Guðmundar á Glæsisvöllum og færðu hann Ingibjörgu, dóttur Guðmundar.	He told then the-king first from accordingly, and he found women in the-forest, then from accordingly, that they The-Grims (name) made a-storm that they the-brothers, and they wished to-save the-ship, and afterwards had they The-Grims (name) him along himself to Gudmund (name) of Glasir-Plains (place) and travelled he Ingibjorg (name), daughter-of Gudmund (name).	He told the king accordingly from the beginning, how he found the women in the forest, that the Grims who were brothers had made a storm come upon the brothers, and how they wishes to save their ship, and afterwards how they took him to Gudmund of Glasir Plains and delivered him to Ingibjorg, daughter of Gudmund.
Þá mælti konungur:	Then spoke the-king:	Then the king spoke:
"Hversu þótti þér það að vera?"	"How-so thought you there to be?"	"How did you find it there?",
"Allgott", svarar hann, "og hvergi hefir mér betra þótt".	"All-good", said he, "and nowhere have I better thought".	"All good", said he, "and nowhere have I thought better".
Þá spurði konungur að um siðu Guðmundar konungs og að fjölmenni eða athöfn.	Then asked the-king that about customs Gudmund (name) the-king and to followers or deeds.	Then the king asked about the customs of Gudmund and his followers and their deeds.

The Tale of Helgi Thórisson (Old Icelandic)

Old Icelandic	Literal	English
En hann lét yfir öllu velkominn og sagði, að hans var miklu fleiri en hann fengi talit.	Then he had over all well and said, that he was much more than he got counted.	Then he had said well about all, and that there was more than he could count to tell them.
konungur mælti:	the-king spoke:	The king spoke:
"Hví fóru þér svo skjótliga í brott í fyrra vetur?"	"Why travelled you so shortly to away the first winter?"	"Why did you travel away so quickly the first winter?",
"Guðmundr konungur sendi þá til að svíkja yður", svarar hann, "en fyrir bænir yðrar lét hann mig lausan, svo að þér mættið viti, hvað er af mér væri orðið.	"Gudmund (name) the-king sent them to of fool you", said he, "but for prayers yours had he me released, so that you may know, what was of me was become.	"King Gudmund sent them to fool you", he said, "but for your prayers he had me released, so that you may know what had become of me.
En því fóru vér svo skjótt í brott næstunni, að þeir Grímar höfðu ei náttúru til að drekka þann drykk, er þér létuð signa.	But because travelled we so shortly to away the-last-time, that they The-Grims (name) had not the-nature to of drink the drink, which you had signed.	But because we travelled so quickly away the last time, the Grims did not have the nature to drink the drink that you had signed.
Urðu þeir þessu reiðir, að þeir sá sig yfirstigna, og því drápu þeir menn yðra, að svo sagði Guðmundr konungur fyrir, ef þeir fengi eigi mein yður gert.	Became they this angry, that they saw themselves surpassed, and therefore killed they people yours, that so told Gudmund (name) the-king before, if they got not harm yours done.	They became angry that you had surpassed them, and therefore they killed your people, because King Gudmund told them to do so, if they could not do harm to you.
En hann sýndi tign sína í því, að hann sendi yður hornin, að þér mundið þá síður eptir mér leita".	But he showed prestige his in because, that he sent you the-horns, that you remember then less afterwards me seeking".	But he showed his prestige in sending you the horns, so that you would remember less about seeking me".
konungur spurði:	the-king asked:	The king asked:
"Hví fórtu nú í brott öðru sinni?"	"Why travelled now to away the-other with?"	"Why did you go away this time?",
Hann svaraði:	He answered:	he answered:
"Ingibjörg olli því.	"Ingibjorg (name) caused therefore.	"Because of Ingibjorg.

The Tale of Helgi Thórisson (Old Icelandic)

Old Icelandic	Literal	English
Hún þóttist ei mega liggja hjá mér nema með meinlætum, ef hún kæmi við mig beran, og því fór eg mest í brott, enda vildi Guðmundr konungur eigi þreyta við yður, þegar hann vissi, að þér vilduð mig í brott hafi.	She thought not may lay beside me without with malignance, if she came with me bare, and because-of travelled I most to away, and wished Gudmund (name) the-king not tired with you, as-soon-as he knew, that you willed me to away at-sea.	She thought that she may no longer lay beside me without feeling uneasy whenever she came into contact with me bare, and for that reason most I travelled away, and King Gudmund did not wise to be tired of you, as soon as he knew that you willed me to go away to sea.
En um tign og risnu Guðmundar konungs má eg ei í fám orðum segja og um fjölmenni það, er með honum er".	But about prestige and hospitality Gudmund (name) the-king may I only of few words to-say and about followers that, are with him are".	But about the prestige and hospitality of King Gudmund I have little words to say about it or the followers that are with him there".
konungur spurði:	the-king asked:	The king asked:
"Hví ertu blindr?"	"Why are-you blind?"	"Why are you blind?"
Hann svaraði:	He answered:	He answered:
"Ingibjörg Guðmundardóttir greip úr mér bæði augun, þá er við skildum, og sagði, að konur í Noregi mundu mín skamma stund njóta".	"Ingibjorg (name) Daughter-of-Gudmund (name) gripped from me both eyes, then when we separated, and said, that women in Norway (place) would my short while enjoy".	"Ingibjorg, daughter of Gudmund, gripped both my eyes from me, and then when we separated, she said that women in Norway would enjoy my company for a short while".
konungur sagði:	the-king said:	The king said:
"Makligr væri Guðmundr meingerða af mér fyrir þau manndráp, er hann gerði, ef guð vildi það vera láta".	"Properly would-be Gudmund (name) harmed of me for those murders, that he did, if God would that be allowed".	"Gudmund would be properly harmed by me for those murders that he did, if God would allow it".
Síðan var sent eptir Þóri, föður Helga, og þakkaði hann honum velkominn, er sonur hans var aptr kominn úr trölla höndum.	Afterwards was sent after Thori (name), father Helga's (name), and thanked he him well, that son his was returned come from monsters hands.	Afterwards Helgi's father Thorri was sent for and he thanked him well that his son was returned from the hands of such monsters.
fer hann síðan heim, en Helgi er eptir með konungi og lifir til annarrar jafnlengdar.	travelled he then home, but Helgi (name) was after with the-king and lived until another equal-length.	He then travelled home, but Helgi was thereafter with the king and lived another year.

The Tale of Helgi Thórisson (Old Icelandic)

Old Icelandic	Literal	English
En konungur hefir hornin Gríma með sért, þá er hann fór síðasta sinn úr landi.	Then the-king had the-horns Grims' (name) with him, then when he travelled last his out-of land.	Then the king had the Grim horns with him, when he travelled last out of the land.
En það segja menn, þá er Óláfr konungur hvarf af Orminum langa, að hyrfi og hornin og hafi engi maður þau séð síðan.	Is it said people, then that Olaf (name) the-king disappeared from Serpent long, that disappeared also the-horns and has no man them seen since.	It is said by people, that then King Olaf disappeared from The Long Serpent, and that the horns also disappeared and no man has seen them since.
og lýkr hér frá Grímum að segja.	and concludes here from The-Grims (name) to say.	And here concludes what may be said about the Grims.

Word List (Old Icelandic to English)

Word List (Old Icelandic to English)

Old Icelandic	English	*Old Icelandic*	English
		bæði	both
		bænir	prayers
		bær	farm

A, a

Old Icelandic	English
að	at, in, of, that, the, to
aðrar	others
af	from, of, out-of
aflat	surplus
alla	all
allar	all
allgóðir	all-gold
allgóður	all-good
Allgott	all-good
allir	all
Allr	all
allra	all
allt	all
Alreksstöðum	Alreksstead (place)
annar	another, one
annarra	other
annarrar	another
annat	another
aptni	after
aptr	returned
atburð	events
athöfn	deeds
augun	eyes
austan	east

Á, á

á	about, an, and, by, in, it, of, on, out, so, to
áður	before
áliðnu	late
ár	year
átti	eighth, had

B, b

bað	bid, prayed
báðir	both
bæ	a-farm
bæði	both
bænir	prayers
bær	farm
baki	horseback
bar	surpassed
báru	bore
beiddi	asked, bids
beran	bare
betra	better
betri	better
betur	better
biður	asked
bjarga	to-save
bjart	bright
bjó	settled
blessa	bless
blindr	blind
borð	a-table, tables
borða	the-table
borðum	the-table
bræðrum	the-brothers
bræður	brothers
brest	a-crash
bresti	crash
bróðir	brother
bróður	brother
brott	away
brottu	away
búa	prepared
búin	prepared
búizt	prepared
búnar	prepared
burt	away
byskup	bishop, the-bishop
býsna	extreme

D, d

dag	a-day
dagr	day
dauðum	dead
dimma	darkness
dóttir	daughter, daughter-of

Word List (Old Icelandic to English)

Old Icelandic	English
dóttur	daughter-of
drápu	killed
drekahálsinum	the-dragon's-neck
drekahöfuð	dragon's-head
drekka	drank, drink
drekki	drink
drepna	killed
drykk	drink
drykki	drank
drykkinum	drinks, the-drinks
drykkr	drink
dugir	enough
dvaldist	dwelled

E, e

eða	and, or
ef	if
eg	I
ei	not, only
eigi	not
Ein	one
eina	one
einn	alone, one
einu	one
eitt	one
en	and, but, is, than, that, then, was
enda	and
engi	no
engra	no
engum	none
Eptir	after, afterwards
er	am, and, are, as, is, that, then, was, were, when, where, which, who
ertu	are-you
eru	are, there-are, they-are
Erum	we-are

F, f

Old Icelandic	English
Faðir	father
fæðsla	feast
færðu	travelled
færi	brought
færir	bring
færum	travelled
Fagna	welcomed
fagrt	fair
fám	few
fann	found
fara	travel, travelled
farið	travelled
fast	fastened
fé	wealth
Fellr	fell
félögum	company
fengi	got
Fengu	got
fer	travel, travelled
Finna	Sámi (name)
Finnmerkr	Finnmark (place)
fjár	wealth
fjarri	far-away
fjölkunnigr	skilled-in-magic
fjölmenni	followers
fleiri	more
flesk	bacon
föður	father
fór	travelled
fórtu	travelled
fóru	travelled
frá	from
frændum	kinsman
fram	from, from
framar	above
Frétti	inquired
fríður	beautiful
fullr	full
fund	meet
fylla	filled
fyrir	before, for
fyrra	first
fyrst	first

G, g

Word List (Old Icelandic to English)

Old Icelandic	English
gæta	guard
gaf	gave
gakk	come
ganga	went
gat	could
gefast	give
gefi	to-give
gegn	directly
gegndi	reason
gengið	going
gengu	going, went
gengur	went
gera	did, do, done
gerði	be, did
gerðu	did, made
gerir	did
gert	done
gervar	fashioned
Gestir	the-guests
Glæsisvöllum	Glasir-Plains (place)
glóaði	shone
góð	good
góða	good
góðum	good
gólfinu	the-floor
gott	good
gras	graze
greip	gripped
Gretti	Gretti (name)
Gríma	Grim (name), Grims' (name)
Grímar	Grims (name), the-Grims (name), the-Grims' (name)
Grímaskarð	Grim-Pass (place)
Grímr	Grim (name)
Grímum	Grims (name), the-Grims (name)
gripir	treasures
guð	God
Guðmundar	Gudmund (name)
Guðmundardóttir	daughter-of-Gudmund (name)
Guðmundi	Gudmund (name)
Guðmundr	Gudmund (name)
gull	gold
gullbúin	gold-inlaid
gulli	gold
gullknappr	golden-ball
gullskotit	gold-laid

H, h

Old Icelandic	English
hafði	had
hafi	at-sea, had, has
hag	circumstances
Halda	held
hana	her
handlaugar	hand-washing
Hann	he, him
hans	he, him, his
harðla	greatly
hark	noise, racket
héðan	hence
hef	have
hefðu	had
hefir	had, have
heilsar	greeted
heim	home
heita	was-named
heiti	am-named
heitir	named
heldu	busy
heldur	rather
Helga	Helga's (name), Helgi (name)
Helgi	Helgi (name)
helst	keep
henni	her
hér	here
herbergi	room
herra	lord
hersir	a-local-chief
hestanna	horses
Hestar	horses
hestum	horses
hét	named, was-named
heyra	heard
heyrðu	heard
heyrt	heard

Word List (Old Icelandic to English)

Old Icelandic	English
hina	the
hingað	here
hirð	retainers
hittir	found
hjá	beside
hlýða	attending
höfðu	had
höfuðin	heads
höllina	the-hall
höndum	hands
honum	he, him, to-him
horfði	looked
horn	horns
hornin	horns, the-horns
hornum	horns
hornunum	the-horns
hugr	thought
Hún	she
hvað	what
hvaðan	from-where
hvar	were, what, where
hvarf	disappeared
hvárrtveggi	each
hver	any
hvergi	nowhere
hverju	each
Hversu	how-so
Hví	why
hvílast	rest
hvílur	beds
hvort	either
hyrfi	disappeared
Hyrningar	Hyrnings (name)

I, i

Old Icelandic	English
illa	evil
illu	evil
Ingibjörg	Ingibjorg (name)
Ingibjörgu	Ingibjorg (name)
inni	the
inum	the

Í, í

Old Icelandic	English
í	in, of, the, to
íþróttir	sports

J, j

Old Icelandic	English
jafnlengdar	equal-length
jól	Yule
jóla	Yule

K, k

Old Icelandic	English
kæmi	came
kallaðir	called
kallat	called
kann	can
kastar	cast
kaupferð	trade, trading-voyage
kaups	trade
kemur	came
kenna	knew
ker	vessels
kirkju	church
kirkjudyra	church-door
kistlar	chests
kistlunum	chests
klæðast	clothed
kom	came
koma	came
komið	came
kominn	become, came, come
komnir	comes
kómu	came
kona	the-woman
konar	kinds-of
konu	woman
konung	the-king
konunga	kings
konungi	the-king
konungs	the-king, the-king's
konungur	king, the-King
konur	women
konurnar	women
krásir	food

Word List (Old Icelandic to English)

Old Icelandic	English
kvað	spoke
kveðja	greeted
kveðju	greetings
kveðst	said
kveldið	evening

L, l

Old Icelandic	English
læsti	locked
lætur	had
land	land
landi	land
landtjaldinu	land-tent
langa	long
láta	allowed
látit	made
látum	have
laugat	bathed
launa	repay
lausan	released
leita	seeking
lengra	longer
lesit	read
lét	had
létuð	had
líður	passed, passes
lifir	lived
liggja	laid, lay, to-lay
litum	colours
ljós	lights
login	lights
lýkr	concludes

M, m

Old Icelandic	English
má	may
maður	a-man, man
mæla	spoke
mælti	spoke
mættið	may
mættum	may
Makligr	properly
manna	people, peoples
manndráp	murders
manni	person
margs	many
mat	food
með	along, as-well, with
meðan	while
mega	may
megi	may
mein	harm
meingerða	harmed
meinlætum	malignance
meir	more
menn	men, people
mér	I, me
messu	mass
mest	most
mestu	most
mig	me
mikið	much
mikil	much
mikill	large
mikils	much
mikinn	great
miklu	great, much
mín	my
mjög	a-great
mönnum	people
mösurtré	maple-tree
móti	return
mundi	should
mundið	remember
mundu	would
munnlaugar	mouth-basins
munum	shall
myrkri	darkness

N, n

Old Icelandic	English
nær	when
nærri	near
næstunni	the-last-time
nætr	nights
nafnbót	rank
nafni	name, names
náttúru	the-nature
nema	without

Word List (Old Icelandic to English)

Old Icelandic	English
nes	headland
niður	down, son
njóta	enjoy
nokkurt	some
nokkut	anything
norður	north
Noregi	Norway (place)
nótt	night
nú	now
nyt	use

O, o

Old Icelandic	English
ofan	above, down, over
og	also, and
okkart	ours
olli	caused
orðið	become
orðum	words
Orminum	serpent
oss	us

Ó, ó

Old Icelandic	English
Óláf	Olaf (name)
Óláfr	Olaf (name)
Óláfs	Olaf (name)
óvíst	uncertain

Ö, ö

Old Icelandic	English
öðru	the-other
öðrum	other
öl	ale
öll	all
öllu	all
öllum	all
öngu	not
önnur	also

P, p

Old Icelandic	English
prettóttr	deceitful

R, r

Old Icelandic	English
Rauðabergi	Raudaberg (place)
rauðum	red
reiðingr	riding
reiðir	angry
reiðklæðum	riding-clothes
reistu	raised
ríða	riders, riding, rode
risnu	hospitality

S, s

Old Icelandic	English
sá	saw
sæmiliga	well-enough
sængr	beds
sætis	seats
sagði	said, told
sagt	said
sama	the-same
saman	together
samnafna	same-name
samt	together
sat	sat
sé	is
séð	seen
seg	say
segist	said
segja	said, say, to-say
sem	as, that-which
sendi	sends, sent
sendir	sent
sent	sent
sért	him, himself, saw, them
settu	set
Síðan	after, afterwards, since, then
síðasta	last
siðu	customs
síður	less
sig	themselves

Word List (Old Icelandic to English)

Old Icelandic	English
signa	signed
silfri	silver
sína	his
sinn	his
sinni	with
síns	his, theirs
sínum	his, theirs
situr	sat
Sjá	saw
sjaldan	seldom
sjó	the-sea
skal	shall
skamma	short
skammt	short-distance
skildum	separated
skilja	separate
skip	ship
skipinu	the-ship
skips	ships
skipsins	ship
skipta	divide
skjótliga	shortly
skjótt	away, quickly, shortly
skóginn	the-forest
skóginum	the-forest
skógr	forests
sköruligu	bold-like
skrautligri	splendid
skulu	shall
skulum	should
slík	such
slógu	threw
slökktu	put-out
smjör	butter
sonur	son
spurði	asked
spyr	asked
spyrja	asked
stafat	staved
stafnana	ship's-prow
standa	stand, stood
stigu	stepped
stóð	stood
stöðva	stop
stofunni	the-room
Stöndum	stand
stöngin	the-pole
stóra	great
stund	time, while
Sú	so
suður	south
sumri	summer
sumt	some
svaraði	answered
svarar	said, told
svíkja	fool
svo	so
sýndi	showed
syni	sons

T, t

Old Icelandic	English
taka	take, took
tala	spoke
talit	counted
tekin	taken
tekur	took
tendruð	lit
tíðendi	news
tign	prestige
til	to, until
tjald	tent
tjaldi	tent
tók	received
tóku	took
tólf	twelve
trölla	monsters
tvá	two
tveir	two
tvö	two

Þ, þ

Old Icelandic	English
þá	them, then
það	it, it-was, that, the, there
þær	these, they
þakkaði	thanked
þangað	from-there

Word List (Old Icelandic to English)

Old Icelandic	English
þann	the
þau	them, they, those
þegar	as-soon-as, straight-away
þegn	thane
þeim	that, them, then, they
þeir	the, they
þeirra	theirs, they
þenna	these, they
þér	to-you, you, you-to
Þess	this
þessa	this
Þessi	this
þessu	this
þetta	that, they, this
þigg	accept
þjóna	served
þó	though
Þóri	Thori (name)
Þórir	Thorir (name)
Þorsteinn	Thorstein (name)
þótt	thought
þótti	thinks, thought
þóttist	thought
þreyta	tired
þrifligir	thriving
þrír	three
þrjá	three
þrjár	three
þú	you
því	accordingly, because, because-of, therefore
þykir	thought
þykjast	realised
þykkju	things

U, u

um	about, in
undir	under
undr	strange
upp	up
Urðu	became

Ú, ú

úr	from, out-of, through
úti	outside

V, v

væn	fair
vænleik	beauty
væri	should-be, was, were, would-be
værið	become
valdi	control
var	was, were
varða	warrant
varðveita	preserved
varir	aware
vatnskarl	basins
veðrit	a-storm, weather
veður	weather
veg	way
Veit	knew
velkominn	well
vér	we
vera	be
verða	became, become, to-become, were
verðum	have
Verður	became
verið	been
vetur	winter
veturinn	winter
við	to, we, with
víða	widely
Víkinni	the-bay
vil	will, wish
vildi	wished, would
vildu	wished
vilduð	willed
vilt	wished
Vímund	Vimund (name)
vináttu	friendship
vinir	friend
vísa	directed

Word List (Old Icelandic to English)

Old Icelandic	English
vissan	knowledge
vissi	knew
víst	certain
vísu	a-verse
viti	certainly, know
vor	aware, ours
voru	was, were

Y, y

yðar	you
yðra	yours
yðrar	yours
yður	to-you, you, yours
yfir	over
yfirstigna	surpassed
yrði	becomes

Ý, ý

ýmsum	various

Word List (English to Old Icelandic)

Word List (English to Old Icelandic)

English	Old Icelandic

A, a

English	Old Icelandic
about	á, um
above	framar, ofan
accept	þigg
accordingly	því
a-crash	brest
a-day	dag
a-farm	bæ
after	aptni, Eptir, Síðan
afterwards	eptir, Síðan
a-great	mjög
ale	öl
all	alla, allar, allir, Allr, allra, allt, öll, öllu, öllum
all-gold	allgóðir
all-good	allgóður, Allgott
allowed	láta
a-local-chief	hersir
alone	einn
along	með
Alreksstead (place)	Alreksstöðum
also	og, önnur
am	er
a-man	maður
am-named	heiti
an	á
and	á, eða, en, enda, er, og
angry	reiðir
another	annar, annarrar, annat
answered	svaraði
any	hver
anything	nokkut
are	er, eru
are-you	ertu
as	er, sem
asked	beiddi, biður, spurði, spyr, spyrja
as-soon-as	þegar
a-storm	veðrit
as-well	með
at	að
a-table	borð
at-sea	hafi
attending	hlýða
a-verse	vísu
aware	varir, vor
away	brott, brottu, burt, skjótt

B, b

English	Old Icelandic
bacon	flesk
bare	beran
basins	vatnskarl
bathed	laugat
be	gerði, vera
beautiful	fríður
beauty	vænleik
became	Urðu, verða, Verður
because	því
because-of	því
become	kominn, orðið, værið, verða
becomes	yrði
beds	hvílur, sængr
been	verið
before	áður, fyrir
beside	hjá
better	betra, betri, betur
bid	bað
bids	beiddi
bishop	byskup
bless	blessa
blind	blindr
bold-like	sköruligu
bore	báru
both	báðir, bæði
bright	bjart
bring	færir
brother	bróðir, bróður
brothers	bræður
brought	færi
busy	heldu

Word List (English to Old Icelandic)

English	Old Icelandic
but	en
butter	smjör
by	á

C, c

English	Old Icelandic
called	kallaðir, kallat
came	kæmi, kemur, kom, koma, komið, kominn, kómu
can	kann
cast	kastar
caused	olli
certain	víst
certainly	viti
chests	kistlar, kistlunum
church	kirkju
church-door	kirkjudyra
circumstances	hag
clothed	klæðast
colours	litum
come	gakk, kominn
comes	komnir
company	félögum
concludes	lýkr
control	valdi
could	gat
counted	talit
crash	bresti
customs	siðu

D, d

English	Old Icelandic
darkness	dimma, myrkri
daughter	dóttir
daughter-of	dóttir, dóttur
daughter-of-Gudmund (name)	Guðmundardóttir
day	dagr
dead	dauðum
deceitful	prettóttr
deeds	athöfn
did	gera, gerði, gerðu, gerir
directed	vísa
directly	gegn
disappeared	hvarf, hyrfi
divide	skipta
do	gera
done	gera, gert
down	niður, ofan
dragon's-head	drekahöfuð
drank	drekka, drykki
drink	drekka, drekki, drykk, drykkr
drinks	drykkinum
dwelled	dvaldist

E, e

English	Old Icelandic
each	hvárrtveggi, hverju
east	austan
eighth	átti
either	hvort
enjoy	njóta
enough	dugir
equal-length	jafnlengdar
evening	kveldið
events	atburð
evil	illa, illu
extreme	býsna
eyes	augun

F, f

English	Old Icelandic
fair	fagrt, væn
far-away	fjarri
farm	bær
fashioned	gervar
fastened	fast
father	Faðir, föður
feast	fæðsla
fell	Fellr
few	fám
filled	fylla
Finnmark (place)	Finnmerkr
first	fyrra, fyrst
followers	fjölmenni

Word List (English to Old Icelandic)

English	Old Icelandic
food	krásir, mat
fool	svíkja
for	fyrir
forests	skógr
found	fann, hittir
friend	vinir
friendship	vináttu
from	af, frá, fram, fram, úr
from-there	þangað
from-where	hvaðan
full	fullr

G, g

English	Old Icelandic
gave	gaf
give	gefast
Glasir-Plains (place)	Glæsisvöllum
God	guð
going	gengið, gengu
gold	gull, gulli
golden-ball	gullknappr
gold-inlaid	gullbúin
gold-laid	gullskotit
good	góð, góða, góðum, gott
got	fengi, Fengu
graze	gras
great	mikinn, miklu, stóra
greatly	harðla
greeted	heilsar, kveðja
greetings	kveðju
Gretti (name)	Gretti
Grim (name)	Gríma, Grímr
Grim-Pass (place)	Grímaskarð
Grims (name)	Grímar, Grímum
Grims' (name)	Gríma
gripped	greip
guard	gæta
Gudmund (name)	Guðmundar, Guðmundi, Guðmundr

H, h

English	Old Icelandic
had	átti, hafði, hafi, hefðu, hefir, höfðu, lætur, lét, létuð
hands	höndum
hand-washing	handlaugar
harm	mein
harmed	meingerða
has	hafi
have	hef, hefir, látum, verðum
he	Hann, hans, honum
headland	nes
heads	höfuðin
heard	heyra, heyrðu, heyrt
held	Halda
Helga's (name)	Helga
Helgi (name)	Helga, Helgi
hence	héðan
her	hana, henni
here	hér, hingað
him	hann, hans, honum, sért
himself	sért
his	hans, sína, sinn, síns, sínum
home	heim
horns	horn, hornin, hornum
horseback	baki
horses	hestanna, Hestar, hestum
hospitality	risnu
how-so	Hversu
Hyrnings (name)	Hyrningar

I, i

English	Old Icelandic
I	eg, mér
if	ef
in	á, að, í, um
Ingibjorg (name)	Ingibjörg, Ingibjörgu
inquired	Frétti
is	En, er, sé
it	á, það
it-was	það

Word List (English to Old Icelandic)

English	Old Icelandic

K, k

English	Old Icelandic
keep	helst
killed	drápu, drepna
kinds-of	konar
king	konungur
kings	konunga
kinsman	frændum
knew	kenna, Veit, vissi
know	viti
knowledge	vissan

L, l

English	Old Icelandic
laid	liggja
land	land, landi
land-tent	landtjaldinu
large	mikill
last	síðasta
late	áliðnu
lay	liggja
less	síður
lights	ljós, login
lit	tendruð
lived	lifir
locked	læsti
long	langa
longer	lengra
looked	horfði
lord	herra

M, m

English	Old Icelandic
made	gerðu, látit
malignance	meinlætum
man	maður
many	margs
maple-tree	mösurtré
mass	messu
may	má, mættið, mættum, mega, megi
me	mér, mig
meet	fund
men	menn
monsters	trölla
more	fleiri, meir
most	mest, mestu
mouth-basins	munnlaugar
much	mikið, mikil, mikils, miklu
murders	manndráp
my	mín

N, n

English	Old Icelandic
name	nafni
named	heitir, hét
names	nafni
near	nærri
news	tíðendi
night	nótt
nights	nætr
no	engi, engra
noise	hark
none	engum
north	norður
Norway (place)	Noregi
not	ei, eigi, öngu
now	nú
nowhere	hvergi

O, o

English	Old Icelandic
of	á, að, af, í
Olaf (name)	Óláf, Óláfr, Óláfs
on	á
one	annar, Ein, eina, einn, einu, eitt
only	ei
or	eða
other	annarra, öðrum
others	aðrar
ours	okkart, vor
out	á
out-of	af, úr
outside	úti
over	ofan, yfir

Word List (English to Old Icelandic)

English	Old Icelandic
P, p	
passed	líður
passes	líður
people	manna, menn, mönnum
peoples	manna
person	manni
prayed	bað
prayers	bænir
prepared	búa, búin, búizt, búnar
preserved	varðveita
prestige	tign
properly	Makligr
put-out	slökktu
Q, q	
quickly	skjótt
R, r	
racket	hark
raised	reistu
rank	nafnbót
rather	heldur
Raudaberg (place)	Rauðabergi
read	lesit
realised	þykjast
reason	gegndi
received	tók
red	rauðum
released	lausan
remember	mundið
repay	launa
rest	hvílast
retainers	hirð
return	móti
returned	aptr
riders	ríða
riding	reiðingr, ríða
riding-clothes	reiðklæðum
rode	ríða
room	herbergi
S, s	
said	kveðst, sagði, sagt, segist, segja, svarar
same-name	samnafna
Sámi (name)	Finna
sat	sat, situr
saw	sá, sért, Sjá
say	seg, segja
seats	sætis
seeking	leita
seen	séð
seldom	sjaldan
sends	sendi
sent	sendi, sendir, sent
separate	skilja
separated	skildum
serpent	Orminum
served	þjóna
set	settu
settled	bjó
shall	munum, skal, skulu
she	Hún
ship	skip, skipsins
ships	skips
ship's-prow	stafnana
shone	glóaði
short	skamma
short-distance	skammt
shortly	skjótliga, skjótt
should	mundi, skulum
should-be	væri
showed	sýndi
signed	signa
silver	silfri
since	síðan
skilled-in-magic	fjölkunnigr
so	á, Sú, svo
some	nokkurt, sumt
son	niður, sonur
sons	syni

Word List (English to Old Icelandic)

English	Old Icelandic
south	suður
splendid	skrautligri
spoke	kvað, mæla, mælti, tala
sports	íþróttir
stand	standa, Stöndum
staved	stafat
stepped	stigu
stood	standa, stóð
stop	stöðva
straight-away	þegar
strange	undr
such	slík
summer	sumri
surpassed	bar, yfirstigna
surplus	aflat

T, t

English	Old Icelandic
tables	borð
take	taka
taken	tekin
tent	tjald, tjaldi
than	en
thane	þegn
thanked	þakkaði
that	að, en, er, það, þeim, þetta
that-which	sem
the	að, hina, í, inni, inum, það, þann, þeir
the-bay	Víkinni
the-bishop	byskup
the-brothers	bræðrum
the-dragon's-neck	drekahálsinum
the-drinks	drykkinum
the-floor	gólfinu
the-forest	skóginn, skóginum
the-Grims (name)	Grímar, Grímum
the-Grims' (name)	Grímar
the-guests	Gestir
the-hall	höllina
the-horns	hornin, hornunum
theirs	síns, sínum, þeirra
the-king	konung, konungi, konungs, konungur
the-king's	konungs
the-last-time	næstunni
them	sért, þá, þau, þeim
themselves	sig
then	En, Er, Síðan, Þá, þeim
the-nature	náttúru
the-other	öðru
the-pole	stöngin
there	það
there-are	Eru
therefore	því
the-room	stofunni
the-same	sama
these	þær, þenna
the-sea	sjó
the-ship	skipinu
the-table	borða, borðum
the-woman	kona
they	Þær, þau, þeim, þeir, þeirra, þenna, Þetta
they-are	eru
things	þykkju
thinks	þótti
this	Þess, þessa, Þessi, þessu, þetta
Thori (name)	Þóri
Thorir (name)	Þórir
Thorstein (name)	Þorsteinn
those	þau
though	þó
thought	hugr, þótt, þótti, þóttist, þykir
three	þrír, þrjá, þrjár
threw	slógu
thriving	þrifligir
through	úr
time	stund
tired	þreyta
to	á, að, í, til, við
to-become	verða
together	saman, samt
to-give	gefi
to-him	honum

Word List (English to Old Icelandic)

English	Old Icelandic	English	Old Icelandic
to-lay	liggja	well-enough	sæmiliga
told	sagði, svarar	went	ganga, Gengu, gengur
took	taka, tekur, tóku	were	er, hvar, væri, var, verða, voru
to-save	bjarga	what	hvað, hvar
to-say	segja	when	er, nær
to-you	þér, yður	where	er, hvar
trade	kaupferð, kaups	which	er
trading-voyage	kaupferð	while	meðan, stund
travel	fara, fer	who	er
travelled	færðu, færum, fara, farið, fer, fór, fórtu, fóru	why	Hví
treasures	gripir	widely	víða
twelve	tólf	will	vil
two	tvá, tveir, tvö	willed	vilduð
		winter	vetur, veturinn
		wish	vil
		wished	vildi, vildu, vilt
		with	með, sinni, við
		without	nema
		woman	konu
		women	konur, konurnar
		words	orðum
		would	mundu, vildi
		would-be	væri

U, u

English	Old Icelandic
uncertain	óvíst
under	undir
until	til
up	upp
us	oss
use	nyt

V, v

various	ýmsum	year	ár
vessels	ker	you	þér, þú, yðar, yður
Vimund (name)	Vímund	yours	yðra, yðrar, yður
		you-to	þér
		Yule	jól, jóla

Y, y

W, w

English	Old Icelandic
warrant	varða
was	en, er, væri, var, voru
was-named	heita, hét
way	veg
we	vér, við
wealth	fé, fjár
we-are	Erum
weather	veðrit, veður
welcomed	Fagna
well	velkominn

A Word Comparison of Old Norse and Old Icelandic Words

A Word Comparison of Old Norse and Old Icelandic Words

Old Norse	Old Icelandic	English	Old Norse	Old Icelandic	English
áðr	áður	before	líðr	líður	passed
allgóðr	allgóður	all-good	líðr	líður	passes
annarr	annar	another	maðr	maður	a-man
annarr	annar	one	maðr	maður	man
at	að	at	mik	mig	me
at	að	in	mikit	mikið	much
at	að	of	mjök	mjög	a-great
at	að	that	niðr	niður	down
at	að	the	niðr	niður	son
at	að	to	norðr	norður	north
betr	betur	better	ok	og	also
biðr	biður	asked	ok	og	and
bræðr	bræður	brothers	ór	úr	from
eigi	ei	not	ór	úr	out-of
eigi	ei	only	ór	úr	through
ek	eg	I	orðit	orðið	become
ekki	eigi	not	segir	svarar	said
engu	öngu	not	segir	svarar	told
færa	færi	brought	sér	sért	him
farit	farið	travelled	sér	sért	himself
ferr	fer	travel	sér	sért	saw
Ferr	fer	travelled	sér	sért	them
fríðr	fríður	beautiful	sét	séð	seen
gefa	gefi	to-give	síðr	síður	less
gengit	gengið	going	sik	sig	themselves
gengr	gengur	went	sitr	situr	sat
hafa	hafi	at-sea	sonr	sonur	son
hafa	hafi	had	spyrr	spyr	asked
heðan	héðan	hence	suðr	suður	south
hefði	hefðu	had	svá	svo	so
heldr	heldur	rather	svarar	svaraði	answered
helzt	helst	keep	tekr	tekur	took
hingat	hingað	here	þangat	þangað	from-there
hvárt	hvort	either	Þar	það	there
hvat	hvað	what	Þat	það	it
kemr	kemur	came	þat	það	it-was
komit	komið	came	þat	það	that
konungr	konungur	king	þat	það	the
Konungr	konungur	the-King	þeira	þeirra	theirs
kveldit	kveldið	evening	þeira	þeirra	they
lætr	lætur	had	þykkir	þykir	thought

A Word Comparison of Old Norse and Old Icelandic Words

Old Norse	Old Icelandic	English
þykkjast	þykjast	realised
tvau	tvö	two
várr	vor	aware
várr	vor	ours
váru	voru	was
váru	voru	were
veðr	veður	weather
vel	velkominn	well
Verðr	Verður	became
verit	verið	been
vetr	vetur	winter
vetrinn	veturinn	winter
vill	vilt	wished
vit	við	we
vit	við	with
vita	viti	certainly
vita	viti	know
yðr	yður	to-you
yðr	yður	you
yðr	yður	yours

The Tale of Auðun of the West Fjords (Old Norse)

The Tale of Auðun of the West Fjords (*Old Norse*)

Auðunar þáttr vestfirzka, from the Morkinskinna Book (GKS[1] 1009 fol., c. 1275, Royal Danish Library in Copenhagen)

Old Norse	Literal	English
1	**1**	**1**
MAÐR hét Auðunn, vestfirzkr at kyni ok félítill.	Man named Audun, Westfjords by kin and fee-little.	There was a man named Audun, from the West Fjords by kin, and he was poor.
Hann fór útan vestr þar í fjörðum með umbráði Þorsteins, búanda góðs, ok Þóris stýrimanns, er þar hafði þegit vist of vetrinn með Þorsteini.	He travelled out west there in fields with managed Thorstein, farmer good, and Thorir skipper, who there had received hospitality over winter with Thorstein.	He travelled west to the fields which were managed by Thorstein, a good farmer, and Thorir who was a skipper, and they received hospitality from Thorstein over the winter.
Auðunn var ok þar ok starfaði fyrir honum Þóri ok þá þessi laun af honum, útanferðina ok hans umsjá.	Audun was also there and worked for him Thorir and then this reward of him, out-travelling and him about-see.	Audun was also there and worked for Thorir, and was rewarded by him with a place on his voyage, and taking care of him.
Hann Auðunn lagði mestan hluta fjár þess, er var, fyr móður sína, áðr hann stigi á skip, ok var kveðit á þriggja vetra björg.	He Audun laid most lot wealth this, that was, for mother his, after he climbed on the-ship, and was said of three winters aid.	Audun gave most of his wealth that was for his mother, once he had gone aboard the ship, and it was said to be three winters' worth of aid.
Ok nú fara þeir út heðan, ok ferst þeim vel, ok var Auðunn of vetrinn eftir með Þóri stýrimanni.	And now travelled they out hence, and travelled they well, and was Audun of winter afterwards with Thorir skipper.	And now they travelled out from there, and they travelled well, and Audun spent the winter afterwards with the skipper Thorir.
Hann átti bú á Mæri.	He had a-farm in Moer.	He had a farm in Moer.
Ok um sumarit eftir fara þeir út til Grænlands ok eru þar of vetrinn.	And about summer afterwards travelled they out to Greenland and were there of winter.	And around the summer afterwards they travelled out to Greenland and were there for the winter.
Þess er við getit, at Auðunn kaupir þar bjarndýri eitt, gersimi mikla, ok gaf þar fyrir alla eigu sína.	This is with told-of, that Audun bought there a-bear one, treasured much, and gave there for all owned his.	It is told that Audun bought a bear there, which was much treasured, and gave all that he owned for it.

The Tale of Auðun of the West Fjords (Old Norse)

Old Norse	Literal	English
Ok nú of sumarit eftir þá fara þeir aftr til Nóregs ok verða vel reiðfara.	And now of summer afterwards then travelled they returning to Norway and was well voyage.	And now about the summer afterwards then they travelled returning to Norway and the voyage went well.
Hefir Auðunn dýr sitt með sér ok ætlar nú at fara suðr til Danmerkr á fund Sveins konungs ok gefa honum dýrit.	Had Audun wild-animal his with him and intended now to travel south to Denmark to meet Svein the-king and give him the-beast.	Audun had his wild-animal with him and intended now to travel south to Denmark to meet King Svein and give him the beast.
Ok er hann kom suðr í landit, þar sem konungr var fyrir, þá gengr hann upp af skipi ok leiðir eftir sér dýrit ok leigir sér herbergi.	And as he came south to land, there as the-king was present, then went he up off the-ship and took behind him the-beast and rented himself a-room.	And as he came south to land, where the king was present, he then went up off the ship and took the beast with him and rented himself a room.
Haraldi konungi var sagt brátt, at þar var komit bjarndýri, gersimi mikil, ok á íslenzkr maðr.	Harald the-king was told soon, that there was come a-bear, treasured much, and an Icelander man.	King Harald was soon told, that a bear had come, which was much treasured, and an Icelander.
Konungr sendir þegar menn eftir honum,	The-king sent straight-away people after him,	The king sent people to fetch him straight away,
ok er Auðunn kom fyrir konung, kveðr hann konung vel.	and as Audun came before the-king, greeted he the-king well.	and when Audun came before the king, he greeted the king well.
Konungr tók vel kveðju hans ok spurði síðan:	The-king took well greeting his and asked afterwards:	The king received his greeting well and afterwards asked:
"Áttu gersimi mikla í bjarndýri?"	"Have-you treasured much a bear?"	"Do you have a bear which is much treasured?".
Hann svarar ok kveðst eiga dýrit eitthvert.	He answered and said owned a-beast some-kind.	He answered and said that he owned a beast of some kind.
Konungr mælti:	The-king spoke:	The king spoke:
"Villtu selja oss dýrit við slíku verði sem þú keyptir?"	"Will-you sell us the-beast with such worth as you bought?"	"Will you sell us the beast for the same worth as you bought it?".
Hann svarar:	He answered:	He answered:
"Eigi vil ek þat, herra?"	"Not wish I that, lord?"	"I do not wish to do that, lord".

The Tale of Auðun of the West Fjords (Old Norse)

Old Norse	Literal	English
"Villtu þá", segir konungr, "at ek gefa þér tvau verð slík, ok mun þat réttara, ef þú hefir þar við gefit alla þína eigu?"	"Will-you then", said the-king, "that I give to-you twice worth such, and should that righter, if you have there with given all you own?"	"Do you wish then", said the king, "that I give you twice the worth, and that should be right, if you have given all you own for it?".
"Eigi vil ek þat, herra", segir hann.	"Not wish I that, lord", said he.	"I do not wish to do that, lord", he said.
Konungr mælti:	The-king spoke:	The king spoke:
"Villtu gefa mér þá?"	"Will-you give me then?"	"Will you give it to me then?".
Hann svarar:	He answered:	He answered:
"Eigi, herra".	"Not lord".	"I will not, lord".
Konungr mælti:	The-king spoke:	The king spoke:
"Hvat villtu þá af gera?"	"What will-you then of do?"	"What do you wish to do then?".
Hann svarar:	He answered:	He answered:
"Fara", segir hann, "til Danmerkr ok gefa Sveini konungi".	Travel", said he, "to Denmark and give Svein the-king".	"Travel", said he, to Denmark and give it to King Svein".
Haraldr konungr segir:	Harald the-king said:	King Harald said:
"Hvárt er, at þú ert maðr svá óvitr, at þú hefir eigi heyrt ófrið þann, er í milli er landa þessa, eða ætlar þú giftu þína svá mikla, at þú munir þar komast með gersimar, er aðrir fá eigi komizt klaklaust, þó at nauðsyn eigi til?"	"Whether is, that you are a-man so unwise, that you have none heard un-peace then, that is between the land this, or suppose you gift yours so much, that you would there come with treasure, that others get none coming unhurt, though that necessary not to?"	"Is it possible, that you are an unwise man, that you have not heard of the state of war that is between these lands, or you suppose that you are so gifted that you would come there with treasure, where others have not gone unhurt though it was necessary?".
Auðunn svarar:	Audun answered:	Audun answered:
"Herra, þat er á yðru valdi, en engu játum vér öðru en þessu, er vér höfum áðr ætlat".	"Lord that is for your will, but none profess we other than this, that we have before intended".	"That is for your will lord, but I cannot agree to anything other than what I have previously intended".
Þá mælti konungr:	Then spoke the-king:	Then the king spoke:

The Tale of Auðun of the West Fjords (Old Norse)

Old Norse	Literal	English

"Hví mun eigi þat til, at þú farir leið þína, sem þú vill, ok kom þá til mín, er þú ferr aftr, ok seg mér, hversu Sveinn konungr launar þér dýrit, ok kann þat vera, at þú sér gæfumaðr".

"Why should not that to, that you travel journey yours, as you wish, and come then to me, when you travel back, and say to-me, how-so Svein the-king repays your beast, and can that be, that you yourself gifted-man".

"Then why should you not, to travel on your journey, as you wish, and then come to me, when you travel back, and tell me how King Svein repays you for the beast, and can it be, that you will be a gifted man".

"Því heit ek þér", sagði Auðunn.

"Accordingly promise I to-you", said Audun.

"I promise this to you accordingly", said Audun.

Hann ferr nú síðan suðr með landi ok í Vík austr ok þá til Danmerkr, ok er þá uppi hverr penningr fjárins, ok verðr hann þá biðja matar bæði fyr sik ok fyr dýrit.

He travelled now afterwards south along land and to Vik east and then to Denmark, and was then up every penny of-wealth, and was he then begging food both for himself and for the-beast.

He now travelled afterwards south along the land and to Vik east and then to Denmark, and then every penny of his wealth was spent, and he was then begging for food both for himself and for the beast.

Hann kemr á fund ármanns Sveins konungs, þess er Áki hét, ok bað hann vista nökkurra bæði fyr sik ok fyr dýrit,

He came to meet steward Svein's the-king, this was Aki named, and asked him provisions some asked for himself and for the-beast,

He came to meet a steward of King Svein, who was named Aki, and he asked him for some provisions for himself and for the beast,

"ek ætla", segir hann, "at gefa Sveini konungi dýrit".

"I intend", said he, "to give Svein the-king the-beast".

I intend, he said, "to give this beast to King Svein".

Áki lézt selja mundu honum vistir, ef hann vildi.

Aki said sell would him provisions, if he wished.

Aki said that he would sell him provisions if he wished.

Auðunn kveðst ekki til hafa fyrir at gefa, "en ek vilda þó", segir hann, "at þetta kæmist til leiðar, at ek mætta dýrit færa konungi".

Audun said not to have for to give, "and I wish though", said he, "that this comes to the-way, that I might the-beast bring the-king".

Audun said that he did not have anything to give, "and though I wish", he said, "that I may be able t bring this beast to the king".

"Ek mun fá þér vistir, sem þit þurfuð til konungs fundar, en þar í móti vil ek eiga hálft dýrit, ok máttu á þat líta, at dýrit mun deyja fyrir þér, þars þit þurfuð vistir miklar, en fé sé farit, ok er búit við, at þú hafir þá ekki dýrsins".

"I shall give you provisions, that you need to-the-king meet, then there on meeting will I own half the-beast, and might be that look, that the-beast could die for you, there you need provisions much, but money is gone, and is settled with, that you have then not the-beast".

"I shall give you provisions, that you need to meet the king, then on meeting him I will own half the beast, otherwise it might be, that the beast could die before you, there you will need many provisions, but your money is gone, and it shall be that you will then not have the beast".

The Tale of Auðun of the West Fjords (Old Norse)

Old Norse	Literal	English
Ok er hann lítr á þetta, sýnist honum nökkut eftir sem ármaðrinn mælti fyrir honum, ok sættast þeir á þetta, at hann selr Áka hálft dýrit, ok skal konungr síðan meta allt saman.	And when he looked a this, considered he sometime afterwards what steward spoke before him, and reconciled they to this, that he sell Aki half the-beast, and shall the-king afterwards value all the-same.	And when he looked at this, he considered for some time afterwards what the steward had said to him, and they reconciled to this, that he would sell Aki half of the beast, and the king would afterwards value it all the same.
Skulu þeir fara báðir nú á fund konungs, ok svá gera þeir, fara nú báðir á fund konungs ok stóðu fyr borðinu.	Shall they travel both now and meet the-king, and so did they, travelled now both to meet the-king and stood before table.	And should they now both travel and meet the king, and they did so, they both travelled to meet the king and stood before his tables.
Konungr íhugaði, hverr þessi maðr myndi vera, er hann kenndi eigi, ok mælti síðan til Auðunar:	The-king considered, who this man should be, that he knew not, and spoke then to Audun:	The king considered, who this man should be, that he did not know, and then spoke to Audun:
"Hverr ertu?" segir hann.	"Who are-you?" said he.	"Who are you?" he said.
Hann svarar:	He answered:	He answered:
"Ek em íslenzkr maðr, herra", segir hann, "ok kominn nú útan af Grænlandi ok nú af Nóregi, ok ætlaðak at færa yðr bjarndýr þetta.	"I am Icelander man, lord", said he, "and coming now out out-of Greenland and now from Norway, and intended to bring your bear this.	"I am an Icelander, lord", he said, "and I have come from Greenland and from Norway intending to bring you this bear.
Keyptak þat með allri eigu minni, ok nú er þó á orðit mikit fyrir mér, ek á nú hálft eitt dýrit", ok segir konungi síðan, hversu farit hafði með þeim Áka, ármanni hans.	Purchased that with all own mine, and now is though that become much for me, I of not half one beast", and told the-king then, how-so fared had with them Aki, the-steward his.	I purchased it with all that I own, and now though it has become much for me, I do not own half of the beast", and he then told the king, how it had gone with Aki, his steward.
Konungr mælti:	The-king spoke:	The king spoke:
"Er þat satt, Áki, er hann segir?"	"Is that true, Aki, what he says?"	"Is that true, Aki, what he says?".
"Satt er þat", segir hann.	"True is that", said he.	"That is true", he said.
Konungr mælti:	The-king spoke:	The king spoke:

The Tale of Auðun of the West Fjords (Old Norse)

Old Norse	Literal	English
"Ok þótti þér þat til liggja, þar sem ek settak þik mikinn mann, at hefta þat eða tálma, er maðr gerðist til at færa mér gersimi ok gaf fyrir alla eign ok sá þat Haraldr konungr at ráði at láta hann fara í friði, ok er hann várr óvinr?	"And thought you that to lay-out, then since I intended you a-great man, to stop that or prevent, as a-man did to that bring to-me treasure and gave because all owned and so that Harald the-king that decided to let him travel in peace, and that he our un-friend	"And you thought to let this happen, even though I intended you to be a great man, to stop or prevent, as a man made to bring this treasure and give to me all that he owned, and even though King Harald decided to let him travel in peace, even though he is our enemy?
Hygg þú at þá, hvé sannligt þat var þinnar handar, ok þat væri makligt, at þú værir drepinn.	Think you that then, how true-like that was your hand, and that should-be proper, that you would-be killed.	Think then how true your hand was, and it would be right, that you should be killed.
En ek mun nú eigi þat gera, en braut skaltu fara þegar ór landinu ok koma aldrigi aftr síðan mér í augsýn.	But I should now not that do, but away shall travel straight-away out-of this-land and come never back after to-me in eyesight.	I will not do what I should, but you shall travel away immediately out of this land and never come back in my sight.
En þér, Auðunn, kann ek slíka þökk sem þú gefir mér allt dýrit, ok ver hér með mér".	But you, Audun, can I such thanks as you gave me all animal, and be here with me".	But you, Audun, can I thank such as you gave me the whole animal, and be here with me".
Þat þekkist hann ok er með Sveini konungi um hríð.	That knew he and was with Svein the-king about awhile.	That he knew, and he was with King Svein for a while.

2

Ok er liðu nökkurar stundir, þá mælti Auðunn við konung:	And as passed some time, then spoke Audun with the-king:	And as some time has passed, then Audun spoke with the king:
"Braut fýsir mik nú, herra".	"Away desire me now, lord".	"I desire now to travel away, lord".
Konungr svarar heldr seint:	The-king answered rather coldly:	The king answered rather coldly:
"Hvat villtu þá", segir hann, "ef þú vill eigi með oss vera?"	"What will-you then", said he, "if you wish not with us be?"	"What do you wish for then", he said, "if not to be with us?".
Hann segir:	He said:	He said:

The Tale of Auðun of the West Fjords (Old Norse)

Old Norse	Literal	English
"Suðr vil ek ganga".	"South wish I to-go".	"I wish to go south".
"Ef þú vildir eigi svá gott ráð taka", segir konungr, "þá myndi mér fyr þykkja í, er þú fýsist í brott".	"If you wish not so good course take", said the-king, "then would me for think it, that you desire to away".	"If you did not wish to take such a good course", said the king, "I would mind it to think that you desire to go away".
Ok nú gaf konungr honum silfr mjök mikit, ok fór hann suðr síðan með Rúmferlum, ok skipaði konungr til um ferð hans, bað hann koma til sín, er hann kæmi aftr.	And now gave the-king him silver much great, and travelled he south afterwards with Rome-travellers, and directed the-king to about travel his, asked him come to him, when he came returning.	And now the king gave him much great silver, and he travelled south afterwards with pilgrims, and the king made arrangements for his journey, and asked him to come to him when he returned.
Nú fór hann ferðar sinnar, unz hann kemr suðr í Rómaborg.	Now travelled he journey his, until he came south to Rome-city.	Now he travelled on his journey, until he came south to Rome.
Ok er hann hefir þar dvalizt, sem hann tíðir, þá ferr hann aftr, tekr þá sótt mikla, gerir hann þá ákafliga magran.	And when he had there dwelled, such he a-time, then travelled he returning, took then sickness much, made him then extremely thin.	And when he had dwelled there for such a time, he travelled to return, and took to much sickness, which made him extremely thin.
Gengr þá upp allt féit, þat er konungr hafði gefit honum til ferðarinnar, tekr síðan upp stafkarlsstíg ok biðr sér matar.	Went then up all treasure, that which the-king had given him to travelling, taking afterwards up begging and asked he food.	Gone was all his treasure, which the king had given him for travelling, and afterwards he took to begging and he asked for food.
Hann er þá kollóttr ok heldr ósælligr.	He was then bald and rather unhappy.	He was then bald and rather unhappy.
Hann kemr aftr í Danmörk at páskum, þangat sem konungr er þá staddr, en eigi þorði hann at láta sjá sik ok var í kirkjuskoti ok ætlaði þá til fundar við konung, er hann gengi til kirkju um kveldit.	He came back to Denmark at Easter, there as the-king was then standing, but not dared he to let seen himself and was in church-wing and intended then to meet with the-king, when he went to church around evening.	He came back to Denmark at Easter, there where the king was standing, but he dared not to let himself be seen, and was in the church wing and intended to meet with the king, when he went to church in the evening.
Ok nú er hann sá konunginn ok hirðina fagrliga búna, þá þorði hann eigi at láta sjá sik.	And now when he saw the-king and guardsmen beautifully prepared, then dared he not to let seen himself.	And now when he saw the king and the guardsmen so beautifully dressed, then he dared not to let himself be seen.

The Tale of Auðun of the West Fjords (Old Norse)

Old Norse	Literal	English
Ok er konungr gekk til drykkju í höllina, þá mataðist Auðunn úti, sem siðr er til Rúmferla, meðan þeir hafa eigi kastat staf ok skreppu.	And when the-king went to drinking in the-hall, then ate Audun outside, as custom is for Rome-travellers, while they have not cast staff and pouch.	And when the king went drinking in the hall, Audun ate outside, which was the custom for pilgrims, while they have cast aside their staff and pouch.
Ok nú of aftaninn, er konungr gekk til kveldsöngs, ætlaði Auðunn at hitta hann, ok svá mikit sem honum þótti fyrr fyr, jók nú miklu á, er þeir váru drukknir hirðmenninir.	And now of evening, as the-king going to evensong, intended Audun to meet him, and so much as he thought for before, increased now much for, that they were in-drink the-courtiers.	And now in the evening, as the king was going to evensong, Audun intended to meet him, and as much as he had thought before was now increased, because the courtiers were drunk.
Ok er þeir gengu inn aftr, þá þekkði konungr mann ok þóttist finna, at eigi hafði frama til at ganga fram at hitta hann.	And as they went inside back, then noticed the-king a-man and thought found, that not had confidence to that going from to meet him.	And as they went back inside, then the king thought he noticed a man thought he found, that he did not have the confidence in going to meet him.
Ok nú er hirðin gekk inn, þá veik konungr út ok mælti:	And now as the-courtiers going inside, then turned-to the-king out and spoke:	And now as the courtiers were going inside, then the king turned and spoke out:
"Gangi sá nú fram, er mik vill finna.	"Come so now forth, who me wishes to-meet.	"Come forth now, who wishes to meet me.
Mik grunar, at sá muni vera maðrinn".	I suspect, that so shall be a-man".	For I suspect that there is such a man".
Þá gekk Auðunn fram ok fell til fóta konungi, ok varla kenndi konungr hann.	Then went Audun forth and fell to feet the-king's, and hardly recognised the-king him.	Then Audun went forth and fell at the king's feet, and the king hardly recognised him.
Ok þegar er konungr veit, hverr hann er, tók konungr í hönd honum Auðuni ok bað hann vel kominn, "ok hefir þú mikit skipazt", segir hann, "síðan vit sáumst", leiðir hann eftir sér inn.	And as-soon-as that the-king knew, who he was, took the-king in hand him Audun and bid him well come, "and have you much changed", said he, "since we saw", led he after him inside.	And as soon as the king knew who he was, the king took Audun in hand and bid him welcome, "and you have changed much", he said, "since we last saw each other", and after he led him inside.
Ok er hirðin sá hann, hlógu þeir at honum, en konungr sagði:	And when courtiers saw him, laughed they at him, but the-king said:	And when the courtiers saw him, they laughed at him, but the king said:

The Tale of Auðun of the West Fjords (Old Norse)

Old Norse	Literal	English
"Eigi þurfuð þér at honum at hlæja, því at betr hefir hann sét fyrir sinni sál heldr en þér".	"None need you that him to laugh, because that better has he himself seen for his soul rather than you".	"None of you need to laugh at him, because he has seen better for his soul than any of you".
Þá lét konungr gera honum laug ok gaf honum síðan klæði, ok er hann nú með honum.	Then had the-king made him bath and gave him afterwards clothes, and was he now with him.	Then the king had a bath made for him, and afterwards gave him clothes, and he was now with him.

3

Old Norse	Literal	English
Þat er nú sagt, einhverju sinni of várit, at konungr býðr Auðuni at vera með sér álengðar ok kveðst mundu gera hann skutilsvein sinn ok leggja til hans góða virðing.	It is now said, one-such on-the-way to spring, that the-king bid Audun to be with him all-longer and said would make him cup-bearer his and grant to him good worth.	It is now said, that on the way to spring, the king invited Audun to be with him for all of his days, and said that he would make him his cup-bearer and grant him good worthiness.
Auðunn segir:	Audun said:	Audun said:
"Guð þakki yðr, herra, sóma þann allan, er þér vilið til mín leggja, en hitt er mér í skapi, at fara út til Íslands".	"God thank you, lord, honour this all, that you wish to me grant, but find I to-me of mind, to travel out to Iceland".	"God thank you, lord, for all this honour that you wish to grant me, but I find in my mind, to travel out to Iceland".
Konungr segir:	The-king said:	The king said:
"Þetta sýnist mér undarliga kosit".	"This seems to-me strange choice".	"This seems a strange choice to me".
Auðunn mælti:	Audun spoke:	Audun spoke:
"Eigi má ek þat vita, herra", segir hann, "at ek hafa hér mikinn sóma með yðr, en móðir mín troði stafkarls stíg út á Íslandi, því at nú er lokit björg þeiri, er ek lagða til, áðr ek færa af Íslandi".	"Not may I that know, lord", said he, "that I have here much honour with you, but mother mine treads the-beggar's path out in Iceland, for that now is ended help there, that I enriched to, before I travelled from Iceland".	"Not may I know, lord", said he, "that I have much honour here with you, but my mother treads the beggar's path out in Iceland, for now my help there is ended, that which I enriched her with, before I travelled out from Iceland".
Konungr svarar:	The-king answered:	The king answered:
"Vel er mælt", segir hann, "ok mannliga, ok muntu verða giftumaðr.	"Well is spoken", said he, "and man-like, and shall-you be gifted-man.	"It is well spoken", said he, "and like a man, and you shall be a gifted man.

The Tale of Auðun of the West Fjords (Old Norse)

Old Norse	Literal	English
Sjá einn var svá hlutrinn, at mér myndi eigi mislíka, at þú færir í braut heðan, ok ver nú með mér, þar til er skip búast".	So one as such thing, that to-me should not mislike, that you travel to away from-here, and be now with me, then until that ship prepared".	So there is one such thing, that I should not dislike, that you travel away from here, and be now with me, then until a ship is prepared".
Hann gerir svá.	He did so.	He did so.
Einn dag, er á leið várit, gekk Sveinn konungr ofan á bryggjur, ok váru menn þá at at búa skip til ýmissa landa, í Austrveg eða Saxland, til Svíþjóðar eða Nóregs.	One day, when it passed spring, went Svein the-king over-to the quay, and were people then about that prepared ships to various lands, in Eastern-lands or Saxon-lands, to Sweden or Norway.	One day, when spring had passed, King Svein went over to the quay, and there were people about preparing ships for various lands, Eastern-lands, Saxon-lands, to Sweden or Norway.
Þá koma þeir Auðunn at einu skipi fögru, ok váru menn at at búa skipit.	Then came there Audun to one ship beautiful, and were people that it prepared ship.	Then Audun came to a beautiful ship, and there were people that were preparing the ship.
Þá spurði konungr:	Then asked the-king:	Then the king asked:
"Hversu lízt þér, Auðunn, á þetta skip?"	"How-so appears to-you, Audun, about this ship?"	"How does this ship appear to you, Audun?"
Hann svarar:	He answered:	He answered:
"Vel, herra".	"Well lord".	"Well lord".
Konungr mælti:	The-king spoke:	The king spoke:
"Þetta skip vil ek þér gefa ok launa bjarndýrit".	"This ship wish I to-you give and reward the-bear".	"I wish to give you this ship as a reward for the bear".
Hann þakkaði gjöfina eftir sinni kunnustu.	He thanked the-gift after he knew-how.	He thanked him for the gift as well as he knew how.
Ok er leið stund ok skipit var albúit, þá mælti Sveinn konungr við Auðun:	And when passed awhile and ship was all-prepared, then spoke Svein the-king with Audun:	And when a while had passed and the ship was all prepared, then King Svein spoke with Audun:

The Tale of Auðun of the West Fjords (Old Norse)

Old Norse	Literal	English
"Þó villtu nú á braut, þá mun ek nú ekki letja þik, en þat hefi ek spurt, at illt er til hafna fyrir landi yðru, ok eru víða öræfi ok hætt skipum.	"Though will now to away, then should I now not discourage you, but it have I heard, that ill is to harbour for land yours, and they-are widely wild and at-risk ships.	"Though you now wish to go away, then I should not now discourage you, but I have heard that bad are the harbours in your land, and they are widely wild and ships are at risk.
Nú brýtr þú ok týnir skipinu ok fénu.	Now wrecked you and lose the-ship and cargo.	Now should your ship be wrecked and you lose your ship and cargo.
Lítt sér þat þá á, at þú hafir fundit Svein konung ok gefit honum gersimi".	Little to-you that then be, that you have met Svein the-king and gave him treasure".	You shall have little to say that you have met King Svein and gave him treasure".
Síðan seldi konungr honum leðrhosu fulla af silfri, "ok ertu þá enn eigi félauss með öllu, þótt þú brjótir skipit, ef þú fær haldit þessu.	Afterwards handed-over the-king to-him leather-purse full of silver, "and are-you then one not money-less with all, though you wrecked ship, if you go holding this.	Afterwards the king handed over to him a leather purse full of silver, "and are you then not penniless, even though your ship is wrecked, if you hold on to this.
Verða má svá enn", segir konungr, "at þú týnir þessu fé. Lítt nýtr þú þá þess, er þú fannt Svein konung ok gaft honum gersimi".	Become may so then", said the-king, "that you lose this money. Little benefit you then this, that you found Svein the-king and gave him treasure".	But if it becomes then", said the king, "that you lose this money. It will benefit you little then, that you have met King Svein and given him treasure".
Síðan dró konungr hring af hendi sér ok gaf Auðuni ok mælti:	Then drew the-king a-ring of hand his and gave Audun and spoke:	Then the king drew a ring from his hand and gave it to Audun saying:
"Þó at svá illa verði, at þú brjótir skipit ok týnir fénu, eigi ertu félauss, ef þú kemst á land, því at margir menn hafa gull á sér í skipsbrotum, ok sér þá, at þú hefir fundit Svein konung, ef þú heldr hringinum.	"Though that so ill be, that you wrecked ship and lose money, not are-you money-less, if you came to land, therefore that many people have gold about themselves for ship-wreck, and yourself then, that you have met Svein the-king, if you hold the-ring.	"Even though it would be so bad if your ship was wrecked, and you lose all the money, you shall not be penniless, therefore many people have gold about themselves in case of being shipwrecked, and you shall have met King Svein, if you hold on to this ring.

The Tale of Auðun of the West Fjords (Old Norse)

Old Norse	Literal	English
En þat vil ek ráða þér", segir hann, "at þú gefir eigi hringinn, nema þú þykkist eiga svá mikit gott at launa nökkurum göfgum manni, þá gef þeim hringinn, því at tígnum mönnum sómir at þiggja.	But that wish I advise to-you", said he, "that you give not the-ring, except you think not so much good to reward some noble man, then give them the-ring, for that dignified people honourable that accept.	But I wish to advise you", he said, "that you do not give the ring to anyone, unless you think it will be good to reward some noble man, then give them the ring, for dignified and honourable people will accept.
Ok far nú heill".	And travel now whole".	And now travel whole".

4

Old Norse	Literal	English
Síðan lætr hann í haf ok kemr í Nóreg ok lætr flytja upp varnað sinn, ok þurfti nú meira við þat en fyrr, er hann var í Nóregi.	Afterwards laid he to sea and came to Norway and had carried up wares his, and needed now more with that than before, when he was in Norway.	Afterwards he put to sea and came to Norway and had his wares carried up, which he needed more now than before, when he was in Norway.
Hann ferr nú síðan á fund Haralds konungs ok vill efna þat, er hann hét honum, áðr hann fór til Danmerkr, ok kveðr konung vel.	He travelled not afterwards to meet Harald the-king and wished carry-out that, which he promised him, before he travelled to Denmark, and greeted the-king well.	He travelled now afterwards to meet King Harald, as he wished to carry out what he had promised him, before he travelled to Denmark, and he greeted the king well.
Haraldr konungr tók vel kveðju hans, "ok sezt niðr", segir hann, "ok drekk hér með oss".	Harald the-king received well greeting his, "and sit down", said he, "and drink here with us".	King Harald received his greeting well, "and sit down", he said, "and drink here with us".
Ok svá gerir hann.	And so did he.	And so he did.
Þá spurði Haraldr konungr:	Then asked Harald the-king:	Then King Harald asked:
"Hverju launaði Sveinn konungr þér dýrit?"	"How rewarded Svein the-king you the-beast?"	"How did King Svein reward you for the beast?".
Auðunn svarar:	Audun answered:	Audun answered:
"Því, herra, at hann þá at mér".	"Because lord, that he then at me".	"Because lord, that he accepted it of me".
Konungr sagði:	The-king said:	The king said:

The Tale of Auðun of the West Fjords (Old Norse)

Old Norse	Literal	English
"Launat mynda ek þér því hafa. Hverju launaði hann enn?"	"Repaid would I you accordingly have. How rewarded he then?"	"I would have repaid you accordingly. How did he reward you then?".
Auðunn svarar:	Audun answered:	Audun answered:
"Gaf hann mér silfr til suðrgöngu".	"Gave he me silver to south-going".	"He gave me silver to go south".
Þá segir Haraldr konungr:	Then said Harald the-king:	Then King Harald said:
"Mörgum manni gefr Sveinn konungr silfr til suðrgöngu eða annarra hluta, þótt ekki færi honum gersimar.	"Many people gives Svein the-king silver to south-going or others lots, though not bring him treasure.	"King Svein gives many people silver to go south, lots of others, though they do not bring him treasure".
Hvat er enn fleira?"	What was it more?"	What was it more?".
"Hann bauð mér", segir Auðunn, "at gerast skutilsveinn hans ok mikinn sóma til mín at leggja".	"He bid me", said Audun, "to be cup-bearer his and much honour to me that granted".	"He invited me", said Audun, "to be his cup-bearer and to grant me much honour".
"Vel var þat mælt", segir konungr, "ok launa myndi hann enn fleira".	"Well was that said", said the-king, "and rewarded would he then more".	"That was well said", said the king, "and he would reward you more".
Auðunn segir:	Audun said:	Audun said:
"Gaf hann mér knörr með farmi þeim, er hingat er bezt varit í Nóreg".	"Gave he me a-ship with cargo then, that there was best wares in Norway".	"He then gave me a ship with cargo, of wares that sell best in Norway".
"Þat var stórmannligt", segir konungr, "en launat mynda ek þér því hafa. Launaði hann því fleira?"	"That was great-man-like", said the-king, "but rewarded would I you accordingly have. Rewarded he then more?"	"That was generous", said the king, "but I would have rewarded you accordingly. Did he reward you then more?".
Auðunn segir:	Audun said:	Audun said:
"Gaf hann mér leðrhosu fulla af silfri ok kvað mik þá eigi félausan, ef ek helda því, þó at skip mitt bryti við Ísland".	"Gave he to-me leather-purse full of silver and said to-me then not money-less, if I held therefore, though that ship mine break at Iceland".	"He gave me a leather purse full of silver, and said to me that if I held it I would therefore not be penniless, even if my ship was wrecked in Iceland".
Konungr segir:	The-king said:	The king said:

The Tale of Auðun of the West Fjords (Old Norse)

Old Norse	Literal	English
"Þat var ágætliga gert, ok þat mynda ek ekki gert hafa. Lauss mynda ek þykkjast, ef ek gæfa þér skipit. Hvárt launaði hann fleira?"	"That was greatly done, and that would I not done have. Less should I seem, if I gave you the-ship. How rewarded he more?"	"That was greatly done, and I would not have done that. Less would I think, if I gave you the ship. How did he reward you more?".
"Svá var víst, herra", segir Auðunn, "at hann launaði. Hann gaf mér hring þenna, er ek hefi á hendi, ok kvað svá mega at berast, at ek týnda fénu öllu, ok sagði mik þá eigi félausan, ef ek ætta hringinn, ok bað mik eigi lóga, nema ek ætta nökkurum tígnum manni svá gott at launa, at ek vilda gefa.	"So was certainly, lord", said Audun, "that he rewarded. He gave me ring this, that I have in hand, and said so may it bear, that I lose money all, and said to-me then not money-less, if I had the-ring, and bid me not lose, except I have some noble man so good to repay, that I wish give.	"So it certainly was, lord", said Audun, "that he rewarded. He gave me this ring, that I have in hand, and so it may bear, though I lose all my money, it is said to me that I would not be penniless, if I had the ring, and he asked me not to part with it, unless I have some noble man so good to repay, that I wish to give it to.
En nú hefi ek þann fundit, því at þú áttir kost at taka hvárttveggja frá mér, dýrit ok svá líf mitt, en þú lézt mik fara þangat í friði, sem aðrir náðu eigi".	But now have I then found, because that you have benefit to take either-way from me, the-beast and so life mine, but you let me travel from-here in peace, as others reached not".	But now then I have found, because you could have taken away from me, the beast or my life, but you let me travel from here in peace, as others could not".
Konungr tók við gjöfinni með blíðu ok gaf Auðuni í móti góðar gjafar, áðr en þeir skildist.	The-king received with the-gift with joyfulness and gave Audun in return good gifts, before that they separated.	The king received the gift with joyfulness and gave Audun good gifts in return, before they separated.
Auðunn varði fénu til Íslandsferðar ok fór út þegar um sumarit til Íslands ok þótti vera inn mesti gæfumaðr.	Audun was wealth to Iceland-journey and travelled out from-there about summer to Iceland and thought was the most gifted-man.	Audun used his wealth to travel to Iceland and travelled out from there around summer to Iceland and he was thought of as the most gifted man.
Frá þessum manni, Auðuni, var kominn Þorsteinn Gyðuson.	From this people, Audun, was descended Thorstein Gyduson.	From these people, Audun, were descended Thorstein Gyduson.

Word List (Old Norse to English)

Word List (Old Norse to English)

Old Norse	English

A, a

Old Norse	English
aðrir	others
af	from, of, off, out-of
aftaninn	evening
aftr	back, returning
albúit	all-prepared
aldrigi	never
alla	all
allan	all
allri	all
allt	all
annarra	others
at	about, at, by, it, that, to
Auðun	Audun (name)
Auðunar	Audun (name)
Auðuni	Audun (name)
Auðunn	Audun (name)
augsýn	eyesight
austr	east
Austrveg	Eastern-lands (place)

Á, á

Old Norse	English
á	a, about, an, and, be, for, in, it, of, on, that, the, to
áðr	after, before
ágætliga	greatly
Áka	Aki (name)
ákafliga	extremely
Áki	Aki (name)
álengðar	all-longer
ármaðrinn	steward
ármanni	the-steward
ármanns	steward
átti	had
áttir	have
áttu	have-you

Æ, æ

Old Norse	English
ætla	intend
ætlaðak	intended
ætlaði	intended
ætlar	intend, intended
ætlat	intended
ætta	had, have

B, b

Old Norse	English
bað	asked, bid
báðir	both
bæði	asked, both
bauð	bid
berast	bear
betr	better
bezt	best
biðja	begging
biðr	asked
bjarndýr	bear
bjarndýri	a-bear, bear
bjarndýrit	the-bear
björg	aid, help
blíðu	joyfulness
borðinu	table
brátt	soon
braut	away
brjótir	wrecked
brott	away
bryggjur	quay
bryti	break
brýtr	wrecked
bú	a-farm
búa	prepared
búanda	farmer
búast	prepared
búit	settled
búna	prepared
býðr	bid

D, d

Word List (Old Norse to English)

Old Norse	English
dag	day
Danmerkr	Denmark (place)
Danmörk	Denmark (place)
deyja	die
drekk	drink
drepinn	killed
dró	drew
drukknir	in-drink
drykkju	drinking
dvalizt	dwelled
dýr	wild-animal
dýrit	a-beast, animal, beast, the-beast
dýrsins	the-beast

E, e

Old Norse	English
eða	or
ef	if
efna	carry-out
eftir	after, afterwards, behind
eiga	not, own, owned
eigi	none, not
eign	owned
eigu	own, owned
einhverju	one-such
einn	one
einu	one
eitt	one
eitthvert	some-kind
ek	I
ekki	not
em	am
en	and, but, than, that, then
engu	none
enn	it, one, then
er	as, I, is, that, the, was, what, when, which, who
ert	are
ertu	are-you
eru	they-are, were

F, f

Old Norse	English
fá	get, give
fær	go
færa	bring, travelled
færi	bring
færir	travel
fagrliga	beautifully
fannt	found
far	travel
fara	travel, travelled
farir	travel
farit	fared, gone
farmi	cargo
fé	money
féit	treasure
félausan	money-less
félauss	money-less
félítill	fee-little
fell	fell
fénu	cargo, money, wealth
ferð	travel
ferðar	journey
ferðarinnar	travelling
ferr	travel, travelled
ferst	travelled
finna	found, to-meet
fjár	wealth
fjárins	of-wealth
fjörðum	fields
fleira	more
flytja	carried
fögru	beautiful
fór	travelled
fóta	feet
frá	from
fram	forth, from
frama	confidence
friði	peace
fulla	full
fund	meet
fundar	meet
fundit	found, met
fyr	before, for
fyrir	because, before, for, present
fyrr	before, for

Word List (Old Norse to English)

Old Norse	English
fýsir	desire
fýsist	desire

G, g

Old Norse	English
gæfa	gave
gæfumaðr	gifted-man
gaf	gave, have
gaft	gave
ganga	going, to-go
gangi	come
gef	give
gefa	give
gefir	gave, give
gefit	gave, given
gefr	gives
gekk	going, went
gengi	went
gengr	went
gengu	went
gera	did, do, made, make
gerast	be
gerðist	did
gerir	did, made
gersimar	treasure
gersimi	treasure, treasured
gert	done
getit	told-of
giftu	give
giftumaðr	gifted-man
gjafar	gifts
gjöfina	the-gift
gjöfinni	the-gift
góða	good
góðar	good
góðs	good
göfgum	noble
gott	good
Grænlandi	Greenland (place)
Grænlands	Greenland (place)
grunar	suspect
Guð	God (name)
gull	gold
Gyðuson	Gyduson (name)

H, h

Old Norse	English
hætt	at-risk
haf	sea
hafa	have
hafði	had
hafir	have
hafna	harbour
haldit	holding
hálft	half
handar	hand
hann	he, he himself, him
hans	him, his
Haraldi	Harald (name)
Haraldr	Harald (name)
Haralds	Harald (name)
heðan	from-here, hence
hefi	have
hefir	had, has, have
hefta	stop
heill	whole
heit	promise
helda	held
heldr	hold, rather
hendi	hand
hér	here
herbergi	a-room
herra	lord
hét	named, promised
heyrt	heard
hingat	there
hirðin	courtiers, the-courtiers
hirðina	guardsmen
hirðmenninir	the-courtiers
hitt	find
hitta	meet
hlæja	laugh
hlógu	laughed
hluta	lot, lots
hlutrinn	thing
höfum	have
höllina	the-hall
hönd	hand
honum	he, him, to-him
hríð	awhile

Word List (Old Norse to English)

Old Norse	English
hring	a-ring, ring
hringinn	the-ring
hringinum	the-ring
hvárt	how, whether
hvárttveggja	either-way
hvat	what
hvé	how
hverju	how
hverr	every, who
hversu	how-so
hví	why
hygg	think

I, i

illa	ill
illt	ill
inn	inside, the

Í, í

í	a, for, in, is, it, of, on, to
íhugaði	considered
Ísland	Iceland (place)
Íslandi	Iceland (place)
Íslands	Iceland (place)
íslandsferðar	Iceland-journey
Íslenzkr	Icelander (name)

J, j

játum	profess
jók	increased

K, k

kæmi	came
kæmist	comes
kann	can
kastat	cast
kaupir	bought
kemr	came
kemst	came
kenndi	knew, recognised
keyptak	purchased
keyptir	bought
kirkju	church
kirkjuskoti	church-wing
klæði	clothes
klaklaust	unhurt
knörr	a-ship
kollóttr	bald
kom	came, come
koma	came, come
komast	come
kominn	come, coming, descended
komit	come
komizt	coming
konung	the-king
konungi	the-king, the-king's
konunginn	the-king
konungr	the-king
konungs	the-king
kosit	choice
kost	benefit
kunnustu	knew-how
kvað	said
kveðit	said
kveðju	greeting
kveðr	greeted
kveðst	said
kveldit	evening
kveldsöngs	evensong
kyni	kin

L, l

lætr	had, laid
lagða	enriched
lagði	laid
land	land
landa	land, lands
landi	land
landinu	this-land
landit	land
láta	let

Word List (Old Norse to English)

Old Norse	English
laug	bath
laun	reward
launa	repay, reward, rewarded
launaði	rewarded
launar	repays
launat	repaid, rewarded
lauss	less
leðrhosu	leather-purse
leggja	grant, granted
leið	journey, passed
leiðar	the-way
leiðir	led, took
leigir	rented
lét	had
letja	discourage
lézt	let, said
liðu	passed
líf	life
liggja	lay-out
líta	look
lítr	looked
lítt	little
lízt	appears
lóga	lose
lokit	ended

M, m

Old Norse	English
má	may
maðr	a-man, man
maðrinn	a-man
mælt	said, spoken
mælti	spoke
Mæri	Moer (place)
mætta	might
magran	thin
makligt	proper
mann	a-man, man
manni	man, people
mannliga	man-like
margir	many
mataðist	ate
matar	food
máttu	might
með	along, with
meðan	while
mega	may
meira	more
menn	people
mér	me, to-me
mestan	most
mesti	most
meta	value
mik	I, me, to-me
mikil	much
mikinn	a-great, much
mikit	great, much
mikla	much
miklar	much
miklu	much
milli	between
mín	me, mine
minni	mine
mislíka	mislike
mitt	mine
mjök	much
móðir	mother
móður	mother
mönnum	people
mörgum	many
móti	meeting, return
mun	could, shall, should
mundu	would
muni	shall
munir	should
muntu	shall-you
mynda	should, would
myndi	should, would

N, n

Old Norse	English
náðu	reached
nauðsyn	necessary
nema	except
niðr	down
nökkurar	some
nökkurra	some
nökkurum	some
nökkut	sometime

Word List (Old Norse to English)

Old Norse	English
Nóreg	Norway (place)
Nóregi	Norway (place)
Nóregs	Norway (place)
nú	not, now
nýtr	benefit

O, o

Old Norse	English
of	of, over, to
ofan	over-to
ok	also, and
orðit	become
oss	us

Ó, ó

Old Norse	English
ófrið	un-peace
ór	out-of
ósælligr	unhappy
óvinr	un-friend
óvitr	unwise

Ö, ö

Old Norse	English
öðru	other
öllu	all
öræfi	wild

P, p

Old Norse	English
páskum	Easter
penningr	penny

R, r

Old Norse	English
ráð	course
ráða	advise
ráði	decided
reiðfara	voyage
réttara	righter
Rómaborg	Rome-city (place)
rúmferla	Rome-travellers
rúmferlum	Rome-travellers

S, s

Old Norse	English
sá	saw, so
sættast	reconciled
sagði	said, said
sagt	said, told
sál	soul
saman	the-same
sannligt	true-like
satt	TRUE
sáumst	saw
Saxland	Saxon-lands (place)
sé	is
seg	say
segir	said, says, told
seint	coldly
seldi	handed-over
selja	sell
selr	sell
sem	as, since, such, that, what
sendir	sent
sér	he, him, himself, his, themselves, to-you, yourself
sét	seen
settak	intended
sezt	sit
síðan	after, afterwards, since, then
siðr	custom
sik	himself
silfr	silver
silfri	silver
sín	him
sína	his
sinn	his
sinnar	his
sinni	he, his, on-the-way
sitt	his
sjá	seen, so
skal	shall

Word List (Old Norse to English)

Old Norse	English
skaltu	shall
skapi	mind
skilðist	separated
skip	ship, ships, the-ship
skipaði	directed
skipazt	changed
skipi	ship, the-ship
skipinu	the-ship
skipit	ship, the-ship
skipsbrotum	ship-wreck
skipum	ships
skreppu	pouch
skulu	shall
skutilsvein	cup-bearer
skutilsveinn	cup-bearer
slík	such
slíka	such
slíku	such
sóma	honour
sómir	honourable
sótt	sickness
spurði	asked
spurt	heard
staddr	standing
staf	staff
stafkarls	the-beggar's
stafkarlsstíg	beggar's-path
starfaði	worked
stíg	path
stigi	climbed
stóðu	stood
stórmannligt	great-man-like
stund	awhile
stundir	time
stýrimanni	skipper
stýrimanns	skipper
suðr	south
suðrgöngu	south-going
sumarit	summer
svá	so, such
svarar	answered
Svein	Svein (name)
Sveini	Svein (name)
Sveinn	Svein (name)
Sveins	Svein (name), Svein's (name)
Svíþjóðar	Sweden (place)
sýnist	considered, seems

T, t

Old Norse	English
taka	take
tálma	prevent
tekr	taking, took
tíðir	a-time
tígnum	dignified, noble
til	for, to, until
tók	received, took
troði	treads
tvau	twice
týnda	lose
týnir	lose

Þ, þ

Old Norse	English
þá	then
þakkaði	thanked
þakki	thank
þangat	from-here, there
þann	then, this
þar	then, there
þars	there
þat	it, that
þegar	as-soon-as, from-there, straight-away
þegit	received
þeim	them, then, they
þeir	there, they
þeiri	there
þekkði	noticed
þekkist	knew
þenna	this
þér	to-you, you, your
þess	this
þessa	this
þessi	this
þessu	this
þessum	this
þetta	this
þiggja	accept

Word List (Old Norse to English)

Old Norse	English
þik	you
þína	you, yours
þinnar	your
þit	you
þó	though
þökk	thanks
þorði	dared
Þóri	Thorir (name)
Þóris	Thorir (name)
Þorsteini	Thorstein (name)
Þorsteinn	Thorstein (name)
Þorsteins	Thorstein (name)
þótt	though
þótti	thought
þóttist	thought
þriggja	three
þú	you
þurfti	needed
þurfuð	need
því	accordingly, because, for, then, therefore
þykkist	think
þykkja	think
þykkjast	seem

U, u

um	about, around
umbráði	managed
umsjá	about-see
undarliga	strange
unz	until
upp	up
uppi	up

Ú, ú

út	out
útan	out
útanferðina	out-travelling
úti	outside

V, v

Old Norse	English
væri	should-be
værir	would-be
valdi	will
var	as, was
varði	was
varit	wares
várit	spring
varla	hardly
varnað	wares
várr	our
váru	were
veik	turned-to
veit	knew
vel	well
ver	be
vér	we
vera	be, was
verð	worth
verða	be, become, was
verði	be, worth
verðr	was
Vestfirzkr	Westfjords (place)
vestr	west
vetra	winters
vetrinn	winter
við	at, with
víða	widely
Vík	Vik (place)
vil	will, wish
vilda	wish
vildi	wished
vildir	wish
vilið	wish
vill	wish, wished, wishes
villtu	will, will-you
virðing	worth
vist	hospitality
víst	certainly
vista	provisions
vistir	provisions
vit	we
vita	know

Y, y

Word List (Old Norse to English)

Old Norse | *English*

yðr — you, your
yðru — your, yours

Ý, ý

ýmissa — various

Word List (English to Old Norse)

Word List (English to Old Norse)

English	Old Norse	English	Old Norse

A, a

a	*á, á*
about	*á, á, á*
an	*á*
and	*á, á, á*
after	*áðr, áðr, ætla*
Aki (name)	*Áka, ákafliga*
all-prepared	*albúit*
all-longer	*álengðar*
all	*alla, allan, allri, allt, at*
at	*at, at*
Audun (name)	*Auðun, Auðunar, Auðuni, Auðunn*
asked	*bað, bað, báðir, bæði*
a-bear	*bjarndýri*
aid	*björg*
away	*braut, brott*
a-farm	*bú*
a-beast	*dýrit*
animal	*dýrit*
afterwards	*eftir, eftir*
am	*em*
as	*er, er, er*
are	*ert*
are-you	*ertu*
at-risk	*hætt*
a-room	*herbergi*
awhile	*hríð, hring*
a-ring	*hring*
a-ship	*knörr*
appears	*lízt*
a-man	*maðr, maðr, maðrinn*
ate	*mataðist*
along	*með*
a-great	*mikinn*
also	*ok*
advise	*ráða*
answered	*svarar*
as-soon-as	*þegar*
accept	*þiggja*
accordingly	*því*
a-time	*tíðir*

around	*um*
about-see	*umsjá*

B, b

be	*á, á, á, á, áðr, áðr*
before	*áðr, ætla, ætlaðak, ætlaði*
back	*aftr*
by	*at*
bid	*bað, báðir, bæði*
both	*báðir, bæði*
bear	*berast, betr, bezt*
better	*betr*
best	*bezt*
begging	*biðja*
break	*bryti*
beast	*dýrit*
behind	*eftir*
but	*en*
bring	*færa, færi*
beautifully	*fagrliga*
beautiful	*fögru*
because	*fyrir, fyrir*
bought	*kaupir, kemr*
bald	*kollóttr*
benefit	*kost, kunnustu*
bath	*laug*
between	*milli*
become	*orðit, páskum*
beggar's-path	*stafkarlsstíg*

C, c

carry-out	*efna*
cargo	*farmi, fé*
carried	*flytja*
confidence	*frama*
come	*gangi, gef, gefa, gefir, gefir, gefit*
courtiers	*hirðin*
considered	*íhugaði, illa*

Word List (English to Old Norse)

English	*Old Norse*
came	*kæmi, kæmist, kann, kastat, kaupir*
comes	*kæmist*
can	*kann*
cast	*kastat*
church	*kirkju*
church-wing	*kirkjuskoti*
clothes	*klæði*
coming	*kominn, kominn*
choice	*kosit*
could	*mun*
course	*ráð*
coldly	*seint*
custom	*siðr*
changed	*skipazt*
cup-bearer	*skutilsvein, skutilsveinn*
climbed	*stigi*
certainly	*víst*

D, d

English	*Old Norse*
day	*dag*
Denmark (place)	*Danmerkr, Danmörk*
die	*deyja*
drink	*drekk*
drew	*dró*
drinking	*drykkju*
dwelled	*dvalizt*
desire	*fýsir, fýsist*
did	*gera, gera, gera*
do	*gera*
done	*gert*
descended	*kominn*
discourage	*letja*
down	*niðr*
decided	*ráði*
directed	*skipaði*
dared	*þorði*
dignified	*tígnum*

E, e

English	*Old Norse*
evening	*aftaninn, aftr*
extremely	*ákafliga*
eyesight	*augsýn*
east	*austr*
Eastern-lands (place)	*Austrveg*
either-way	*hvárttveggja*
every	*hverr*
evensong	*kveldsöngs*
enriched	*lagða*
ended	*lokit*
except	*nema*
Easter	*páskum*

F, f

English	*Old Norse*
for	*á, á, á, áðr, áðr, ætla, ætlaðak*
from	*af, aftaninn, aftr*
farmer	*búanda*
found	*fannt, farit, farit*
fared	*farit*
fee-little	*félítill*
fell	*fell*
fields	*fjörðum*
feet	*fóta*
forth	*fram*
full	*fulla*
from-here	*heðan, heðan*
find	*hitt*
food	*matar*
from-there	*þegar*

G, g

English	*Old Norse*
greatly	*ágætliga*
get	*fá*
give	*fá, fær, færa, færi, fagrliga*
go	*fær*
gone	*farit*
gave	*gæfa, gæfumaðr, gaf, gaf, gaft*
gifted-man	*gæfumaðr, gaf*
going	*ganga, gangi*

Word List (English to Old Norse)

English	*Old Norse*	English	*Old Norse*
given	*gefit*	heard	*heyrt, hirðin*
gives	*gefr*	how	*hvárt, hvárttveggja, hvé*
gifts	*gjafar*		
good	*góða, góðar, góðs, gott*	how-so	*hversu*
		handed-over	*seldi*
Greenland (place)	*Grænlandi, Grænlands*	himself	*sér, sér*
		honour	*sóma*
God (name)	*Guð*	honourable	*sómir*
gold	*gull*	hardly	*varla*
Gyduson (name)	*Gyðuson*	hospitality	*vist*
guardsmen	*hirðina*		
greeting	*kveðju*		
greeted	*kveðr*		
grant	*leggja*		
granted	*leggja*		
great	*mikit*		
great-man-like	*stórmannligt*		

H, h

I, i

English	*Old Norse*
in	*á, á*
it	*á, áðr, áðr, ætla, ætlaðak*
intend	*ætla, ætlaðak*
intended	*ætlaðak, ætlaði, ætlar, ætlar, ætlat*
in-drink	*drukknir*
if	*ef*
I	*ek, em, en*
is	*er, ert, ertu*
ill	*illa, illt*
inside	*inn*
Iceland (place)	*Ísland, Íslandi, Íslands*
Iceland-journey	*Íslandsferðar*
Icelander (name)	*Íslenzkr*
increased	*jók*

English	*Old Norse*
had	*ætta, ætta, af, aftaninn, aftr, ágætliga*
have	*ætta, af, aftaninn, aftr, ágætliga, Áka, ákafliga, Áki*
have-you	*áttu*
help	*björg*
harbour	*hafna*
holding	*haldit*
half	*hálft*
hand	*handar, hann, hann*
he	*hann, hann, hann, hans*
he himself	*hann*
him	*hann, hans, hans, Haraldi, Haraldr*
his	*hans, Haraldi, Haraldr, Haralds, heðan, heðan, hefi*
Harald (name)	*Haraldi, Haraldr, Haralds*
hence	*heðan*
has	*hefir*
held	*helda*
hold	*heldr*
here	*hér*

J, j

English	*Old Norse*
joyfulness	*blíðu*
journey	*ferðar, finna*

K, k

English	*Old Norse*
killed	*drepinn*
knew	*kenndi, keyptir, kirkju*
knew-how	*kunnustu*
kin	*kyni*
know	*vita*

Word List (English to Old Norse)

English	*Old Norse*

L, l

lord	*herra*
laugh	*hlæja*
laughed	*hlógu*
lot	*hluta*
lots	*hluta*
laid	*lætr, lagða*
land	*land, landa, landa, landi*
lands	*landa*
let	*láta, laug*
less	*lauss*
leather-purse	*leðrhosu*
led	*leiðir*
life	*líf*
lay-out	*liggja*
look	*líta*
looked	*lítr*
little	*lítt*
lose	*lóga, lokit, má*

M, m

money	*fé, félausan*
money-less	*félausan, félauss*
more	*fleira, flytja*
meet	*fund, fundar, fundit*
met	*fundit*
made	*gera, gera*
make	*gera*
may	*má, maðr*
man	*maðr, maðrinn, Mæri*
Moer (place)	*Mæri*
might	*mætta, mann*
man-like	*mannliga*
many	*margir, mataðist*
me	*mér, mestan, mesti*
most	*mestan, mesti*
much	*mikil, mikinn, mikinn, mikit, mikit, mikla, miklar*
mine	*mín, minni, mislíka*
mislike	*mislíka*
mother	*móðir, móður*
meeting	*móti*
mind	*skapi*
managed	*umbráði*

N, n

never	*aldrigi*
not	*eiga, eiga, eiga, eigi*
none	*eigi, eigi*
noble	*göfgum, grunar*
named	*hét*
necessary	*nauðsyn*
Norway (place)	*Nóreg, Nóregi, Nóregs*
now	*nú*
noticed	*þekkði*
needed	*þurfti*
need	*þurfuð*

O, o

of	*á, á, á, á*
on	*á, á*
others	*aðrir, af*
off	*af*
out-of	*af, aftr*
or	*eða*
own	*eiga, eiga*
owned	*eiga, eigi, eigi*
one-such	*einhverju*
one	*einn, einu, eitt, eitthvert*
of-wealth	*fjárins*
other	*öðru*
over	*of*
over-to	*ofan*
on-the-way	*sinni*
out	*út, útan*
out-travelling	*útanferðina*
outside	*úti*
our	*várr*

Word List (English to Old Norse)

English	*Old Norse*	English	*Old Norse*
P, p		**S, s**	
prepared	*búa, búast, búit*	steward	*ármaðrinn, ármanni*
peace	*friði*	soon	*brátt*
present	*fyrir*	settled	*búit*
promise	*heit*	some-kind	*eitthvert*
promised	*hét*	suspect	*grunar*
profess	*játum*	sea	*haf*
purchased	*keyptak*	stop	*hefta*
passed	*leið, leiðar*	said	*kvað, kveðit, kveðst, landinu, laun, launa, launa, launa, launaði*
proper	*makligt*		
people	*manni, með, meðan*		
penny	*penningr*	spoken	*mælt*
pouch	*skreppu*	spoke	*mælti*
path	*stíg*	shall	*mun, mun, mundu, muni, munir*
prevent	*tálma*		
provisions	*vista, vistir*	should	*mun, mundu, muni, munir*
Q, q		shall-you	*muntu*
quay	*bryggjur*	some	*nökkurar, nökkurra, nökkurum*
R, r		sometime	*nökkut*
returning	*aftr*	saw	*sá, sá*
rather	*heldr*	so	*sá, sættast, sagði*
ring	*hring*	soul	*sál*
recognised	*kenndi*	Saxon-lands (place)	*Saxland*
reward	*laun, launa*	say	*seg*
repay	*launa*	says	*segir*
rewarded	*launa, launaði, launar*	sell	*selja, selr*
repays	*launar*	since	*sem, sem*
repaid	*launat*	such	*sem, sem, sem, sendir, sér*
rented	*leigir*	sent	*sendir*
return	*móti*	seen	*sét, sezt*
reached	*náðu*	sit	*sezt*
righter	*réttara*	silver	*silfr, silfri*
Rome-city (place)	*Rómaborg*	separated	*skilðist*
Rome-travellers	*rúmferla, rúmferlum*	ship	*skip, skip, skip*
reconciled	*sættast*	ships	*skip, skip*
received	*þegit, þeim*	ship-wreck	*skipsbrotum*
		sickness	*sótt*
		standing	*staddr*
		staff	*staf*
		stood	*stóðu*
		skipper	*stýrimanni, stýrimanns*
		south	*suðr*

Word List (English to Old Norse)

English	Old Norse	English	Old Norse
south-going	suðrgöngu	the-king	konung, konungi, konungi, konunginn, konungr
summer	sumarit		
Svein (name)	Svein, Sveini, Sveinn, Sveins		
		the-king's	konungi
Svein's (name)	Sveins	this-land	landinu
Sweden (place)	Svíþjóðar	the-way	leiðar
seems	sýnist	took	leiðir, leigir, lézt
straight-away	þegar	thin	magran
seem	þykkjast	to-me	mér, meta
strange	undarliga	told	sagt, sál
should-be	væri	the-same	saman
spring	várit	true-like	sannligt
		true	
		themselves	sér
		to-you	sér, sér
		the-ship	skip, skipi, skipi, skipinu

T, t

English	Old Norse	English	Old Norse
that	á, á, á, aðrir, af, af	the-beggar's	stafkarls
the	á, á, aðrir	time	stundir
to	á, aðrir, af, af, af	take	taka
the-steward	ármanni	taking	tekr
the-bear	bjarndýrit	thanked	þakkaði
table	borðinu	thank	þakki
the-beast	dýrit, dýrsins	this	þann, þar, þar, þars, þat, þegar, þegit, þeim
than	en		
then	en, engu, enn, enn, er, er, er, er	them	þeim
		they	þeim, þeir
they-are	eru	though	þó, þökk
travelled	færa, færir, far, fara, fara	thanks	þökk
		Thorir (name)	Þóri, Þóris
travel	færir, far, fara, fara, farir, féit	Thorstein (name)	Þorsteini, Þorsteinn, Þorsteins
treasure	féit, fénu, ferð	thought	þótti, þóttist
travelling	ferðarinnar	three	þriggja
to-meet	finna	therefore	því
to-go	ganga	treads	troði
treasured	gersimi	twice	tvau
told-of	getit	turned-to	veik
the-gift	gjöfina, gjöfinni		
there	hingat, hirðin, hirðmenninir, hlutrinn, höllina, honum		

U, u

English	Old Norse
unhurt	klaklaust
un-peace	ófrið
unhappy	ósælligr
us	oss

the-courtiers	hirðin, hirðmenninir
thing	hlutrinn
the-hall	höllina
to-him	honum
the-ring	hringinn, hringinum
think	hygg, í, í

Word List (English to Old Norse)

English	Old Norse	English	Old Norse
un-friend	*óvinr*	wish	*vil, vilda, vildi, vildir, vilið*
unwise	*óvitr*	wished	*vildi, vildir*
until	*til, tók*	wishes	*vill*
up	*upp, uppi*	will-you	*villtu*

V, v

value	*meta*
voyage	*reiðfara*
Vik (place)	*Vík*
various	*ýmissa*

Y, y

yourself	*sér*
you	*þér, þér, þess, þessa, þessi, þessu*
your	*þér, þess, þessa, þessi*
yours	*þína, þinnar*

W, w

wrecked	*brjótir, bryggjur*
wild-animal	*dýr*
was	*er, er, er, er, er, eru*
what	*er, er, er*
when	*er*
which	*er*
who	*er, eru*
were	*eru, færa*
wealth	*fénu, ferð*
went	*gekk, gengi, gengr, gengu*
whole	*heill*
whether	*hvárt*
why	*hví*
with	*með, meðan*
while	*meðan*
would	*mundu, muni, munir*
wild	*öræfi*
worked	*starfaði*
would-be	*værir*
will	*valdi, var, varði*
wares	*varit, várit*
well	*vel*
we	*vér, vera*
worth	*verð, verða, verði*
Westfjords (place)	*Vestfirzkr*
west	*vestr*
winters	*vetra*
winter	*vetrinn*
widely	*víða*

The Tale of Auðun of the West Fjords (*Old Icelandic*)

Auðunar þáttur vestfirska, from the Flateyjarbók (GkS 1005 fol., c. 1390, Árni Magnússon Institute for Icelandic Studies)

Old Icelandic	Literal	English
1	**1**	**1**
Maður hét Auðun, vestfirskur að kyni og félítill.	Man named Audun, Westfjords by kin and fee-little.	There was a man named Audun, from the West Fjords by kin, and he was poor.
Hann fór utan vestur þar í fjörðum með umráði Þorsteins búanda góðs og Þóris stýrimanns er þar hafði þegið vist of veturinn með Þorsteini.	He travelled out west there in fields with managed Thorstein farmer good and Thorir skipper who there had received hospitality over winter with Thorstein.	He travelled west to the fields which were managed by Thorstein, a good farmer, and Thorir who was a skipper, and they received hospitality from Thorstein over the winter.
Auðun var og þar og starfaði fyrir honum Þóri og þá þessi laun af honum, utanferðina og hans umsjá.	Audun was also there and worked for him Thorir and then this reward of him, out-travelling and him about-see.	Audun was also there and worked for Thorir, and was rewarded by him with a place on his voyage, and taking care of him.
Hann Auðun lagði mestan hluta fjár þess er var fyrir móður sína áður hann stigi á skip og var kveðið á þriggja vetra björg.	He Audun laid most lot wealth this that was for mother his after he climbed on the-ship and was said of three winters aid.	Audun gave most of his wealth that was for his mother, once he had gone aboard the ship, and it was said to be three winters' worth of aid.
Og nú fara þeir út héðan og ferst þeim vel og var Auðun of veturinn eftir með Þóri stýrimanni.	And now travelled they out hence and travelled they well and was Audun of winter afterwards with Thorir skipper.	And now they travelled out from there, and they travelled well, and Audun spent the winter afterwards with the skipper Thorir.
Hann átti bú á Mæri.	He had a-farm in Moer.	He had a farm in Moer.
Og um sumarið eftir fara þeir út til Grænlands og eru þar of veturinn.	And about summer afterwards travelled they out to Greenland and were there of winter.	And around the summer afterwards they travelled out to Greenland and were there for the winter.

The Tale of Auðun of the West Fjords (Old Icelandic)

Old Icelandic	Literal	English
Þess er við getið að Auðun kaupir þar bjarndýri eitt, gersemi mikla, og gaf þar fyrir alla eigu sína.	This is with told-of that Audun bought there a-bear one, treasured much, and have there for all owned his.	It is told that Audun bought a bear there, which was much treasured, and gave all that he owned for it.
Og nú of sumarið eftir þá fara þeir aftur til Noregs og verða vel reiðfara.	And now of summer afterwards then travelled they returning to Norway and was well voyage.	And now about the summer afterwards then they travelled returning to Norway and the voyage went well.
Hefir Auðun dýr sitt með sér og ætlar nú að fara suður til Danmerkur á fund Sveins konungs og gefa honum dýrið.	Had Audun wild-animal his with him and intended now to travel south to Denmark to meet Svein the-king and give him the-beast.	Audun had his wild-animal with him and intended now to travel south to Denmark to meet King Svein and give him the beast.
Og er hann kom suður í landið þar sem konungur var fyrir þá gengur hann upp af skipi og leiðir eftir sér dýrið og leigir sér herbergi.	And as he came south to land there as the-king was present then went he up off the-ship and took behind him the-beast and rented himself a-room.	And as he came south to land, where the king was present, he then went up off the ship and took the beast with him and rented himself a room.
Haraldi konungi var sagt brátt að þar var komið bjarndýri, gersemi mikil, og á íslenskur maður.	Harald the-king was told soon that there was come a-bear, treasured much, and an Icelander man.	King Harald was soon told, that a bear had come, which was much treasured, and an Icelander.
Konungur sendir þegar menn eftir honum.	The-king sent straight-away people after him.	The king sent people to fetch him straight away,
Og er Auðun kom fyrir konung kveður hann konung vel.	And as Audun came before the-king greeted he the-king well.	and when Audun came before the king, he greeted the king well.
Konungur tók vel kveðju hans og spurði síðan:	The-king took well greeting his and asked afterwards:	The king received his greeting well and afterwards asked:
"Áttu gersemi mikla í bjarndýri?"	"Have-you treasured much a bear?"	"Do you have a bear which is much treasured?".
Hann svarar og kveðst eiga dýrið eitthvert.	He answered and said owned a-beast some-kind.	He answered and said that he owned a beast of some kind.
Konungur mælti:	The-king spoke:	The king spoke:
"Viltu selja oss dýrið við slíku verði sem þú keyptir?"	"Will-you sell us the-beast with such worth as you bought?"	"Will you sell us the beast for the same worth as you bought it?".
Hann svarar:	He answered:	He answered:

The Tale of Auðun of the West Fjords (Old Icelandic)

Old Icelandic	Literal	English
"Eigi vil eg það herra".	"Not wish i that lord".	"I do not wish to do that, lord".
"Viltu þá", segir konungur, "að eg gefi þér tvö verð slík og mun það réttara ef þú hefir þar við gefið alla þína eigu?"	"Will-you then" said the-king, "that i give to-you twice worth such and should that righter if you have there with given all you own?"	"Do you wish then", said the king, "that I give you twice the worth, and that should be right, if you have given all you own for it?".
"Eigi vil eg það herra", segir hann.	"Not wish i that lord" said he.	"I do not wish to do that, lord", he said.
Konungur mælti:	The-king spoke:	The king spoke:
"Viltu gefa mér þá?"	"Will-you give me then?"	"Will you give it to me then?".
Hann svarar:	He answered:	He answered:
"Eigi herra".	"Not lord".	"I will not, lord".
Konungur mælti:	The-king spoke:	The king spoke:
"Hvað viltu þá af gera?"	"What will-you then of do?"	"What do you wish to do then?".
Hann svarar:	He answered:	He answered:
"Fara suður til Danmerkur og gefa Sveini konungi".	"Travel south to Denmark and give Svein the-king".	"Travel", said he, to Denmark and give it to King Svein".
Haraldur konungur segir:	Harald the-king said:	King Harald said:
"Hvort er að þú ert maður svo óvitur að þú hefir eigi heyrt ófrið þann er í milli er landa þessa eða ætlar þú giftu þína svo mikla að þú munir þar komast með gersemar er aðrir fá eigi komist klakklaust þó að nauðsyn eigi til?"	"Whether is that you are a-man so unwise that you have none heard un-peace then that is between the land this or intend you give yours so much that you should there come with treasure that others get none coming unhurt though that necessary not to?"	"Is it possible, that you are an unwise man, that you have not heard of the state of war that is between these lands, or you suppose that you are so gifted that you would come there with treasure, where others have not gone unhurt though it was necessary?".
Auðun svarar:	Audun answered:	Audun answered:
"Herra það er á yðru valdi en öngu játum vér öðru en þessu er vér höfum áður ætlað".	"Lord that is for your will but none profess we other than this that we have before intended".	"That is for your will lord, but I cannot agree to anything other than what I have previously intended".

The Tale of Auðun of the West Fjords (Old Icelandic)

Old Icelandic	Literal	English
Þá mælti konungur:	Then spoke the-king:	Then the king spoke:
"Hví mun eigi það til að þú farir leið þína sem þú vilt og kom þá til mín er þú ferð aftur og seg mér hversu Sveinn konungur launar þér dýrið. Og kann það vera að þú sért gæfumaður".	"Why should not that to that you travel journey yours as you wish and come then to me that you travel back and say to-me how-so Svein the-king repays your beast. And can that be that you yourself gifted-man".	"Then why should you not, to travel on your journey, as you wish, and then come to me, when you travel back, and tell me how King Svein repays you for the beast, and can it be, that you will be a gifted man".
"Því heiti eg þér", sagði Auðun.	"Accordingly promise i to-you" said Audun.	"I promise this to you accordingly", said Audun.
Hann fer nú síðan suður með landi og í Vík austur og þá til Danmerkur og er þá uppi hver peningur fjárins og verður hann þá biðja matar bæði fyrir sig og fyrir dýrið.	He travelled now afterwards south along land and to Vik east and then to Denmark and was then up every penny of-wealth and was he then begging food both for himself and for the-beast.	He now travelled afterwards south along the land and to Vik east and then to Denmark, and then every penny of his wealth was spent, and he was then begging for food both for himself and for the beast.
Hann kemur á fund ármanns Sveins konungs þess er Áki hét og bað hann vista nakkvarra bæði fyrir sig og fyrir dýrið.	He came to meet steward Svein's the-king this was Aki named and asked him provisions some asked for himself and for the-beast.	He came to meet a steward of King Svein, who was named Aki, and he asked him for some provisions for himself and for the beast,
"Eg ætla", segir hann, "að gefa Sveini konungi dýrið".	"I intend" said he, "to give Svein the-king the-beast".	I intend, he said, "to give this beast to King Svein".
Áki lést selja mundu honum vistir ef hann vildi.	Aki said sell would him provisions if he wished.	Aki said that he would sell him provisions if he wished.
Auðun kveðst ekki til hafa fyrir að gefa "en eg vildi þó", segir hann, "að þetta kæmist til leiðar að eg mætti dýrið færa konungi".	Audun said not to have for to give "and i wish though" said he, "that this comes to-the-way that i might the-beast bring the-king".	Audun said that he did not have anything to give, "and though I wish", he said, "that I may be able t bring this beast to the king".
"Eg mun fá þér vistir sem þið þurfið til konungs fundar en þar í móti vil eg eiga hálft dýrið og máttu á það líta að dýrið mun deyja fyrir þér þars þið þurfið vistir miklar en fé sé farið og er búið við að þú hafir þá ekki dýrsins".	"I shall give you provisions that you need to-the-king meet then there on meeting will i own half the-beast and might be that look that the-beast could die for you there you need provisions much but money is gone and is settled with that you have then not the-beast".	"I shall give you provisions, that you need to meet the king, then on meeting him I will own half the beast, otherwise it might be, that the beast could die before you, there you will need many provisions, but your money is gone, and it shall be that you will then not have the beast".

The Tale of Auðun of the West Fjords (Old Icelandic)

Old Icelandic	Literal	English
Og er hann lítur á þetta sýnist honum nokkuð eftir sem ármaðurinn mælti fyrir honum og sættast þeir á þetta að hann selur Áka hálft dýrið og skal konungur síðan meta allt saman.	And when he looked a this considered he sometime afterwards what steward spoke before him and reconciled they to this that he sell Aki half the-beast and shall the-king afterwards value all the-same.	And when he looked at this, he considered for some time afterwards what the steward had said to him, and they reconciled to this, that he would sell Aki half of the beast, and the king would afterwards value it all the same.
Skulu þeir fara báðir nú á fund konungs. Og svo gera þeir, fara nú báðir á fund konungs og stóðu fyrir borðinu.	Shall they travel both now and meet the-king. And so did they, travelled now both to meet the-king and stood before table.	And should they now both travel and meet the king, and they did so, they both travelled to meet the king and stood before his tables.
Konungur íhugaði hver þessi maður mundi vera er hann kenndi eigi og mælti síðan til Auðunar:	The-king considered who this man should be that he knew not and spoke then to Audun:	The king considered, who this man should be, that he did not know, and then spoke to Audun:
"Hver ertu?" segir hann.	"Who are-you?" said he.	"Who are you?" he said.
Hann svarar:	He answered:	He answered:
"Eg em íslenskur maður herra", segir hann, "og kominn nú utan af Grænlandi og nú af Noregi og ætlaði eg að færa yður bjarndýr þetta.	"I am Icelander man lord" said he, "and coming now out out-of Greenland and now from Norway and intended I to bring your bear this.	"I am an Icelander, lord", he said, "and I have come from Greenland and from Norway intending to bring you this bear.
Keypti eg það með allri eigu minni og nú er þó á orðið mikið fyrir mér, eg á nú hálft eitt dýrið" og segir síðan konungi hversu farið hafði með þeim Áka ármanni hans.	Purchased I it with all own mine and now is though that become much for me, i of not half one beast" and told after the-king how-so fared had with them Aki the-steward his.	I purchased it with all that I own, and now though it has become much for me, I do not own half of the beast", and he then told the king, how it had gone with Aki, his steward.
Konungur mælti:	The-king spoke:	The king spoke:
"Er það satt Áki er hann segir?"	"Is that true Aki what he says?"	"Is that true, Aki, what he says?".
"Satt er það", segir hann.	"True is that" said he.	"That is true", he said.
Konungur mælti:	The-king spoke:	The king spoke:

The Tale of Auðun of the West Fjords (Old Icelandic)

Old Icelandic	Literal	English
"Og þótti þér það til liggja þar sem eg setti þig mikinn mann að hefta það eða tálma er maður gerðist til að færa mér gersemi og gaf fyrir alla eign og sá það Haraldur konungur að ráði að láta hann fara í friði og er hann vor óvinur?	"And thought you that to lay-out then since i intended you a-great man to stop that or prevent as a-man did to that bring to-me treasure and gave because all owned and so that Harald the-king that decided to let him travel in peace and that he our un-friend?	"And you thought to let this happen, even though I intended you to be a great man, to stop or prevent, as a man made to bring this treasure and give to me all that he owned, and even though King Harald decided to let him travel in peace, even though he is our enemy?
Hygg þú að þá hve sannlegt það var þinnar handar og það væri maklegt að þú værir drepinn.	Think you that then how true-like that was your hand and that should-be proper that you would-be killed.	Think then how true your hand was, and it would be right, that you should be killed.
En eg mun nú eigi það gera en braut skaltu fara þegar úr landinu og koma aldregi aftur síðan mér í augsýn.	But i should now not that do but away shall travel straight-away out-of this-land and come never back after to-me in eyesight.	I will not do what I should, but you shall travel away immediately out of this land and never come back in my sight.
En þér Auðun kann eg slíka þökk sem þú gefir mér allt dýrið og ver hér með mér".	But you Audun can i such thanks as you gave me all animal and be here with me".	But you, Audun, can I thank such as you gave me the whole animal, and be here with me".
Það þekkist hann og er með Sveini konungi um hríð.	That knew he and was with Svein the-king about awhile.	That he knew, and he was with King Svein for a while.

2   2   2

Old Icelandic	Literal	English
Og er liðu nakkverjar stundir þá mælti Auðun við konung:	And as passed some time then spoke Audun with the-king:	And as some time has passed, then Audun spoke with the king:
"Braut fýsir mig nú herra".	"Away desire me now lord".	"I desire now to travel away, lord".
Konungur svarar heldur seint:	The-king answered rather coldly:	The king answered rather coldly:
"Hvað viltu þá", segir hann, "ef þú vilt eigi með oss vera?"	"What will-you then" said he, "if you wish not with us be?"	"What do you wish for then", he said, "if not to be with us?".
Hann svarar:	He answered:	He said:
"Suður vil eg ganga".	"South wish i to-go".	"I wish to go south".

The Tale of Auðun of the West Fjords (Old Icelandic)

Old Icelandic	Literal	English
"Ef þú vildir eigi svo gott ráð taka", segir konungur, "þá mundi mér fyrir þykja í er þú fýsist í brott".	"If you wish not so good course take" said the-king, "then would me for think it that you desire to away".	"If you did not wish to take such a good course", said the king, "I would mind it to think that you desire to go away".
Og nú gaf konungur honum silfur mjög mikið og fór hann suður síðan með Rúmferlum og skipaði konungur til um ferð hans, bað hann koma til sín er hann kæmi aftur.	And now gave the-king him silver much great and travelled he south afterwards with Rome-travellers and directed the-king to about travel his, asked him come to him when he came returning.	And now the king gave him much great silver, and he travelled south afterwards with pilgrims, and the king made arrangements for his journey, and asked him to come to him when he returned.
Nú fór hann ferðar sinnar uns hann kemur suður í Rómaborg.	Now travelled he journey his until he came south to Rome-city.	Now he travelled on his journey, until he came south to Rome.
Og er hann hefir þar dvalist sem hann tíðir þá fer hann aftur, tekur þá sótt mikla. Gerir hann þá ákaflega magran.	And as he had there dwelled such he a-time then travelled he returning, took then sickness much. Made him then extremely thin.	And when he had dwelled there for such a time, he travelled to return, and took to much sickness, which made him extremely thin.
Gengur þá upp allt féið það er konungur hafði gefið honum til ferðarinnar, tekur síðan upp stafkarls stíg og biður sér matar.	Went then up all treasure that which the-king had given him to travelling, taking afterwards up beggar's-path path and asked he food.	Gone was all his treasure, which the king had given him for travelling, and afterwards he took to begging and he asked for food.
Hann er þá kollóttur og heldur ósællegur.	He was then bald and rather unhappy.	He was then bald and rather unhappy.
Hann kemur aftur í Danmörk að páskum þangað sem konungur er þá staddur en ei þorði hann að láta sjá sig og var í kirkjuskoti og ætlaði þá til fundar við konung er hann gengi til kirkju um kveldið.	He came back to Denmark at easter there as the-king was then standing but not dared he to let seen himself and was in church-wing and intended then to meet with the-king when he went to church around evening.	He came back to Denmark at Easter, there where the king was standing, but he dared not to let himself be seen, and was in the church wing and intended to meet with the king, when he went to church in the evening.
Og nú er hann sá konunginn og hirðina fagurlega búna þá þorði hann eigi að láta sjá sig.	And now when he saw the-king and guardsmen beautifully prepared then dared he not to let seen himself.	And now when he saw the king and the guardsmen so beautifully dressed, then he dared not to let himself be seen.

The Tale of Auðun of the West Fjords (Old Icelandic)

Old Icelandic	Literal	English
Og er konungur gekk til drykkju í höllina þá mataðist Auðun úti sem siður er til Rúmferla meðan þeir hafa eigi kastað staf og skreppu.	And when the-king went to drinking in the-hall then ate Audun outside as custom is for Rome-travellers while they have not cast staff and pouch.	And when the king went drinking in the hall, Audun ate outside, which was the custom for pilgrims, while they have cast aside their staff and pouch.
Og nú of aftaninn er konungur gekk til kveldsöngs ætlaði Auðun að hitta hann. Og svo mikið sem honum þótti fyrr fyrir jók nú miklu á er þeir voru drukknir hirðmennirnir.	And now of evening as the-king going to evensong intended Audun to meet him. And so much as he thought for before increased now much for that they were in-drink the-courtiers.	And now in the evening, as the king was going to evensong, Audun intended to meet him, and as much as he had thought before was now increased, because the courtiers were drunk.
Og er þeir gengu inn aftur þá þekkti konungur mann og þóttist finna að eigi hafði frama til að ganga fram að hitta hann.	And as they went inside back then noticed the-king a-man and thought found that not had confidence to that going from to meet him.	And as they went back inside, then the king thought he noticed a man thought he found, that he did not have the confidence in going to meet him.
Og er hirðin gekk inn þá veik konungur út og mælti:	And as the-courtiers going inside then turned-to the-king out and spoke:	And now as the courtiers were going inside, then the king turned and spoke out:
"Gangi sá nú fram er mig vill finna.	"Come so now forth who me wishes to-meet.	"Come forth now, who wishes to meet me.
Mig grunar að sá muni vera maðurinn".	I suspect that so shall be a-man".	For I suspect that there is such a man".
Þá gekk Auðun fram og féll til fóta konungi og varla kenndi konungur hann.	Then went Audun forth and fell to feet the-king's and hardly recognised the-king him.	Then Audun went forth and fell at the king's feet, and the king hardly recognised him.
Og þegar er konungur veit hver hann er tók konungur í hönd honum Auðuni og bað hann velkominn "og hefir þú mikið skipast", segir hann, "síðan við sáumst", leiðir hann eftir sér inn.	And as-soon-as that the-king knew who he was took the-king in hand him Audun and asked him well "and have you much changed" said he, "since we saw" led he after him inside.	And as soon as the king knew who he was, the king took Audun in hand and bid him welcome, "and you have changed much", he said, "since we last saw each other", and after he led him inside.
Og er hirðin sá hann hlógu þeir að honum en konungur sagði:	And when courtiers saw him laughed they at him but the-king said:	And when the courtiers saw him, they laughed at him, but the king said:

The Tale of Auðun of the West Fjords (Old Icelandic)

Old Icelandic	Literal	English
"Eigi þurfið þér að honum að hlæja því að betur hefir hann séð fyrir sinni sál heldur en þér".	"None need you that him to laugh because that better has he himself seen for his soul rather than you".	"None of you need to laugh at him, because he has seen better for his soul than any of you".
Þá lét konungur gera honum laug og gaf honum síðan klæði og er hann nú með honum.	Then had the-king made him bath and gave him afterwards clothes and was he not with him.	Then the king had a bath made for him, and afterwards gave him clothes, and he was now with him.

3

Það er nú sagt einhverju sinni of vorið að konungur býður Auðuni að vera með sér álengdar og kveðst mundu gera hann skutilsvein sinn og leggja til hans góða virðing.	It is now said one-such on-the-way to spring that the-king bid Audun to be with him all-longer and said would make him cup-bearer his and grant to him good worth.	It is now said, that on the way to spring, the king invited Audun to be with him for all of his days, and said that he would make him his cup-bearer and grant him good worthiness.
Auðun segir:	Audun said:	Audun said:
"Guð þakki yður herra sóma þann allan er þér viljið til mín leggja en hitt er mér í skapi að fara út til Íslands".	"God thank you lord honour this all that you wish to me grant but find i to-me of mind to travel out to Iceland".	"God thank you, lord, for all this honour that you wish to grant me, but I find in my mind, to travel out to Iceland".
Konungur segir:	The-king said:	The king said:
"Þetta sýnist mér undarlega kosið".	"This seems to-me strange choice".	"This seems a strange choice to me".
Auðun mælti:	Audun spoke:	Audun spoke:
"Eigi má eg það vita herra", segir hann, "að eg hafi hér mikinn sóma með yður en móðir mín troði stafkarls stíg út á Íslandi því að nú er lokið björg þeirri er eg lagði til áður eg færi af Íslandi".	"Not may i that know lord" said he, "that i have here much honour with you but mother mine treads the-beggar's path out in Iceland for that now is ended help there that i enriched to before i travelled from Iceland".	"Not may I know, lord", said he, "that I have much honour here with you, but my mother treads the beggar's path out in Iceland, for now my help there is ended, that which I enriched her with, before I travelled out from Iceland".
Konungur svarar:	The-king answered:	The king answered:
"Vel er mælt", segir hann, "og mannlega og muntu verða giftumaður.	"Well is spoken" said he, "and man-like and shall-you be gifted-man.	"It is well spoken", said he, "and like a man, and you shall be a gifted man.

The Tale of Auðun of the West Fjords (Old Icelandic)

Old Icelandic	Literal	English
Sjá einn var svo hluturinn að mér mundi eigi mislíka að þú færir í braut héðan og ver nú með mér þar til er skip búast".	So one as such thing that to-me should not mislike that you travel to away from-here and be now with me then until that ship prepared".	So there is one such thing, that I should not dislike, that you travel away from here, and be now with me, then until a ship is prepared".
Hann gerir svo.	He did so.	He did so.
Einn dag er á leið vorið gekk Sveinn konungur ofan á bryggjur og voru menn þá að að búa skip til ýmissa landa, í Austurveg eða Saxland, til Svíþjóðar eða Noregs.	One day when it passed spring went Svein the-king over-to the quay and were people then about that prepared ships to various lands, in Eastern-lands or Saxon-lands, to Sweden or Norway.	One day, when spring had passed, King Svein went over to the quay, and there were people about preparing ships for various lands, Eastern-lands, Saxon-lands, to Sweden or Norway.
Þá koma þeir Auðun að einu skipi fögru og voru menn að að búa skipið.	Then came there Audun to one ship beautiful and were people that it prepared ship.	Then Audun came to a beautiful ship, and there were people that were preparing the ship.
Þá spurði konungur:	Then asked the-king:	Then the king asked:
"Hversu líst þér Auðun á þetta skip?"	"How-so appears to-you Audun about this ship?"	"How does this ship appear to you, Audun?"
Hann svarar:	He answered:	He answered:
"Vel herra".	"Well lord".	"Well lord".
Konungur mælti:	The-king spoke:	The king spoke:
"Þetta skip vil eg þér gefa og launa bjarndýrið".	"This ship wish i to-you give and reward the-bear".	"I wish to give you this ship as a reward for the bear".
Hann þakkaði gjöfina eftir sinni kunnustu.	He thanked the-gift after he knew-how.	He thanked him for the gift as well as he knew how.
Og er leið stund og skipið var albúið þá mælti Sveinn konungur við Auðun:	And when passed awhile and ship was all-prepared then spoke Svein the-king with Audun:	And when a while had passed and the ship was all prepared, then King Svein spoke with Audun:

The Tale of Auðun of the West Fjords (Old Icelandic)

Old Icelandic	Literal	English
"Þó viltu nú á braut þá mun eg nú ekki letja þig en það hefi eg spurt að illt er til hafna fyrir landi yðru og eru víða öræfi og hætt skipum.	"Though will now to away then should i now not discourage you but it have i heard that ill is to harbour for land yours and they-are widely wild and at-risk ships.	"Though you now wish to go away, then I should not now discourage you, but I have heard that bad are the harbours in your land, and they are widely wild and ships are at risk.
Nú brýtur þú og týnir skipinu og fénu.	Now wrecked you and lose the-ship and cargo.	Now should your ship be wrecked and you lose your ship and cargo.
Lítt sér það þá á að þú hafir fundið Svein konung og gefið honum gersemi".	Little to-you that then be that you have met Svein the-king and gave him treasure".	You shall have little to say that you have met King Svein and gave him treasure".
Síðan seldi konungur honum leðurhosu fulla af silfri "og ertu þá enn eigi félaus með öllu þótt þú brjótir skipið ef þú færð haldið þessu.	Afterwards handed-over the-king to-him leather-purse full of silver "and are-you then one not money-less with all though you wrecked ship if you go holding this.	Afterwards the king handed over to him a leather purse full of silver, "and are you then not penniless, even though your ship is wrecked, if you hold on to this.
Verða má svo enn" segir konungur, "að þú týnir þessu fé. Lítt nýtur þú þá þess, er þú fannst Svein konung og gafst honum gersemi".	Become may so then" said the-king, "that you lose this money. Little benefit you then this, that you found Svein the-king and gave him treasure".	But if it becomes then", said the king, "that you lose this money. It will benefit you little then, that you have met King Svein and given him treasure".
Síðan dró konungur hring af hendi sér og gaf Auðuni og mælti:	Then drew the-king a-ring of hand his and gave Audun and spoke:	Then the king drew a ring from his hand and gave it to Audun saying:
"Þó að svo illa verði að þú brjótir skipið og týnir fénu, eigi ertu félaus ef þú kemst á land því að margir menn hafa gull á sér í skipsbrotum og sér þá að þú hefir fundið Svein konung ef þú heldur hringinum.	"Though that so ill be that you wrecked ship and lose money, not are-you money-less if you came to land therefore that many people have gold about themselves for ship-wreck and yourself then that you have met Svein the-king if you hold the-ring.	"Even though it would be so bad if your ship was wrecked, and you lose all the money, you shall not be penniless, therefore many people have gold about themselves in case of being shipwrecked, and you shall have met King Svein, if you hold on to this ring.
En það vil eg ráða þér", segir hann, "að þú gefir eigi hringinn nema þú þykist eiga svo mikið gott að launa nakkverjum göfgum manni, þá gef þeim hringinn því að tignum mönnum sómir að þiggja.	But that wish i advise to-you" said he, "that you give not the-ring except you think not so much good to reward some noble man, then give them the-ring for that dignified people honourable that accept.	But I wish to advise you", he said, "that you do not give the ring to anyone, unless you think it will be good to reward some noble man, then give them the ring, for dignified and honourable people will accept.

The Tale of Auðun of the West Fjords (Old Icelandic)

Old Icelandic	Literal	English
Og far nú heill".	And travel now whole".	And now travel whole".
4	**4**	**4**
Síðan lætur hann í haf og kemur í Noreg og lætur flytja upp varnað sinn og þurfti nú meira við það en fyrr er hann var í Noregi.	Afterwards laid he to sea and came to Norway and had carried up wares his and needed now more with that than before when he was in Norway.	Afterwards he put to sea and came to Norway and had his wares carried up, which he needed more now than before, when he was in Norway.
Hann fer nú síðan á fund Haralds konungs og vill efna það er hann hét honum áður hann fór til Danmerkur og kveður konung vel.	He travelled now afterwards to meet Harald the-king and wished carry-out that which he promised him before he travelled to Denmark and greeted the-king well.	He travelled now afterwards to meet King Harald, as he wished to carry out what he had promised him, before he travelled to Denmark, and he greeted the king well.
Haraldur konungur tók vel kveðju hans "og sest niður", segir hann, "og drekk hér með oss".	Harald the-king received well greeting his "and sit down" said he, "and drink here with us".	King Harald received his greeting well, "and sit down", he said, "and drink here with us".
Og svo gerir hann.	And so did he.	And so he did.
Þá spurði Haraldur konungur:	Then asked Harald the-king:	Then King Harald asked:
"Hverju launaði Sveinn konungur þér dýrið?"	"How rewarded Svein the-king you the-beast?"	"How did King Svein reward you for the beast?".
Auðun svarar:	Audun answered:	Audun answered:
"Því herra að hann þá að mér".	"Because lord that he then at me".	"Because lord, that he accepted it of me".
Konungur sagði:	The-king said:	The king said:
"Launað mundi eg þér því hafa. Hverju launaði hann enn?"	"Repaid should i you accordingly have. How rewarded he then?"	"I would have repaid you accordingly. How did he reward you then?".
Auðun svarar:	Audun answered:	Audun answered:
"Gaf hann mér silfur til suðurgöngu".	"Gave he me silver to south-going".	"He gave me silver to go south".
Þá segir Haraldur konungur:	Then said Harald the-king:	Then King Harald said:

The Tale of Auðun of the West Fjords (Old Icelandic)

Old Icelandic	Literal	English
"Mörgum manni gefur Sveinn konungur silfur til suðurgöngu eða annarra hluta þótt ekki færi honum gersemar.	"Many people gives Svein the-king silver to south-going or others lots though not bring him treasure.	"King Svein gives many people silver to go south, lots of others, though they do not bring him treasure".
Hvað er enn fleira?"	What was it more?"	What was it more?".
"Hann bauð mér", segir Auðun, "að gerast skutilsveinn hans og mikinn sóma til mín að leggja".	"He bid me" said Audun, "to be cup-bearer his and much honour to me that granted".	"He invited me", said Audun, "to be his cup-bearer and to grant me much honour".
"Vel var það mælt", segir konungur, "og launa mundi hann enn fleira".	"Well was that said" said the-king, "and rewarded would he then more".	"That was well said", said the king, "and he would reward you more".
Auðun segir:	Audun said:	Audun said:
"Gaf hann mér knörr með farmi þeim er hingað er best varið í Noreg".	"Gave he me a-ship with cargo then that there was best wares in Norway".	"He then gave me a ship with cargo, of wares that sell best in Norway".
"Það var stórmannlegt", segir konungur, "en launað mundi eg þér því hafa. Launaði hann því fleira?"	"That was great-man-like" said the-king, "but rewarded would i you accordingly have. Rewarded he then more?"	"That was generous", said the king, "but I would have rewarded you accordingly. Did he reward you then more?".
Auðun segir:	Audun said:	Audun said:
"Gaf hann mér leðurhosu fulla af silfri og kvað mig þá eigi félausan ef eg héldi því þó að skip mitt bryti við Ísland".	"Gave he to-me leather-purse full of silver and said to-me then not money-less if i held therefore though that ship mine break at Iceland".	"He gave me a leather purse full of silver, and said to me that if I held it I would therefore not be penniless, even if my ship was wrecked in Iceland".
Konungur segir:	The-king said:	The king said:
"Það var ágætlega gert og það mundi eg ekki gert hafa. Laus mundi eg þykjast ef eg gæfi þér skipið. Hvort launaði hann fleira?"	"That was greatly done and that would i not done have. Less should i seem if i gave you the-ship. How rewarded he more?"	"That was greatly done, and I would not have done that. Less would I think, if I gave you the ship. How did he reward you more?".

The Tale of Auðun of the West Fjords (Old Icelandic)

Old Icelandic	Literal	English
"Svo var víst herra", segir Auðun, "að hann launaði. Hann gaf mér hring þenna er eg hefi á hendi og kvað svo mega að berast að eg týndi fénu öllu og sagði mig þá eigi félausan ef eg ætti hringinn og bað mig eigi lóga nema eg ætti nakkverjum tignum manni svo gott að launa að eg vildi gefa.	"So was certainly lord" said Audun, "that he rewarded. He gave me ring this that i have in hand and said so may it bear that i lose money all and said to-me then not money-less if i had the-ring and bid me not lose except i have some noble man so good to repay that i wish give.	"So it certainly was, lord", said Audun, "that he rewarded. He gave me this ring, that I have in hand, and so it may bear, though I lose all my money, it is said to me that I would not be penniless, if I had the ring, and he asked me not to part with it, unless I have some noble man so good to repay, that I wish to give it to.
En nú hefi eg þann fundið því að þú áttir kost að taka hvorttveggja frá mér, dýrið og svo líf mitt, en þú lést mig fara þangað í friði sem aðrir náðu eigi".	But now have i then found because that you have benefit to take either-way from me, the-beast and so life mine, but you let me travel from-here in peace as others reached not".	But now then I have found, because you could have taken away from me, the beast or my life, but you let me travel from here in peace, as others could not".
Konungur tók við gjöfinni með blíði og gaf Auðuni í móti góðar gjafar áður en þeir skildust.	The-king received with the-gift with joyfulness and gave Audun in return good gifts before that they separated.	The king received the gift with joyfulness and gave Audun good gifts in return, before they separated.
Auðun varði fénu til Íslandsferðar og fór út þegar um sumarið til Íslands og þótti vera hinn mesti gæfumaður.	Audun was wealth to Iceland-journey and travelled out from-there about summer to Iceland and thought was the most gifted-man.	Audun used his wealth to travel to Iceland and travelled out from there around summer to Iceland and he was thought of as the most gifted man.
Frá þessum manni, Auðuni, var kominn Þorsteinn Gyðuson.	From this people, Audun, was descended Thorstein Gyduson.	From these people, Audun, were descended Thorstein Gyduson.

Word List (Old Icelandic to English)

Word List (Old Icelandic to English)

Old Icelandic	English

A, a

að	about, at, by, it, that, to
aðrir	others
af	from, of, off, out-of
aftaninn	evening
aftur	back, returning
albúið	all-prepared
aldregi	never
alla	all
allan	all
allri	all
allt	all
annarra	others
Auðun	Audun (name)
Auðunar	Audun (name)
Auðuni	Audun (name)
augsýn	eyesight
austur	east
Austurveg	Eastern-lands (place)

Á, á

á	a, about, an, and, be, for, in, it, of, on, that, the, to
áður	after, before
ágætlega	greatly
Áka	Aki (name)
ákaflega	extremely
Áki	Aki (name)
álengdar	all-longer
ármaðurinn	steward
ármanni	the-steward
ármanns	steward
átti	had
áttir	have
áttu	have-you

Æ, æ

ætla	intend
ætlað	intended
ætlaði	intended
ætlar	intend, intended
ætti	had, have

B, b

bað	asked, bid
báðir	both
bæði	asked, both
bauð	bid
berast	bear
best	best
betur	better
biðja	begging
biður	asked
bjarndýr	bear
bjarndýri	a-bear, bear
bjarndýrið	the-bear
björg	aid, help
blíði	joyfulness
borðinu	table
brátt	soon
braut	away
brjótir	wrecked
brott	away
bryggjur	quay
bryti	break
brýtur	wrecked
bú	a-farm
búa	prepared
búanda	farmer
búast	prepared
búið	settled
búna	prepared
býður	bid

D, d

dag	day

Word List (Old Icelandic to English)

Old Icelandic	English
Danmerkur	Denmark (place)
Danmörk	Denmark (place)
deyja	die
drekk	drink
drepinn	killed
dró	drew
drukknir	in-drink
drykkju	drinking
dvalist	dwelled
dýr	wild-animal
dýrið	a-beast, animal, beast, the-beast
dýrsins	the-beast

E, e

Old Icelandic	English
eða	or
ef	if
efna	carry-out
eftir	after, afterwards, behind
eg	i
ei	not
eiga	not, own, owned
eigi	none, not
eign	owned
eigu	own, owned
einhverju	one-such
einn	one
einu	one
eitt	one
eitthvert	some-kind
ekki	not
em	am
en	and, but, than, that, then
enn	it, one, then
er	as, i, is, that, the, was, what, when, which, who
ert	are
ertu	are-you
eru	they-are, were

F, f

Old Icelandic	English
fá	get, give
færa	bring
færð	go
færi	bring, travelled
færir	travel
fagurlega	beautifully
fannst	found
far	travel
fara	travel, travelled
farið	fared, gone
farir	travel
farmi	cargo
fé	money
féið	treasure
félaus	money-less
félausan	money-less
félítill	fee-little
féll	fell
fénu	cargo, money, wealth
fer	travelled
ferð	travel
ferðar	journey
ferðarinnar	travelling
ferst	travelled
finna	found, to-meet
fjár	wealth
fjárins	of-wealth
fjörðum	fields
fleira	more
flytja	carried
fögru	beautiful
fór	travelled
fóta	feet
frá	from
fram	forth, from
frama	confidence
friði	peace
fulla	full
fund	meet
fundar	meet
fundið	found, met
fyrir	because, before, for, present
fyrr	before, for
fýsir	desire

106

Word List (Old Icelandic to English)

Old Icelandic	English
fýsist	desire

G, g

Old Icelandic	English
gæfi	gave
gæfumaður	gifted-man
gaf	gave, have
gafst	gave
ganga	going, to-go
gangi	come
gef	give
gefa	give
gefi	give
gefið	gave, given
gefir	gave, give
gefur	gives
gekk	going, went
gengi	went
gengu	went
gengur	went
gera	did, do, made, make
gerast	be
gerðist	did
gerir	did, made
gersemar	treasure
gersemi	treasure, treasured
gert	done
getið	told-of
giftu	give
giftumaður	gifted-man
gjafar	gifts
gjöfina	the-gift
gjöfinni	the-gift
góða	good
góðar	good
góðs	good
göfgum	noble
gott	good
Grænlandi	Greenland (place)
Grænlands	Greenland (place)
grunar	suspect
Guð	God (name)
gull	gold
Gyðuson	Gyduson (name)

H, h

Old Icelandic	English
hætt	at-risk
haf	sea
hafa	have
hafði	had
hafi	have
hafir	have
hafna	harbour
haldið	holding
hálft	half
handar	hand
hann	he, he himself, him
hans	him, his
Haraldi	Harald (name)
Haralds	Harald (name)
Haraldur	Harald (name)
héðan	from-here, hence
hefi	have
hefir	had, has, have
hefta	stop
heill	whole
heiti	promise
héldi	held
heldur	hold, rather
hendi	hand
hér	here
herbergi	a-room
herra	lord
hét	named, promised
heyrt	heard
hingað	there
hinn	the
hirðin	courtiers, the-courtiers
hirðina	guardsmen
hirðmennirnir	the-courtiers
hitt	find
hitta	meet
hlæja	laugh
hlógu	laughed
hluta	lot, lots
hluturinn	thing
höfum	have
höllina	the-hall

107

Word List (Old Icelandic to English)

Old Icelandic	English
hönd	hand
honum	he, him, to-him
hríð	awhile
hring	a-ring, ring
hringinn	the-ring
hringinum	the-ring
hvað	what
hve	how
hver	every, who
hverju	how
hversu	how-so
hví	why
hvort	how, whether
hvorttveggja	either-way
hygg	think

I, i

illa	ill
illt	ill
inn	inside

Í, í

í	a, for, in, is, it, of, on, to
íhugaði	considered
Ísland	Iceland (place)
Íslandi	Iceland (place)
Íslands	Iceland (place)
íslandsferðar	Iceland-journey
Íslenskur	Icelander (name)

J, j

játum	profess
jók	increased

K, k

kæmi	came
kæmist	comes
kann	can
kastað	cast
kaupir	bought
kemst	came
kemur	came
kenndi	knew, recognised
keypti	purchased
keyptir	bought
kirkju	church
kirkjuskoti	church-wing
klæði	clothes
klakklaust	unhurt
knörr	a-ship
kollóttur	bald
kom	came, come
koma	came, come
komast	come
komið	come
kominn	coming, descended
komist	coming
konung	the-king
konungi	the-king, the-king's
konunginn	the-king
konungs	the-king
konungur	the-king
kosið	choice
kost	benefit
kunnustu	knew-how
kvað	said
kveðið	said
kveðju	greeting
kveðst	said
kveður	greeted
kveldið	evening
kveldsöngs	evensong
kyni	kin

L, l

lætur	had, laid
lagði	enriched, laid
land	land
landa	land, lands
landi	land
landið	land

Word List (Old Icelandic to English)

Old Icelandic	English
landinu	this-land
láta	let
laug	bath
laun	reward
launa	repay, reward, rewarded
launað	repaid, rewarded
launaði	rewarded
launar	repays
laus	less
leðurhosu	leather-purse
leggja	grant, granted
leið	journey, passed
leiðar	the-way
leiðir	led, took
leigir	rented
lést	let, said
lét	had
letja	discourage
liðu	passed
líf	life
liggja	lay-out
líst	appears
líta	look
lítt	little
lítur	looked
lóga	lose
lokið	ended

M, m

Old Icelandic	English
má	may
maður	a-man, man
maðurinn	a-man
mælt	said, spoken
mælti	spoke
Mæri	Moer (place)
mætti	might
magran	thin
maklegt	proper
mann	a-man, man
manni	man, people
mannlega	man-like
margir	many
mataðist	ate
matar	food
máttu	might
með	along, with
meðan	while
mega	may
meira	more
menn	people
mér	me, to-me
mestan	most
mesti	most
meta	value
mig	i, me, to-me
mikið	great, much
mikil	much
mikinn	a-great, much
mikla	much
miklar	much
miklu	much
milli	between
mín	me, mine
minni	mine
mislíka	mislike
mitt	mine
mjög	much
móðir	mother
móður	mother
mönnum	people
mörgum	many
móti	meeting, return
mun	could, shall, should
mundi	should, would
mundu	would
muni	shall
munir	should
muntu	shall-you

N, n

Old Icelandic	English
náðu	reached
nakkvarra	some
nakkverjar	some
nakkverjum	some
nauðsyn	necessary
nema	except
niður	down

Word List (Old Icelandic to English)

Old Icelandic	English
nokkuð	sometime
Noreg	Norway (place)
Noregi	Norway (place)
Noregs	Norway (place)
nú	not, now
nýtur	benefit

O, o

of	of, over, to
ofan	over-to
og	also, and
orðið	become
oss	us

Ó, ó

ófrið	un-peace
ósællegur	unhappy
óvinur	un-friend
óvitur	unwise

Ö, ö

öðru	other
öllu	all
öngu	none
öræfi	wild

P, p

páskum	easter
peningur	penny

R, r

ráð	course
ráða	advise
ráði	decided
reiðfara	voyage
réttara	righter

Old Icelandic	English
Rómaborg	Rome-city (place)
rúmferla	rome-travellers
rúmferlum	rome-travellers

S, s

sá	saw, so
sættast	reconciled
sagði	said, said
sagt	said, told
sál	soul
saman	the-same
sannlegt	true-like
satt	true
sáumst	saw
Saxland	Saxon-lands (place)
sé	is
séð	seen
seg	say
segir	said, says, told
seint	coldly
seldi	handed-over
selja	sell
selur	sell
sem	as, since, such, that, what
sendir	sent
sér	he, him, himself, his, themselves, to-you, yourself
sért	yourself
sest	sit
setti	intended
síðan	after, afterwards, since, then
siður	custom
sig	himself
silfri	silver
silfur	silver
sín	him
sína	his
sinn	his
sinnar	his
sinni	he, his, on-the-way
sitt	his

Word List (Old Icelandic to English)

Old Icelandic	English
sjá	seen, so
skal	shall
skaltu	shall
skapi	mind
skildust	separated
skip	ship, ships, the-ship
skipaði	directed
skipast	changed
skipi	ship, the-ship
skipið	ship, the-ship
skipinu	the-ship
skipsbrotum	ship-wreck
skipum	ships
skreppu	pouch
skulu	shall
skutilsvein	cup-bearer
skutilsveinn	cup-bearer
slík	such
slíka	such
slíku	such
sóma	honour
sómir	honourable
sótt	sickness
spurði	asked
spurt	heard
staddur	standing
staf	staff
stafkarls	beggar's-path, the-beggar's
starfaði	worked
stíg	path
stigi	climbed
stóðu	stood
stórmannlegt	great-man-like
stund	awhile
stundir	time
stýrimanni	skipper
stýrimanns	skipper
suður	south
suðurgöngu	south-going
sumarið	summer
svarar	answered
Svein	Svein (name)
Sveini	Svein (name)
Sveinn	Svein (name)
Sveins	Svein (name), Svein's (name)
Svíþjóðar	Sweden (place)
svo	so, such
sýnist	considered, seems

T, t

Old Icelandic	English
taka	take
tálma	prevent
tekur	taking, took
tíðir	a-time
tignum	dignified, noble
til	for, to, until
tók	received, took
troði	treads
tvö	twice
týndi	lose
týnir	lose

Þ, þ

Old Icelandic	English
þá	then
það	it, that
þakkaði	thanked
þakki	thank
þangað	from-here, there
þann	then, this
þar	then, there
þars	there
þegar	as-soon-as, from-there, straight-away
þegið	received
þeim	them, then, they
þeir	there, they
þeirri	there
þekkist	knew
þekkti	noticed
þenna	this
þér	to-you, you, your
þess	this
þessa	this
þessi	this
þessu	this

Word List (Old Icelandic to English)

Old Icelandic	English
þessum	this
þetta	this
þið	you
þig	you
þiggja	accept
þína	you, yours
þinnar	your
þó	though
þökk	thanks
þorði	dared
Þóri	Thorir (name)
Þóris	Thorir (name)
Þorsteini	Thorstein (name)
Þorsteinn	Thorstein (name)
Þorsteins	Thorstein (name)
þótt	though
þótti	thought
þóttist	thought
þriggja	three
þú	you
þurfið	need
þurfti	needed
því	accordingly, because, for, then, therefore
þykist	think
þykja	think
þykjast	seem

U, u

Old Icelandic	English
um	about, around
umráði	managed
umsjá	about-see
undarlega	strange
uns	until
upp	up
uppi	up
utan	out
utanferðina	out-travelling

Ú, ú

Old Icelandic	English
úr	out-of
út	out
úti	outside

V, v

Old Icelandic	English
væri	should-be
værir	would-be
valdi	will
var	as, was
varði	was
varið	wares
varla	hardly
varnað	wares
veik	turned-to
veit	knew
vel	well
velkominn	well
ver	be
vér	we
vera	be, was
verð	worth
verða	be, become, was
verði	be, worth
verður	was
Vestfirskur	Westfjords (place)
vestur	west
vetra	winters
veturinn	winter
við	at, we, with
víða	widely
Vík	Vik (place)
vil	will, wish
vildi	wish, wished
vildir	wish
viljið	wish
vill	wished, wishes
vilt	wish
viltu	will, will-you
virðing	worth
vist	hospitality
víst	certainly
vista	provisions
vistir	provisions
vita	know
vor	our
vorið	spring

Word List (Old Icelandic to English)

Old Icelandic	English
voru	were

Y, y

yðru	your, yours
yður	you, your

Ý, ý

ýmissa	various

Word List (English to Old Icelandic)

Word List (English to Old Icelandic)

English	Old Icelandic

A, a

English	Old Icelandic
a	á, í
a-bear	bjarndýri
a-beast	dýrið
about	á, að, um
about-see	umsjá
accept	þiggja
accordingly	því
advise	ráða
a-farm	bú
after	áður, eftir, síðan
afterwards	eftir, síðan
a-great	mikinn
aid	björg
Aki (name)	Áka, Áki
all	alla, allan, allri, allt, öllu
all-longer	álengdar
all-prepared	albúið
along	með
also	og
am	em
a-man	maður, maðurinn, mann
an	á
and	á, en, og
animal	dýrið
answered	svarar
appears	líst
are	ert
are-you	ertu
a-ring	hring
a-room	herbergi
around	um
as	er, sem, var
a-ship	knörr
asked	bað, bæði, biður, spurði
as-soon-as	þegar
at	að, við
ate	mataðist
a-time	tíðir
at-risk	hætt
Audun (name)	Auðun, Auðunar, Auðuni
away	braut, brott
awhile	hríð, stund

B, b

English	Old Icelandic
back	aftur
bald	kollóttur
bath	laug
be	á, gerast, ver, vera, verða, verði
bear	berast, bjarndýr, bjarndýri
beast	dýrið
beautiful	fögru
beautifully	fagurlega
because	fyrir, því
become	orðið, verða
before	áður, fyrir, fyrr
beggar's-path	stafkarls
begging	biðja
behind	eftir
benefit	kost, nýtur
best	best
better	betur
between	milli
bid	bað, bauð, býður
both	báðir, bæði
bought	kaupir, keyptir
break	bryti
bring	færa, færi
but	en
by	að

C, c

English	Old Icelandic
came	kæmi, kemst, kemur, kom, koma
can	kann
cargo	farmi, fénu
carried	flytja

Word List (English to Old Icelandic)

English	*Old Icelandic*	English	*Old Icelandic*
carry-out	*efna*		
cast	*kastað*	# E, e	
certainly	*víst*		
changed	*skipast*	east	*austur*
choice	*kosið*	easter	*páskum*
church	*kirkju*	Eastern-lands (place)	*Austurveg*
church-wing	*kirkjuskoti*	either-way	*hvorttveggja*
climbed	*stigi*	ended	*lokið*
clothes	*klæði*	enriched	*lagði*
coldly	*seint*	evening	*aftaninn, kveldið*
come	*gangi, kom, koma, komast, komið*	evensong	*kveldsöngs*
		every	*hver*
comes	*kæmist*	except	*nema*
coming	*kominn, komist*	extremely	*ákaflega*
confidence	*frama*	eyesight	*augsýn*
considered	*íhugaði, sýnist*		
could	*mun*	# F, f	
course	*ráð*		
courtiers	*hirðin*	fared	*farið*
cup-bearer	*skutilsvein, skutilsveinn*	farmer	*búanda*
		fee-little	*félítill*
custom	*siður*	feet	*fóta*
		fell	*féll*
# D, d		fields	*fjörðum*
		find	*hitt*
dared	*þorði*	food	*matar*
day	*dag*	for	*á, fyrir, fyrr, í, því, til*
decided	*ráði*	forth	*fram*
Denmark (place)	*Danmerkur, Danmörk*	found	*fannst, finna, fundið*
descended	*kominn*	from	*af, frá, fram*
desire	*fýsir, fýsist*	from-here	*héðan, þangað*
did	*gera, gerðist, gerir*	from-there	*þegar*
die	*deyja*	full	*fulla*
dignified	*tignum*		
directed	*skipaði*	# G, g	
discourage	*letja*		
do	*gera*	gave	*gæfi, gaf, gafst, gefið, gefir*
done	*gert*		
down	*niður*	get	*fá*
drew	*dró*	gifted-man	*gæfumaður, giftumaður*
drink	*drekk*		
drinking	*drykkju*	gifts	*gjafar*
dwelled	*dvalist*	give	*fá, gef, gefa, gefi, gefir, giftu*
		given	*gefið*

115

Word List (English to Old Icelandic)

English	Old Icelandic	English	Old Icelandic
gives	*gefur*	himself	*sér, sig*
go	*færð*	his	*hans, sér, sína, sinn, sinnar, sinni, sitt*
God (name)	*Guð*	hold	*heldur*
going	*ganga, gekk*	holding	*haldið*
gold	*gull*	honour	*sóma*
gone	*farið*	honourable	*sómir*
good	*góða, góðar, góðs, gott*	hospitality	*vist*
grant	*leggja*	how	*hve, hverju, hvort*
granted	*leggja*	how-so	*hversu*
great	*mikið*		
greatly	*ágætlega*		
great-man-like	*stórmannlegt*		
Greenland (place)	*Grænlandi, Grænlands*		

I, i

English	Old Icelandic
greeted	*kveður*
greeting	*kveðju*
guardsmen	*hirðina*
Gyduson (name)	*Gyðuson*

English	Old Icelandic
i	*eg, er, mig*
Iceland (place)	*Ísland, Íslandi, Íslands*
Icelander (name)	*Íslenskur*
Iceland-journey	*íslandsferðar*
if	*ef*
ill	*illa, illt*
in	*á, í*
increased	*jók*
in-drink	*drukknir*
inside	*inn*
intend	*ætla, ætlar*
intended	*ætlað, ætlaði, ætlar, setti*
is	*er, í, sé*
it	*á, að, enn, í, það*

H, h

English	Old Icelandic
had	*ætti, átti, hafði, hefir, lætur, lét*
half	*hálft*
hand	*handar, hendi, hönd*
handed-over	*seldi*
Harald (name)	*Haraldi, Haralds, Haraldur*
harbour	*hafna*
hardly	*varla*
has	*hefir*
have	*ætti, áttir, gaf, hafa, hafi, hafir, hefi, hefir, höfum*
have-you	*áttu*
he	*hann, honum, sér, sinni*
he himself	*hann*
heard	*heyrt, spurt*
held	*héldi*
help	*björg*
hence	*héðan*
here	*hér*
him	*hann, hans, honum, sér, sín*

J, j

English	Old Icelandic
journey	*ferðar, leið*
joyfulness	*blíði*

K, k

English	Old Icelandic
killed	*drepinn*
kin	*kyni*
knew	*kenndi, þekkist, veit*
knew-how	*kunnustu*
know	*vita*

L, l

Word List (English to Old Icelandic)

English	*Old Icelandic*
laid	*lætur, lagði*
land	*land, landa, landi, landið*
lands	*landa*
laugh	*hlæja*
laughed	*hlógu*
lay-out	*liggja*
leather-purse	*leðurhosu*
led	*leiðir*
less	*laus*
let	*láta, lést*
life	*líf*
little	*lítt*
look	*líta*
looked	*lítur*
lord	*herra*
lose	*lóga, týndi, týnir*
lot	*hluta*
lots	*hluta*

M, m

English	*Old Icelandic*
made	*gera, gerir*
make	*gera*
man	*maður, mann, manni*
managed	*umráði*
man-like	*mannlega*
many	*margir, mörgum*
may	*má, mega*
me	*mér, mig, mín*
meet	*fund, fundar, hitta*
meeting	*móti*
met	*fundið*
might	*mætti, máttu*
mind	*skapi*
mine	*mín, minni, mitt*
mislike	*mislíka*
Moer (place)	*Mæri*
money	*fé, fénu*
money-less	*félaus, félausan*
more	*fleira, meira*
most	*mestan, mesti*
mother	*móðir, móður*

English	*Old Icelandic*
much	*mikið, mikil, mikinn, mikla, miklar, miklu, mjög*

N, n

English	*Old Icelandic*
named	*hét*
necessary	*nauðsyn*
need	*þurfið*
needed	*þurfti*
never	*aldregi*
noble	*göfgum, tignum*
none	*eigi, öngu*
Norway (place)	*Noreg, Noregi, Noregs*
not	*ei, eiga, eigi, ekki, nú*
noticed	*þekkti*
now	*nú*

O, o

English	*Old Icelandic*
of	*á, af, í, of*
off	*af*
of-wealth	*fjárins*
on	*á, í*
one	*einn, einu, eitt, enn*
one-such	*einhverju*
on-the-way	*sinni*
or	*eða*
other	*öðru*
others	*aðrir, annarra*
our	*vor*
out	*út, utan*
out-of	*af, úr*
outside	*úti*
out-travelling	*utanferðina*
over	*of*
over-to	*ofan*
own	*eiga, eigu*
owned	*eiga, eign, eigu*

P, p

Word List (English to Old Icelandic)

English	Old Icelandic	English	Old Icelandic
passed	*leið, liðu*	said	*kvað, kveðið, kveðst, lést, mælt, sagði, sagði, sagt, segir*
path	*stíg*		
peace	*friði*		
penny	*peningur*	saw	*sá, sáumst*
people	*manni, menn, mönnum*	Saxon-lands (place)	Saxland
		say	*seg*
pouch	*skreppu*	says	*segir*
prepared	*búa, búast, búna*	sea	*haf*
present	*fyrir*	seem	*þykjast*
prevent	*tálma*	seems	*sýnist*
profess	*játum*	seen	*séð, sjá*
promise	*heiti*	sell	*selja, selur*
promised	*hét*	sent	*sendir*
proper	*maklegt*	separated	*skildust*
provisions	*vista, vistir*	settled	*búið*
purchased	*keypti*	shall	*mun, muni, skal, skaltu, skulu*

Q, q

		shall-you	*muntu*
quay	*bryggjur*	ship	*skip, skipi, skipið*
		ships	*skip, skipum*

R, r

		ship-wreck	*skipsbrotum*
		should	*mun, mundi, munir*
		should-be	*væri*
		sickness	*sótt*
rather	*heldur*	silver	*silfri, silfur*
reached	*náðu*	since	*sem, síðan*
received	*þegið, tók*	sit	*sest*
recognised	*kenndi*	skipper	*stýrimanni, stýrimanns*
reconciled	*sættast*		
rented	*leigir*	so	*sá, sjá, svo*
repaid	*launað*	some	*nakkvarra, nakkverjar, nakkverjum*
repay	*launa*		
repays	*launar*	some-kind	*eitthvert*
return	*móti*	sometime	*nokkuð*
returning	*aftur*	soon	*brátt*
reward	*laun, launa*	soul	*sál*
rewarded	*launa, launað, launaði*	south	*suður*
		south-going	*suðurgöngu*
righter	*réttara*	spoke	*mælti*
ring	*hring*	spoken	*mælt*
Rome-city (place)	*Rómaborg*	spring	*vorið*
rome-travellers	*rúmferla, rúmferlum*	staff	*staf*
		standing	*staddur*

S, s

		steward	*ármaðurinn, ármanns*
		stood	*stóðu*
		stop	*hefta*

Word List (English to Old Icelandic)

English	*Old Icelandic*	English	*Old Icelandic*
straight-away	þegar	they	þeim, þeir
strange	undarlega	they-are	eru
such	sem, slík, slíka, slíku, svo	thin	magran
		thing	hluturinn
summer	sumarið	think	hygg, þykist, þykja
suspect	grunar	this	þann, þenna, þess, þessa, þessi, þessu, þessum, þetta
Svein (name)	Svein, Sveini, Sveinn, Sveins		
Svein's (name)	Sveins	this-land	landinu
Sweden (place)	Svíþjóðar	Thorir (name)	Þóri, Þóris
		Thorstein (name)	Þorsteini, Þorsteinn, Þorsteins

T, t

		though	þó, þótt
table	borðinu	thought	þótti, þóttist
take	taka	three	þriggja
taking	tekur	time	stundir
than	en	to	á, að, í, of, til
thank	þakki	to-go	ganga
thanked	þakkaði	to-him	honum
thanks	þökk	told	sagt, segir
that	á, að, en, er, sem, það	told-of	getið
the	á, er, hinn	to-me	mér, mig
the-bear	bjarndýrið	to-meet	finna
the-beast	dýrið, dýrsins	took	leiðir, tekur, tók
the-beggar's	stafkarls	to-you	sér, þér
the-courtiers	hirðin, hirðmennirnir	travel	færir, far, fara, farir, ferð
the-gift	gjöfina, gjöfinni	travelled	færi, fara, fer, ferst, fór
the-hall	höllina		
the-king	konung, konungi, konunginn, konungs, konungur	travelling	ferðarinnar
		treads	troði
		treasure	féið, gersemar, gersemi
the-king's	konungi	treasured	gersemi
them	þeim	true	
themselves	sér	true-like	sannlegt
then	en, enn, síðan, þá, þann, þar, þeim, því	turned-to	veik
		twice	tvö
there	hingað, þangað, þar, þars, þeir, þeirri		

U, u

therefore	því		
the-ring	hringinn, hringinum	un-friend	óvinur
the-same	saman	unhappy	ósællegur
the-ship	skip, skipi, skipið, skipinu	unhurt	klakklaust
		un-peace	ófrið
the-steward	ármanni	until	til, uns
the-way	leiðar		

Word List (English to Old Icelandic)

English	*Old Icelandic*	English	*Old Icelandic*
unwise	*óvitur*	worked	*starfaði*
up	*upp, uppi*	worth	*verð, verði, virðing*
us	*oss*	would	*mundi, mundu*
		would-be	*værir*
		wrecked	*brjótir, brýtur*

V, v

value	*meta*
various	*ýmissa*
Vik (place)	*Vík*
voyage	*reiðfara*

Y, y

you	*þér, þið, þig, þína, þú, yður*
your	*þér, þinnar, yðru, yður*
yours	*þína, yðru*
yourself	*sér, sért*

W, w

wares	*varið, varnað*
was	*er, var, varði, vera, verða, verður*
we	*vér, við*
wealth	*fénu, fjár*
well	*vel, velkominn*
went	*gekk, gengi, gengu, gengur*
were	*eru, voru*
west	*vestur*
Westfjords (place)	*Vestfirskur*
what	*er, hvað, sem*
when	*er*
whether	*hvort*
which	*er*
while	*meðan*
who	*er, hver*
whole	*heill*
why	*hví*
widely	*víða*
wild	*öræfi*
wild-animal	*dýr*
will	*valdi, vil, viltu*
will-you	*viltu*
winter	*veturinn*
winters	*vetra*
wish	*vil, vildi, vildir, viljið, vilt*
wished	*vildi, vill*
wishes	*vill*
with	*með, við*

A Word Comparison of Old Norse and Old Icelandic Words

A Word Comparison of Old Norse and Old Icelandic Words

Old Norse	Old Icelandic	English
áðr	áður	after
áðr	áður	before
ætlaðak	ætlaði	intended
ætlat	ætlað	intended
ætta	ætti	had
ætta	ætti	have
aftr	aftur	back
aftr	aftur	returning
ágætliga	ágætlega	greatly
ákafliga	ákaflega	extremely
albúit	albúið	all-prepared
aldrigi	aldregi	never
álengðar	álengdar	all-longer
ármaðrinn	ármaðurinn	steward
at	að	about
at	að	at
at	að	by
at	að	it
at	að	that
at	að	to
Auðunn	Auðun	Audun (name)
austr	austur	east
Austrveg	Austurveg	Eastern-lands (place)
betr	betur	better
bezt	best	best
biðr	biður	asked
bjarndýrit	bjarndýrið	the-bear
blíðu	blíði	joyfulness
brýtr	brýtur	wrecked
búit	búið	settled
býðr	býður	bid
Danmerkr	Danmerkur	Denmark (place)
dvalizt	dvalist	dwelled
dýrit	dýrið	a-beast
dýrit	dýrið	animal
dýrit	dýrið	beast
dýrit	dýrið	the-beast
eigi	ei	not
ek	eg	i
engu	öngu	none
fær	færð	go
færa	færi	travelled
fagrliga	fagurlega	beautifully
fannt	fannst	found
farit	farið	fared
farit	farið	gone
féit	féið	treasure
félauss	félaus	money-less
fell	féll	fell
ferr	fer	travelled
ferr	ferð	travel
fundit	fundið	found
fundit	fundið	met
fyr	fyrir	before
fyr	fyrir	for
gæfa	gæfi	gave
gæfumaðr	gæfumaður	gifted-man
gaft	gafst	gave
gefa	gefi	give
gefit	gefið	gave
gefit	gefið	given
gefr	gefur	gives
gengr	gengur	went
gersimar	gersemar	treasure
gersimi	gersemi	treasure
gersimi	gersemi	treasured
getit	getið	told-of
giftumaðr	giftumaður	gifted-man
hafa	hafi	have
haldit	haldið	holding
Haraldr	Haraldur	Harald (name)
heðan	héðan	from-here
heðan	héðan	hence
heit	heiti	promise
helda	héldi	held
heldr	heldur	hold
heldr	heldur	rather
hingat	hingað	there
hirðmenninir	hirðmennirnir	the-courtiers

121

A Word Comparison of Old Norse and Old Icelandic Words

Old Norse	Old Icelandic	English
hlutrinn	hluturinn	thing
hvárt	hvort	how
hvárt	hvort	whether
hvárttveggja	hvorttveggja	either-way
hvat	hvað	what
hvé	hve	how
hverr	hver	every
hverr	hver	who
inn	hinn	the
Íslenzkr	Íslenskur	Icelander (name)
kastat	kastað	cast
kemr	kemur	came
keyptak	keypti	purchased
klaklaust	klakklaust	unhurt
kollóttr	kollóttur	bald
komit	komið	come
komizt	komist	coming
konungr	konungur	the-king
kosit	kosið	choice
kveðit	kveðið	said
kveðr	kveður	greeted
kveldit	kveldið	evening
lætr	lætur	had
lætr	lætur	laid
lagða	lagði	enriched
landit	landið	land
launat	launað	repaid
launat	launað	rewarded
lauss	laus	less
leðrhosu	leðurhosu	leather-purse
lézt	lést	let
lézt	lést	said
lítr	lítur	looked
lízt	líst	appears
lokit	lokið	ended
maðr	maður	a-man
maðr	maður	man
maðrinn	maðurinn	a-man
mætta	mætti	might
makligt	maklegt	proper
mannliga	mannlega	man-like
mik	mig	i
mik	mig	me
mik	mig	to-me
mikit	mikið	great
mikit	mikið	much
mjök	mjög	much
mynda	mundi	should
mynda	mundi	would
myndi	mundi	should
myndi	mundi	would
niðr	niður	down
nökkurar	nakkverjar	some
nökkurra	nakkvarra	some
nökkurum	nakkverjum	some
nökkut	nokkuð	sometime
Nóreg	Noreg	Norway (place)
Nóregi	Noregi	Norway (place)
Nóregs	Noregs	Norway (place)
nýtr	nýtur	benefit
ok	og	also
ok	og	and
ór	úr	out-of
orðit	orðið	become
ósælligr	ósællegur	unhappy
óvinr	óvinur	un-friend
óvitr	óvitur	unwise
penningr	peningur	penny
sannligt	sannlegt	true-like
segir	svarar	answered
selr	selur	sell
sér	sért	yourself
sét	séð	seen
settak	setti	intended
sezt	sest	sit
siðr	siður	custom
sik	sig	himself
silfr	silfur	silver
skilðist	skildust	separated
skipazt	skipast	changed
skipit	skipið	ship
skipit	skipið	the-ship
staddr	staddur	standing

A Word Comparison of Old Norse and Old Icelandic Words

Old Norse	Old Icelandic	English
stafkarlsstíg	stafkarls	beggar's-path
stórmannligt	stórmannlegt	great-man-like
suðr	suður	south
suðrgöngu	suðurgöngu	south-going
sumarit	sumarið	summer
svá	svo	so
svá	svo	such
tekr	tekur	taking
tekr	tekur	took
þangat	þangað	from-here
þangat	þangað	there
þat	það	it
þat	það	that
þegit	þegið	received
þeiri	þeirri	there
þekkði	þekkti	noticed
þik	þig	you
þit	þið	you
þurfuð	þurfið	need
þykkist	þykist	think
þykkja	þykja	think
þykkjast	þykjast	seem
tígnum	tignum	dignified
tígnum	tignum	noble
tvau	tvö	twice
týnda	týndi	lose
umbráði	umráði	managed
undarliga	undarlega	strange
unz	uns	until
útan	utan	out
útanferðina	utanferðina	out-travelling
varit	varið	wares
várit	vorið	spring
várr	vor	our
váru	voru	were
vel	velkominn	well
verðr	verður	was
Vestfirzkr	Vestfirskur	Westfjords (place)
vestr	vestur	west
vetrinn	veturinn	winter
vilda	vildi	wish
vilið	viljið	wish
vill	vilt	wish
villtu	viltu	will
villtu	viltu	will-you
vit	við	we
yðr	yður	you
yðr	yður	your

The Tale of Thorstein Staff-Struck (*Old Norse*)

Old Norse	Literal	English
1	**1**	**1**
Þórarinn hét maðr, er bjó í Sunnudal, gamall maðr ok sjónlitill.	Thorarin was-named a-man, who lived in Sunnudal, old man and seeing-little.	There was a man named Thorarin who lived in Sunnudal, he was an old man and nearly blind.
Hann hafði verit víkingr mikill í œsku sinni.	He had been viking great in youth his.	He had been a fierce viking in his youth.
Engi var hann dældarmaðr, þótt hann væri gamall.	None was he gentle-man, though he was old.	He was not a gentle man even though he was old.
Son átti hann einn, er Þórsteinn hét.	A-son had he one, who Thorstein was-named.	He had a son who was named Thorstein.
Hann var mikill maðr ok öflugr ok vel stiltr, ok vann svá fyrir búi föður síns, at eigi mundi þriggja manna annarra verk haldkvæmara.	He was great man and powerful and well composed, and worked so for estate father his, that not could three men other work hold-fulfil.	He was a great and powerful man and well composed, and he worked so hard on his father's estate that three other men could not fulfil.
Þórarinn var heldr félitill maðr, enn allmargt átti hann vápna.	Thorarin was rather fee-little man, then all-many had he weapons.	Thorarin was rather a poor man but he had many weapons.
Þeir áttu ok stóðhross feðgar, ok var þeim það helzt til fjár, er þeir seldu undan hestana, því at engir brugðust at reið né dugi.	They had also stud-horses father-and-son, and was their that rather to fee, that they sold away horses, because that none broke that ride nor spirit.	They also had some stud horses and that was their main source of wealth, for the horses they sold were not broken by riding nor broken in spirit.
Þórðr er maðr nefndr;	Thord was a-man named;	There was a man named Thord.
hann var húskarl Bjarna frá Hofi.	he was servant Bjarni's from Hof.	He was a servant of Bjarni from Hof.
Hann varðveitti reiðhesta Bjarna; því var hann kallaðr Þórðr hrossamaðr.	He looked-after riding-horses Bjarni's; accordingly was he called Thord horse-man.	He looked after Bjarni's riding-horses and was therefore called horse-man.
Hann var ójafnaðar maðr mikill, ok lét marga þess kenna, at hann var riks manns húskarl;	He was un-equal-man man great, and had many this be-known, that he was noble man's servant;	Thord was very much an arrogant man and he had it known that he was a nobleman's servant.

The Tale of Thorstein Staff-Struck (Old Norse)

Old Norse	Literal	English
enn eigi var hann sjálfr at meira verðr, ok varð hann eigi at vinsælli.	but not was he himself that more worth, and was he not that popular.	But this did not add to his worth or his popularity.
Þeir menn váru enn á vist með Bjarna, er annarr hét Þórhallr enn annarr Þórvaldr.	They men were then in hospitality with Bjarni, who one named Thorhall and another Thorvald.	There were then men staying with Bjarni, one was named Thorhall, and another Thorvald.
Þeir váru uppaustrarmenn miklir um allt þat, er þeir heyrðu í heraðinu.	They were gossipers much about all that, which they heard in the-district.	They were very much gossipers about all that the heard in the district.
Þeir Þórsteinn ok Þórðr mæltu til hesta-ats ungum hestum,	They Thorstein and Thord spoke-of to horse-fight young horses,	Thorstein and Thord spoke about a horse fight for their young horses.
ok er þeir öttu þeim, vildi hestr Þórðar verr bítast.	and when they matched their, would horse Thord's worst bite.	And when they fought, Thord's horse was bitten the worst.
Þórðr lýstr nú á skoltinn hesti Þórsteins, er honum þótti sinn hestr verr hafa, mikit högg;	Thord struck now to jaw horse Thorstein's, when he thought his horse worse had, much been-struck;	Thord now struck the jaw of Thorstein's horse when he realised that his horse had been struck worse.
enn Þórsteinn sá þat, ok laust á móti best Þórðar heldr meira högg, ok rann nú hestr Þórðar, ok æptu menn nú með kappi.	then Thorstein saw that, and struck to towards the-horse Thord's rather more striking, and ran now horse Thord's, and called-out men now with warriors.	Then Thorstein saw that and struck at Thord's horse rather more, and Thord's horse backed away, and then the warriors who were with them called out.
Þá lýstr Þórðr Þórstein með hestastafnum, ok kom á brúnina, ok hljóp hon ofan fyrir augat.	Then struck Thord Thorstein with horse-staffs, and came to eyebrow, and ran it over before eye.	Then Thord struck Thorstein with his horse staff which came to his eyebrow and ran over his eye.
Þá reist Þórsteinn af skyrtublaði sínu ok batt upp brúnina, ok lætr sem eigi hafi at orðit, ok biðr menn leyna þessu föður hans,	Then carved Thorstein off shirt-sheet his and bound up eyebrow, and behaved as-if not had that worded, and asked people keep-secret this father his,	Then Thorstein carved from his shirt and bandaged his eyebrow and behaved thus that he did not say anything about it, and he asked people to keep this a secret from his father.
ok fell þetta þar nú niðr.	and fell that there now down.	And the matter fell down there.

The Tale of Thorstein Staff-Struck (Old Norse)

Old Norse	Literal	English
Þeir Þórhallr ok Þórvaldr höfðu fyrir kals, ok kölluðu hann Þórstein stangarhögg.	They Thorhall and Thorvald had before taunted, and called him Thorstein Staff-Struck.	Thorvald and Thorhall has thus taunted him and called him Thorstein Staff-Struck.
Litlu fyrir jól um vetrinn rísa konur til verks í Sunnudal.	Little before Yule about winter rose women to work in Sunnudal.	A little before Yule in winter when women got up to work in Sunnudal.
Þá stóð Þórsteinn upp ok bar inn hey, ok lagðist síðan í bekk.	Then stood Thorstein got-up and carried in hay, and laid then on bench.	Then Thorstein got up and carried some hay inside and then lay down on a bench.
Nú kemr Þórarinn karl inn, faðir hans, ok spyrr, hverr þar lægi.	Now came Thorarin old-man in, father his, and asked, why there laying.	Now Thorarin his father, an old man, came in and asked him why he was laying there.
Þórsteinn segir til sín.	Thorstein said to him.	Thorstein told him.
"Hví ertú svá snemma á fótum, sonr?"	"Why are-you so early about feet, son?"	"Why are you up on your feet so early, son?",
segir Þórarinn.	said Thorarin.	said Thorarin the old man.
Þórsteinn svarar:	Thorstein answered:	Thorstein answered:
"Við fá þykkir mér at meta þat er hér þarf at vinna".	"With few seems to-me to meet that which here needs that win".	"With few it seems to me that might help me here",
"Er þér ekki illt í höfuðbeinum, sonr?",	"Are you not ill in head-bone, son?",	"Are you not ill in the head, son?",
segir Þórarinn.	said Thorarin.	said the old man.
"Eigi kenni ek þess",	"Not know I this",	"Not that I have noticed",
segir Þórsteinn.	said Thorstein.	said Thorstein.
"Hvat segir þú mér, sonr", segir Þórarinn, "af hesta-þinginu, því er var í sumar? Vartú eigi lostinn í svima, frændi, sem hundr?"	"What say you to-me, son", said Thorarin, "off horse-fight, which that was in summer? Were-you not struck to dizziness, kinsmen, as a-dog?"	What can you tell me about the horse fight last summer? Were you not struck dizzy by your kinsmen like a dog?"
"Engi þykki mér svivirðing í vera",	"Nothing seems to-me worthy to be",	"It is not worthy to me",

The Tale of Thorstein Staff-Struck (Old Norse)

Old Norse	Literal	English
segir Þórsteinn, "at kalla þat heldr högg enn atburð".	said Thorstein, "to call that rather striking then accident".	said Thorstein, "to call it rather a blow than an incident".
Þórarinn mælti:	Thorarin said:	Thorarin said:
"Eigi mundi mik þess vara, at ek munda eiga ragan son".	"Not thought meet this would-be, that I would have cowardly a-son".	"Not would this be to me, that I would have a coward son".
"Mæl þú þat nú eitt um, faðir",	"Say you that now one-thing about, father",	"Tell me one thing about now, father",
segir Þórsteinn, "er þér þykkir eigi of mælt síðar".	said Thorstein, "that you seem not of speaking afterwards".	said Thorstein, "which you do not think is said-too-much later".
"Eigi man ek hér svá mikit um mæla",	"Not shall I here so much about speak",	"I will not speak so much here",
segir Þórarinn, "sem mér er at skapi".	said Thorarin, "as to-me is to mind".	said Thorarin, "of what I am in the mood to say".

2

Nú reis Þórsteinn upp ok tók vápn sín ok gekk heiman ok fór unz hann kom at hrossahúsi því, er Þórðr gætti hesta Bjarna, ok var hann þar fyrir.	Now rose Thorstein up and took weapon his and went home and travelled until he came to horse-house because, that Thord guarded horses Bjarni's, and was he there before.	Now Thorstein got up and took his weapon, and then went away from home, and went until he came to the horse-house where Thord looked after Bjarni's horses, and he was there before.
Þá hittir Þórsteinn Þórð, ok mælti til hans:	Then found Thorstein Thord, and spoke to him:	Then Thorstein met Thord, and said to him,
"Vita vilda ek þat, Þórðr, hvárt þat var váðaverk, er ek fekk af þér högg í sumar á hestaþingi, eðr hefir þat orðit at vilja þínum; mantú þá vilja bœta yfir".	"Know wish I that, Thord, whether that was accident, that I got of you a-strike in summer at horse-fight, or have that words that wish you; should then will compensation over".	"I wish to know, my Thord, whether it was a tragedy to you when I was beaten by you last summer at a horse meeting, or whether it has been at your will, and whether you will make amends for it".
Þórðr svarar:	Thord answered:	Thord answered:

The Tale of Thorstein Staff-Struck (Old Norse)

Old Norse	Literal	English
"Ef þú átt tvá hváftana, þá bregð þú tungunni sitt í hvárn, ok kalla í öðrum váðaverk, ef þú vilt; enn í öðrum kalla þú alvöru,	"If you had two mouths, then move you tongue yours in each, and call in the-other an-accident, if you wish; but in the-other call you seriously,	"If you had two mouths, then you could move your tongue into each and call it either an accident if you wish but in another call it serious.
ok eru þar svá miklar bœtrnur sem þú mant af mér fá".	and are-you there so much compensation as-if you shall of met get".	And now those are the benefits you'll get from me".
"Bústú þá svá við",	"Settle then so with",	"Settle with that as you will",
segir Þórsteinn,	said Thorstein,	said Thorstein,
"at "at vera má, at ek heimta eigi oftar".	"that to be, may that I claim not". often	"it may be that I don't make this claim often".
Síðan hleypr Þórsteinn at honum ok höggr hann banahögg; gekk síðan til húss at Hofi, ok hitti úti konu eina ok mælti við hana:	Then ran Thorstein at him and struck he death-blow; went afterwards to house at Hof, and met outside woman one and spoke with her:	Then Thorstein ran at him and stuck Thord his death-blow, and went afterwards to the house at Hof and met a woman outside and spoke with her:
"Seg þú Bjarna, at naut hafi stangat Þórð hestasvein hans, ok mun hann bíða þar til þess, er hann kemr, hjá hesthúsinn".	"Tell you Bjarni, that bull had gored Thord horse-boy his, and should he abide there to this, that he comes, beside horse-house".	"Tell Bjarni that a bull has gored Thord horse-man, and he should wait there until he comes to the stable".
"Far þú heim maðr",	"Travel you home man",	"Go back home, man",
segir hon,	said she,	she said,
"enn ek segi þá er mér sýnist".	"then I say then what to-me seems".	"and I will way when it seems to me to do so".
Nú ferr Þórsteinn heim, en konan fór til verks síns.	Now travelled Thorstein home, and the-woman went to work hers.	Now Thorstein travelled home and the woman went to her work.

3

Bjarni reis upp um morguninn; ok er hann var kominn undir borð, þá spyrr hann, hvar Þórðr væri ok svöruðu menn, at hann mundi til hrossa farinn.	Bjarni rose up about morning; and as he was came under the-table, then asked he, where Thord was and answered people, that he would to the-horses gone.	Bjarni got up that morning and was sitting at the table, then Bjarni asked where Thord was, and people answered that he would have travelled to the horses.

The Tale of Thorstein Staff-Struck (Old Norse)

Old Norse	Literal	English
"Heim hugða ek hann þó mundu kominn",	"Home thought I he though would come",	"I thought he would have come home",
segir Bjarni,	said Bjarni,	said Bjarni,
"ef hann væri heill".	"if he was healthy".	"if he was well".
Þá tók kona til orða, sú er Þórsteinn hafði hitta:	Then took the-woman to words, that which Thorstein had met:	Then the woman that Thorsten had met took to words:
"Satt er þat, er oss er oft sagt konum, at þar er lítt til vits at taka, sem vér erum konur.	"True is that, which we are often told women, that there is little to wits to take, which we are women.	"It is true what is told of us women, that there is little to wits taken as we are women.
Hér kom Þórsteinn stangarhögg í morgun, ok kvað naut hafa stangat Þórð, svá at hann mundi eigi sjálfbjarga verða,	Here came Thorstein Staff-Struck in morning, and said a-bull had gored Thord, so it, that, to he could not self-supported be,	Thorstein Staff-Struck came here this morning, and said a bull had struck Thord so that he could not support himself.
enn ek nenta þá ekki at vekja þik, ok hvarf mér ór hug síðan".	but I wanted then not to wake you, and disappeared to-me from thoughts afterwards".	But I didn't want to wake you, and then it disappeared from my thoughts afterwards".
Bjarni sté þá undan borði, gekk til hrossahússins ok fann þar Þórð veginn; ok var hann síðan jarðaðr.	Bjarni stepped then from-under the-table, went to horse-house and found there Thord killed; and was he then earthed.	Bjarni stepped out from under the table, and then went to the stable and found Thord there killed, and he was buried afterwards.
Bjarni býr nú málit til þings ok gerir Þórstein sekan um vigit;	Bjarni prepared now a-case towards the-assembly and make Thorstein guilty about the-killing;	Bjarni now prepared a case to make Thorstein guilty of the killing.
enn Þórsteinn sat heima í Sunnudal, ok vann fyrir föður sínum, ok lét Bjarni þó kyrt vera.	then Thorstein sat home in Sunnudal, and worked for father his, and had Bjarni though still be.	But Thorstein stayed at home in Sunnudal and worked for his father, and Bjarni had little done though.
Um haustit sátu menn við sviðelda at Hofi, enn Bjarni lá úti á eldhúsveggnum, ok hlýddi þaðan til tals manna.	About autumn sat people with bonfires at Hof, when Bjarni lay out on fire-house-wall, and followed from there talk people's.	About autumn the people of Hof had bonfires, and Bjarni lay outside on the fire-house-wall and followed other people's talking.

The Tale of Thorstein Staff-Struck (Old Norse)

Old Norse	Literal	English
Nú taka þeir bræðr tíl orða, Þórhallr ok Þórvaldr, ok mæltu svá:	Now took they brothers to words, Thorhall and Thorvald, and spoke-of so:	Now the brothers Thorhall and Thorvald took to words:
"Eigi varði oss, þá er vér tókum vist með Víga-Bjarna, at vér mundum hér svíða dilka-höfuð, enn Þórsteinn skógarmaðr hans skyldi svíða geldinga-höfuð,	"Not expected us, then when we-are taking provisions with Killer-Bjarni, that we would here singe sheep-heads, then Thorstein outlaw his should singe ram-heads,	"We did not expect when we came to stay with Killer-Bjarni that we would be here singing sheeps" heads when Thorstein the outlaw would be singing rams' heads.
væri eigi verra, at hafa meirr vægt frændum sínum í Böðvarsdal, ok sæti nú eigi skógarmaðrinn jafnhátt honum í Sunnudal,	would not-be worse, than have more mercy kinsmen his in Bodvarsdale, and sat now not outlawed equally him in Sunnudal,	It would not have been worse to have his merciful kinsmen in Bodvarsdale and not sat equally with the outlaw in Sunnudal.
enn hinir verða forlagðir, er fyrir sárunum verða, ok vitum vér eigi, hvenær hann vill þenna flekk má af virðingu sinni".	then they became mislaid, who before injury comes, and know we not, when he will this stain may of worthiness his".	But what is laid becomes mislaid when it becomes faced with injury, and we don't know when he will off this stain from his honour".
Maðr einn svarar:	Man one answered:	One man answered:
"Slíkt er verr mælt enn þagat, oklíklegt, at yðr hafi troll togat tungu ör höfði;	"Such is worse spoken than silence, and-likely, that you have trolls pulled tongue out-of head;	"Such that is spoken is worse than silence, and it's likely that the trolls pulled the tongue out of your head.
ætlum vér, at hann nenni eigi at taka björg frá föður hans sjönlausum ok annarri ómegð þeiri sem er í Sunnudal.	#REF! we, that he bothers not to take help from father his sight-less and another without there as at in Sunnudal.	We think that he does not bother to take help from his blind father and other dependants there at Sunnudal.
Enn kynlegt þykki mér, ef þér sviðit oft lambahöfuðin hér, eðr hrósit því hvat títt var í Böðvarsdal".	Then surprised think I, if you-two singe often lambs-heads here, or praise therefore what reported was in Bodvarsdale".	But I will be surprised if you two singe many more lamb's heads here, or talk about what happened at Bodvarsdale".
Nú fara menn til borða ok síðan til svefns, ok fann eigi á Bjarna, hvat talat hafði verit.	Now travelled men to the-tables and then to sleep, and found not of Bjarni, what told had been.	Now the people went to the tables and then to sleep and Bjarni gave nothing away of what had been told.

The Tale of Thorstein Staff-Struck (Old Norse)

Old Norse	Literal	English
# 4	# 4	# 4
Um morguninn vakti Bjarni þá Þórhall ok Þórvald, ok bað þá fara í Sunnudal ok færa sér höfuð Þórsteins við bolinn skilit at dagmálum.	About morning awoke Bjarni then Thorhall and Thorvald, and asked then to-travel to Sunnudal and travelled themselves head Thorstein's with torso divided that mid-morning.	About morning Bjarni woke Thorhall and Thorvald and asked them to ride to Sunnudal and bring Thorstein's severed head divided from its torso by mid-morning
"Ok þykki mér", segir hann, þit líklegastir til at færa flekk af virðingu minni, er ek hefi eigi þrek til sjálfr".	"And seems to-me", said he, this likeliest to that bring stain of worthiness mine, when I have not strength to myself".	"and it seems to me that you", he said, "will bring the stain off my honour if I have not the strength to myself".
Nú þykkjast þeir víst ofmælt hafa, ok fara þeir nú þó, unz þeir koma í Sunnudal.	Now thought they knew said-too-much had, and travelled they now though, until they came to Sunnudal.	Now they thought that they had said too much, but they travelled until they came to Sunnudal.
Þórsteinn stóð í durum, ok hvatti sax;	Thorstein stood in doorway, and sharpened short-sword;	Thorstein stood in the doorway and sharpened a short-sword.
ok er þeir koma þar, þá spurði hann, hvert þeir ætluðu.	and as they came there, then asked he, what they intended.	And as they came he asked them what their intentions were,
Enn þeir kváðust hrossa leita skyldu.	Then they said horses looking-for should.	and they said that they were looking for some horses,
Enn Þórsteinn kvað þeira mundu skamt at leita, "er þau eru hér við garð".	Then Thorstein said they would short to look-for, "but they were here with fences".	then Thorstein said that they would not have to look far "but they are here by the fence".
"Eigi er víst at vit finnim hrossin, ef þú vísar okkr ekki til", segja þeir.	"Not is-it certain that with finding horses, if you refer us not to", tell they.	"It is not certain that we will find the horses if you do not refer us".
Þórsteinn gengr þá út,	Thorstein went then outside,	Then Thorstein went outside.
ok er þeir koma fyrir garðinu ofan, þá færir Þórvaldr upp öxina ok hleypr at honum; enn Þórsteinn stakk við honum hendi sinni, svá at hann fell fyrir.	and as they came before meadow across, then brought Thorvald up axe and ran at him; but Thorstein pushed against him arms his, so that he fell before.	And as they went across the meadow, Thorvald brought up an axe and ran at him but Thorstein pushed against his arms so that he fell before him.
Þórsteinn lágði saxinu í gegnum hann.	Thorstein laid short-sword in through him.	Thorstein laid his short-sword through him.

The Tale of Thorstein Staff-Struck (Old Norse)

Old Norse	Literal	English
Þá vildi Þórhallr veita honum tilræði ok hafði hann slíka för sem Þórvaldr.	Then willed Thorhall to-give him assault and had he such for as Thorvald.	Then Thorhall wished to assault him, and he had the same as Thorvald.
Þá bindr Þórsteinn á bak báða þá, ok lætr upp taumana á hála hestunum, ok vísar á leið öllu saman, ok ganga hestarnir nú heim til Hofs.	Then tied Thorstein to back both then, and had up reins to neck horses, and saw to pass all together, and went the-horses now home to Hof.	Then Thorstein tied both back and had the reins up to the horses necks and saw them off together, an the horses went home to Hof.
Húskarlar váru úti at Hofi, ok gengu inn ok segja Bjarna, at þeir Þórvaldr váru heim komnir, ok segja þá eigi erindislaust farit hafa.	Servants were out at Hof, and went in and told Bjarni, that they Thorvald were home coming, and told then not errand-lost gone had.	The servants were outside at Hof and went in and told Bjarni that Thorvald and Thorhall had come home, and said that their errand had not gone in vain.
Nú gengr Bjarni út, ok sér nú, hvernig um er búit, ok hefir ekki orð um.	Now went Bjarni out, and himself now, how about was prepared, and had not words about.	Now Bjarni went out himself about what had happened, and had no more words about it, and had them buried.
Lætr hann nú jarða þá, ok er nú kyrt allt, unz jól líðr.	Had he now buried then, and was now peace all, until Yule passed.	And it was now all peaceful until Yule had passed.

5

Þá tekr Rannveig til orða einn aftan, er þau koma í sæng sína, Bjarni ok hon:	Then took Rannveig to words one evening, when they came to bed theirs, Bjarni and her:	Then Rannveig spoke one evening when her and Bjarni came to their bed:
"Hvat ætlar þú at sé tíðast talat í heraðinu?";	"What suppose you that is news talking in the-district?";	"What do you suppose people are talking about in the district?"
segir hon.	said she.	she said.
"Eigi veit ek þat",	"Not know I that",	"I do not know",
segir Bjarni.	said Bjarni.	said Bjarni.
"Margir eru, at því er mér þykkir, ómjúkir í orðum sínum", segir hon;	"Many they-are, that therefore are to-me seeming, unremarkable in words theirs", said she;	"I think many of their words are unremarkable", he said.

The Tale of Thorstein Staff-Struck (Old Norse)

Old Norse	Literal	English
"ok er þat nú tíðast at rœða, at menn þykkjast eigi vita, hvat Þórsteinn stangarhögg muni þess gera, at þér muni þurfa þykkja at hefna;	"and is it now news that discussing, that people consider not known, what Thorstein Staff-Struck would this do, that you would need to-think to revenge;	"This is now what people are talking about, they think they don't know what Thorstein Staff-Struck would have to do for you to take revenge.
hefir hann nú vegit húskarla þína þrjá.	has he now killed servants yours three.	He has now killed three of your servants.
Þykkir þingmönnum þínum eigi vænt til halds, þar er þú ert, ef þessarra er óhefnt, ok eru þér mjök mislagðar hendr í kné".	Think assembly-men yours not expect to hold, there as you are, if this is without-revenge, and are you much misplaced hands on knees".	Your assembly-men do not expect to stay here as you are, if this is without revenge, and you have misplaced your hands on your knees.
Bjarni svarar:	Bjarni answered:	Bjarni answered:
"Hér kemr nú at því sem mælt er, at engi lætr sér annars víti at varnaði verða; enn hlýða mun ek þér, hvat er þú mælir;	"Here comes now that since which spoken is, that no-one has himself another's penalty to warn become; but listen should I to-you, what is you speak;	"Now it comes to what is said, that no one gives himself another's misfortune as a warning, but I will obey you what you say.
hefir Þórsteinn þá ok saklausa drepit".	has Thorstein then and without-cause killed".	Thorstein has killed few without cause".
Hætta þau þessu tali ok sofa af um nóttina.	Concluded then this talking and slept of about the-night.	Then their talking concluded and they slept through the night.
Um morguninn vaknar Rannveig, er Bjarni tók ofan skjöldinn, ok spurði hon, hvert hann skyldi.	About morning awoke Rannveig, as Bjarni took down shield, and asked her, which he should-be.	In the morning Rannveig woke up when Bjarni took down his shield and she asked where he was going.
Hann svarar:	He answered:	He answered:
"Nú skal skifta virðingu með okkr Þórsteini í Sunnudal",	"Now shall exchange honour between us Thorstein in Sunnudal",	"Now we shall exchange honour between us, Thorstein in Sunnudal",
segir hann.	said he.	he said.
"Hversu fjölmennr skaltú vera?"	"How-many followers shall be?"	"How many followers shall you travel with?",
segir hon.	said she.	she said.

The Tale of Thorstein Staff-Struck (Old Norse)

Old Norse	Literal	English
"Eigi mun ek draga fjölmenni at Þórsteini",	"Not shall I drag followers to Thorstein",	"I shall not drag followers to Thorstein",
segir hann,	said he,	he said,
"ok mun ek einn fara".	"and shall I one travelled".	"and I shall travel alone".
"Gerðú eigi þat",	"Do-you not that",	"Do not do that",
segir hon"	said she?"	she said,
"at hætta þér einum undir vápn heljarmannsins".	"to risk to-you one up-to weapons cursed-man-this".	"to risk yourself alone up against the weapons of this cursed man".
Bjarni mælti:	Bjarni spoke:	Bjarni spoke:
"Mun þér nú ekki verða þeira kvenna dœmi, er gráta á annarri stundu, er þær eggja á annarri? Enn ek þoli oft lengr frýju-orð bæði af þér ok öðrum; énn þá stoðar ok eigi at letja mik, er ek vil fara".	"Should you now not become those women judging, who-are weeping at another time, who there encouraging in another? But I tolerate often along taunting both of you and other; but then support and not to discourage me, as I wish to-go".	"Should you not now become one-of-those women who deem to weep at one moment but encourage at another? Before I have tolerated frequently and long enough the taunts of you and others, but then support me and not discourage me as I wish to go".
Bjarni fór nú í Sunnudal, ok stendr Þórsteinn í durum, ok köstuðust þeir á nökkurum orðum.	Bjarni went now to Sunnudal, and standing Thorstein in doorway, and exchanged they of some words.	Bjarni now went to Sunnudal and there was Thorstein standing in the doorway, and they exchanged some words.
Bjarni mælti:	Bjarni spoke:	Bjarni spoke:
"Þú skalt til einvigis ganga við mik í dag, Þórsteinn, á hól þenna, er hér er í tuni".	"You shall to single-combat go with me to day, Thorstein, on hill this, which here is in field".	"You shall go to single combat with me today Thorstein, on this hill which is here in the field.
"Allt er mér til þess vant",	"All is me to this difficulty",	"This is all to my difficulty",
segir Þórsteinn,	say Thorstein,	said Thorstein,
"at berjast við þik; enn ek skal þegar útan, er skip ganga, því at ek kenni drengskap þinn, at þú mant fá föður mínum forverk, er ek ferr frá".	"to fight with you; then I shall straightaway out-travel, with ship going, because that I know honour yours, that you would give father mine for-work, who I travel from".	"to fight with you, but I shall immediately travel out with the first ship going, because I know your honour, that you would give my father labour if I leave".

The Tale of Thorstein Staff-Struck (Old Norse)

Old Norse	Literal	English
"Eigi stoðar nú undan at mælast",	"Not avail now from-under that speak",	"You cannot speak to avail yourself out from under this",
segir Bjarni.	said Bjarni.	said Bjarni.
"Leyfa muntú mér þá at finna föður minn áðr",	"Allow shall-you for-me then that find father mine before",	"Will you allow me that I can find my father before",
segir Þórsteinn.	said Thorstein.	said Thorstein.
"At vísu",	"To-be certain",	"Certainly",
segir Bjarni.	said Bjarni.	said Bjarni.
Þórsteinn gekk inn, ok segir föður sínum, at Bjarni var þar kominn, ok bauð honum til einvígis.	Thorstein went inside, and told father his, that Bjarni was there coming, and invited him to single-combat.	Thorstein went inside and told his father that Bjarni was here and had invited him to single-combat.
Þórarinn karl svarar:	Thorarin old-man answered:	Thorarin, the old man, answered:
"Vera má hverr maðr þess vita, ef hann á við sér ríkara mann, er siti samheraðs honum ok hafi þó gert honum nökkura ósœmd, at hann mun eigi mörgum skyrtum slíta, ok kann ek því eigi at sýta þik, at mér þykkir þú margt hafa tilgert.	"Be may any man this know, if he to against himself more-powerful man, who situated same-district his and has though done him some dishonour, that he should not many shirts wear-out, and know I therefore not to mourn you, that to-me seens you many had to-do.	"Any man may know to expect this, if he has done some discredit against a more powerful man in his own district, that he will not wear out many more shirts, and I know therefore not to mourn you because it seems to me that you have done much.
Tak nú vápn þín ok ver þik sem skörugligast, því at þar mundi hafa verit minnar æfi, at eigi munda ek bograt hafa fyrir slíkum sem Bjarni er, ok er Bjarni þó hinn mesti kappi.	Take now weapons yours and be you as noble, because that there would have been my life, that not would I stoop have before such as Bjarni is, and is Bjarni though the most warriors.	Now take your weapons and be noble, because in my life I would not have stooped before such a man as Bjarni is. Even though he is the best warrior.
Þykki mér ok betra at missa þín enn at eiga ragan son".	Consider I also better to miss you than to have coward a-son".	I consider it better to lose you than to have a coward for a son".

The Tale of Thorstein Staff-Struck (Old Norse)

Old Norse	Literal	English
# 6	# 6	# 6
Nú gengr Þórsteinn út, ok fara þeir síðan út á höllinn ok taka til at herjast með harðfengi, ok hjuggust mjök hlífar fyrir hvárumtveggja;	Now went Thorstein out, and went they afterwards out to the-hill and took to that fighting with toughness, and hewed much protection before each-other;	Now Thorstein went outside and then they went out to the hill and took to fighting with toughness and struck down much of each other's shields.
ok er þeir höfðu mjök lengi barizt, mælti Bjarni til Þórsteins;	and when they had much along carried, spoke Bjarni to Thorstein's;	And then when they had carried on for a long time, Bjarni spoke to Thorstein:
"Þyrstir mik nú, því at ek em óvanari erfiðinu enn þú".	"Thirsty me now, because that I am not-used-to difficulty as you".	"I am thirsty now because I am not used to such difficulty as you".
"Gakk þú þá til lœkjarins",	"Go you then to stream",	"Then go to the stream",
segir Þórsteinn,	said Thorstein,	said Thorstein,
"ok drekk".	"and drink".	"and drink".
Bjarni gerði svá, ok lagði niðr sverðit hjá sér.	Bjarni did so, and had downed the-sword beside himself.	Bjarni did so and put his sword down beside himself.
Þórsteinn tók upp, leit á ok mælti.	Thorstein took up, looked at and spoke.	Thorstein took it up, looked at it, and spoke:
"Eigi mundir þú þetta sverð hafa í Böðvarsdal".	"Not would you this sword have at Bodvarsdale".	"You would not have had this sword at Bodvarsdale".
Bjarni svarar öngu.	Bjarni answered none.	Bjarni did not answer.
Ganga þeir nú enn uppá hólinn, ok berjast um stundarsakir.	Went they now then up hill, and fought about awhile's-sake.	Now they went up the hill and fought awhile,
Þykkir Bjarna maðrinn vígkœnn, ok þykkir fastlegra fyrir enn hann hugði.	Seemed Bjarni the-man battle-cunning, and seemed fixed before then he thought.	and Bjarni seemed convinced that Thorstein was a cunning fighter and the fight seemed more fixed than before.
"Margt hendir mik nú í dag",	"Many happens to-me now this day",	"Everything is happening to me today",
sagði Bjarni,	said Bjarni,	said Bjarni,
"lausir eru skópvengir mínir".	"loose are shoe-thongs mine".	"my shoe-thong is loose".

The Tale of Thorstein Staff-Struck (Old Norse)

Old Norse	Literal	English
"Bind þú þá",	"Tie you then",	"Then tie it",
segir Þórsteinn.	said Thorstein.	said Thorstein.
Nú lýtr Bjarni niðr, enn Þórsteinn gekk inn, ok hefir út skjöldu tvá ok sverð gott; gengr nú á hólinn til Bjarna, ok mælti við hann:	Now stooped Bjarni down, then Thorstein went inside, and had out shields two and sword one; went now in the-hill to Bjarni, and spoke with him:	Now Bjarni stooped down and then Thorstein went inside and brought out two shields and one sword and went to the hill to Bjarni and spoke with him:
"Hér er skjöldr ok sverð, er faðir minn sendi þér, ok mun þetta eigi slæfast meirr í höggunum enn þat er þú hefir áðr.	"Here is shield and sword, that father mine sent you, and should this not blunt more in the-blows than this which you had before.	"Here is a shield and sword that my father has sent you, and this should not be blunt with each blow like the sword you used before.
Nenni ek ok eigi at standa hlífarlauss undir höggum þínum; enn gjarnan vilda ek hætta þessum leik, því at ek er hræddr, at meira megi gæfa þín enn ógifta mín, ok er þó hverr frekr til fjörsins.	Care I also not to stand helpless under blows yours; then gladly will I conclude this sport, because that I am scared, that more may-be gift yours than un-gift mine, and that though each eager to life.	Also I do not care to stand helpless any longer under your blows and I would gladly conclude this sport because I am scared that your good luck shall be greater than my bad luck, and also each of us are eager to struggle to live,
Mun ek nú teljast undan um alla þraut framar meirr, ef ek mætta nökkuru um ráða".	Shall I now tell-you away-from about all struggle from-going more, if I may somewhat about decide".	and I would if I could decide it".
"Eigi man nú stoða at beiðast undan",	"Not should now stand to ask away-from",	"You should not try to ask your way out of it",
sagði Bjarni;	said Bjarni;	said Bjarni,
"berjast skal enn".	"fighting shall still".	"the fight must go on".
"Eigi mundak þá frekt höggva",	"Not would then eagerly strike",	"I wouldn't want to strike the first blow",
segir Þórsteinn.	said Thorstein.	said Thorstein.
Þá höggr Bjarni allan skjöldinn af Þórsteini, ok þá hjó Þórsteinn skjöldinn af Bjarna.	Then struck Bjarni all shield of Thorstein's, and then struck Thorstein shield of Bjarni's.	Then Bjarni struck and destroyed Thorstein's shield, and Thorstein struck and destroyed Bjarni's shield.
"Stórt er nú höggvið",	"Great is now the-blow",	"The striking is greater now",

The Tale of Thorstein Staff-Struck (Old Norse)

Old Norse	Literal	English
segir Bjarni.	said Bjarni.	said Bjarni.
Þórsteinn svarar:	Thorstein answered:	Thorstein answered:
"Eigi hjóstu smærra högg".	"Not have-you-hit a-smaller blow".	"Your strike was no smaller".
Bjarni mælti:	Bjarni spoke:	Bjarni spoke:
"Betr bítr þér nú hit sama sverðit, er þú hefir áðr haft í dag".	"Better bite you now then the-same sword, than you have before had in the-day".	"Now it bites better than the same weapon that you had before in the day".
Þórsteinn mælti:	Thorstein spoke:	Thorstein spoke:
"Spara munda ek mik við óhapp, ef ek mætta svá gera, ok berjumst ek hræddr við þik;	"Spare would I me with mishap, if I might so do, and fight I-am scared against you;	"I wish to spare myself from bad luck if I might do so, and I am scared to fight with you.
vilda ek enn allt á þínu valdi vera láta".	wish I then all to you will be had".	I wish for you to settle all of the matter".
Þá átti Bjarni at höggva, ok var nú hvárrtveggja hlífarlauss.	Then had Bjarni to strike, and was now each helpless.	Then it was Bjarni's turn to strike and now each man was helpless.
Bjarni mælti þá:	Bjarni spoke then:	Then Bjarni spoke:
"Þat mun illt kaup, at taka glœp við miklu happi.	"It should ill purchase, that takes the-wicked with much luck.	"It would ill afford to take much wickedness with luck.
Ætla ek mér fullgoldit fyrir þrjá húskarla mína þik einn, ef þú vilt mér trúr vera".	Suppose I myself fully-golded for three servants mine you alone, if you will to-me true be".	I would suppose myself fully paid for my three servants if you alone will serve me faithfully".
Þórsteinn mælti:	Thorstein said:	Thorstein said:
"Orðit hafa mér svá fœri á þér í dag, at ek mætta svíkja þik, ef ógæfa mín gengi ríkar enn gæfa þín; ok mun ek eigi svíkja þik",	"Words have me so brought in you in day, that I may betray you, if misfortune mine went stronger than gift yours; and should I not betray you",	"I have had many words with you today where I might have betrayed you if my misfortune was stronger than your luck, and so I will not betray you",
sagði Þórsteinn.	said Thorstein.	said Thorstein.

The Tale of Thorstein Staff-Struck (Old Norse)

Old Norse	Literal	English
"Sé ek at þú er afbragðs maðr", sagði Bjarni.	"See I that you are excellent man", said Bjarni.	"I see now that you are an excellent man", said Bjarni.
"Lofa muntú mér, at ek ganga inn til föður þíns",	"Promise shall-you me, that I go inside to father yours",	"You will promise me that I go inside to your father",
segir hann,	said he,	he said,
"ok segi honum slíkt er ek vil".	"and tell him such who I wish".	"and tell him about this as I wish".
"Gakk sem þú vilt fyrir mínum sóknum",	"Go as you wish for my sake",	"Go as you wish, for my sake",
sagði Þorsteinn	said Thorstein	said Thorstein,
"ok far þó varlega".	"and go though warily".	"and go carefully".

7

Old Norse	Literal	English
Þá gekk Bjarni inn, ok at lokhvílu þefri, er Þórarinn karl lá í.	Then went Bjarni in, and to bed-closet there, where Thorarin old-man lay in.	Then Bjarni went in to the bed closet where Thorarin the old man was laying.
Þórarinn spurði, hverr þar færi? Bjarni sagði til sín.	Thorarin asked, who there went? Bjarni told to him.	Thorarin then asked who went there and Bjarni told him.
"Hvat segir þú tíðinda, Bjarni minn?"	"What say you news, Bjarni mine?"	"What news do you speak about, my Bjarni?",
segir Þórarinn.	say Thorarin.	said Thorarin.
"Víg Þórsteins sonar þíns",	"Killing Thorstein son yours",	"The killing of your son",
segir Bjarni.	said Bjarni.	said Bjarni.
"Varðist hann nökkut?"	"Defended he any-at-all?"	"Did he defend himself at all?",
segir Þórarinn.	say Thorarin.	said Thorarin.
"Engan mann ætla ek snarligra verit hafa í vápnaskiftum enn Þórstein son þinn", segir Bjarni.	"None man suppose I speedily have had in weapons-exchange than Thorstein a-son yours", said Bjarni.	"I do not think I have been in such a speedy exchange of weapons as with your son Thorstein".
"Eigi er kynlegt at því",	"Not is wonder that therefore",	"It is no wonder therefore",

The Tale of Thorstein Staff-Struck (Old Norse)

Old Norse	Literal	English
segir karl,	said the-old-man,	said the old man,
"at þungt veitti við þik í Böðvarsdal, er þú bart nú af syni mínum".	"that difficulty granted with you at Bodvarsdale, that you overcome now of son mine".	"that you granted such difficulty to those at Bodvarsdale, that you have now overcome my son".
Þá mælti Bjarni:	Then spoke Bjarni:	Then Bjarni spoke:
"Ek vil bjóða þér til Hofs, ok skaltú sitja þar í öðru öndvegi meðan þá liflr, ok mun ek vera þér í sonar stað".	"I wish to-invite you to Hof, and shall-you settle there in another foremost-seat as-long-as then live, and should I be to-you in son's place".	"I wish to invite you to Hof, and you shall settle there in one of the foremost seats as long as you live, and I shall be in your son's place".
"Svá er mér farit",	"So is to-me going",	"So it goes to me",
segir karl,	said the-old-man,	said the old man,
"sem þeim, er eigi eigu undir sér, ok verðr heitum heimskr maðr feginn.	"which those, who not only submit to-you, and worth called stupid man joyful.	"that those who do not alone accept you and your promise joyfully are stupid.
Enn svá eru heit yðor höfðingja, þá er þér vilit fróa mann eftir slíka atburði, at þat er mánaðar-frá; enn eftir þat eru vér virðir sem aðrir framfœrslumenn, ok fyrnast við þat seint várir harmar.	But so are promises of-you chieftains, then that you wish console people after such events, that it is a-month-from; then after that they-are we valued as-if other paupers, and age with it weak our harm.	But so are the promises of you chieftains whom you wish to console after such events, that a month from then they are valued as paupers and their harm does not weaken with age.
Enn sá maðr þriflst aldregi, er ekki tekr	Then so the-man thrives never, who not takes	Still, the man who takes a pledge with such a man as you may well be deemed to be content with his lot.
handsöl afþér, ok gakk þú nú hingat til min í rekkjugólfit, ok verðr þú nær at ganga, því at karl skelfr nú allr á fótum fyrir elli sakir ok vanheilsu, enn eigi trútt, at mér hafi eigi í skap runnit sonar-dauðinn".	pledge of-you, and come you now here to me in bed-closet, and become you near to going, because that old-man shaking now all on feet for age sake and failing-health, but none truth, to to-me has not in mood slipped son-death".	So I should also take this pledge with you, and now come here to me in the bed closet and come nearer because I am an old man shaking on his feet for the sake of age and ill health, but one truth alone has caused my mood to slip, the death of my son".
Bjarni gekk nú í rekkjugólfit í hendr Þórarins karls.	Bjarni went now into bed-closet in hand Thorarin the-old-man.	Bjarni now went into the bed closet and took Thorarin the old man's hand.

The Tale of Thorstein Staff-Struck (Old Norse)

Old Norse	Literal	English
Hann fann, at hann þuklaði á saxi, ok vildi þá leggja til Bjarna.	He found, that he felt a short-sword, and willed then to-lay to Bjarni.	He then found that he felt a short sword that he wished to lay at Bjarni.
Hann kipti hendinni ok mælti:	He dragged his-hand and spoke:	He drew his hand and spoke:
"Allra fretkarla armastr.	"All contemptible-man miserable.	"You are an all contemptible and miserable man",
Men nú at makligleikum fara með okkr.	But now it serves-you-right going between us.	"How it will serve you right what happens between us.
Þórsteinn sonr þinn lifir, ok skal hann fara heim með mér til Hofs, enn þér skal fá þræla til forverka, ok skal þér engis vant meðan þú lifir".	Thorstein son yours alive, and shall he travel home with me to Hof, then you shall get thralls to working, and shall you nothing want as-long-as you live".	Thorstein your son is alive and he shall travel home with me to Hof, and you shall get servants to work for you and you shall want for nothing as long as you live".
Þórsteinn fór nú heim með Bjarna til Hofs, ok fylgdi honum allt til dauða-dags, ok þótti nær engis manns maki vera at drengskap ok hreysti.	Thorstein travelled now home with Bjarni to Hof, and followed him all until death-day, and thought near only man matched had-been that honour and valour.	Now Thorstein travelled home with Bjarni to Hof and followed him in everything until the day he died, and he was thought the only man near to matching him in honour and valour.

8

Bjarni helt virðingu sinni, ok var hann því vinsælli ok betr stilltr sem hann var ellri, ok var allra manna þrautbeztr ok gerðist trú-maðr mikill hinn siðara hlut ævi sinnar.	Bjarni held worthiness his, and was he therefore popular and better orderly as he was older, and were all men persistent and became true-man great the last part life his.	Bjarni held his standing well and became more popular and more self-controlled as he got older, and he was of all men the most persistent, and he became a great man of true faith for the last part of his life.
Bjarni fór útan ok gekk suðr, ok andaðist í þeiri ferð.	Bjarni travelled out and went south, and died on their journey.	Bjarni travelled abroad and went south and died on that journey.
Hann hvílir í borg þeiri, er Valería heitir, ok er þat mikil borg skamt hingat frá Rúmaborg.	He rested in Borg there, was Sutri named, and was that great Borg short there from Rome-city.	He rested at a city that was named Sutri, and that was a great city, a short distance from the city of Rome.

The Tale of Thorstein Staff-Struck (Old Norse)

Old Norse	Literal	English
Hans son var Skegg-Broddi, er víða kemr við sögur, ok var hinn mesti afbragðsmaðr um sína daga.	His a-son was Skegg-Broddi, who widely came in the-sagas, and was the most outstanding-man about his day.	His son was Beard-Broddi who appears widely in the sagas, and he was the most outstanding man of his day.
Dóttir Bjarna hét Halla, ok Guðríðr, er Kolbeinn lögsögumaðr átti.	Daughter Bjarni's named Halla, and Gudrid, who Kolbein lawspeaker married.	Bjarni had a daughter named Halla, the mother of Gudrid, who married Kolbein the lawspeaker.
Ingveldr var ok dóttir Bjarna, er Þorsteinn Síðu-Hallsson átti, ok var þeira son Magnus, faðir Einars, föður Magnúsar biskups.	Yngvild was also daughter Bjarni's, was Thorstein Sidu-Hallson married, and was their son Magnus, father-of Einar, father-of Magnus the-bishop.	Bjarni had another daughter named Yngvild who married Thorstein Sidu-Hallson, their son was Magnus, the father of Einar, the father of Magnus the bishop.
Ögmundr var ok sonr Þórsteins ok Ingveldra;	Amundi was also son Thorstein's and Yngvild's;	Thorstein and Yngvild also had a son named Amundi.
hann átti Sigríði dóttur Þórgríms blinda,	he married Sigrid daughter Thorgrim's the-blind,	He married Sigrid, the daughter of Thorgrim the blind.
Þeira dóttir (var) Hallfríðr móðir (Ámunda), föður Guðmundar, föður Magnúss góða ok Þóru, móður Gissurar jarls, ok annarrar Þórn, móður Orms Svínfellings.	Their daughter (was) Hallfrid mother-of (Amundi's), father Gudmund's, father-of Magnus the-chieftain and Thora, mother-of Gissurar the-earl, and of-the-other Thora, mother-of Orm Svinafellings.	Amundi also had a daughter named Hallfrid, the mother of Amundi, the father of Gudmund, the father of the chieftain Magnus, and of Thora who married Thorvald Gizurarson, and the other Thora who was the mother of Orm of Svinafell.
Guðrún var ok dóttir Ögmundar, móðir Þórdísar, móður Helgu, móður Guðnýjar, móður Sturlusona: Þórðar, Sighvats og Snorra.	Gudrun was and daughter Ogmund, mother-of Thordis, mother-of Helga, mother-of Gudny, mother-of The-Sturlusons: Thord, Sighvat and Snorri.	Amundi had another daughter called Gudrun, the mother of Thordis, the mother of Helga, the mother of Gudny Bodvar's daughter, the mother of the Sturlusons, Thord, Sighvat, and Snorri.
Rannveig var ok dóttir Ögmundar, móðir Steins, föður Guðrúnar, móður Árnfríðar, er Digr-Helgi átti.	Rannveig was and daughter-of Ogmund, mother-of Stein, father Gudrun, mother-of , who had.	Amundi also had a daughter named Rannveig, the mother of Stein, the father of Gudrun, the mother of Arnfrid, who was married to Stout-Helgi.

The Tale of Thorstein Staff-Struck (Old Norse)

Old Norse	Literal	English
Þórkatla var ok dóttir Ögmundar, móðir Arnbjargar, móður Jóns prests ok Þórgeirs ok Þuríðar,	Thorkatla was and daughter-of Ogmund, mother-of Arnbjorg, mother-of Jon the-priest and Thorgeir and Thorid,	Thorkatla was also a daughter of Amundi, the mother of Arnbjorg, the mother of Fin the priest, and Thorgeir and Thurid.
ok er margt stórmenna frá þeim komit.	and are many prestigious-people from them coming.	And there were many prestigious people descended from them.
Ok lýkr hér sögu-þætti Þórsteins stangarhöggs.	And ends here the-saga-tale Thorstein Staff-Struck.	And there ends the saga of Thorstein Staff-Struck.

Word List (Old Norse to English)

Word List (Old Norse to English)

Old Norse	English

A, a

aðrir	other
af	of, of, off
afbragðs	excellent
afbragðsmaðr	outstanding-man
aftan	evening
afþér	of-you
aldregi	never
alla	all
allan	all
allmargt	all-many
allr	all
allra	all
allt	all, all
alvöru	seriously
andaðist	died
annarr	another, one
annarra	other
annarrar	of-the-other
annarri	another
annars	another's
armastr	miserable
Arnbjargar	Arnbjorg (name)
at	at, it, it, that, to, than, that, to, to-be
atburð	accident
atburði	events
augat	eye

Á, á

á	a, about, at, in, of, on, to
áðr	before
Ámunda	Amundi's (name)
árnfríðar	0
átt	had
átti	had, married
áttu	had

Æ, æ

æfi	life
ætla	suppose
ætlar	suppose
ætluðu	intended
ætlum	suppose
ævi	life

B, b

bað	asked
báða	both
bæði	both
bak	back
banahögg	death-blow
bar	carried
barizt	carried
bart	overcome
batt	bound
bauð	invited
beiðast	ask
bekk	bench
berjast	fight, fighting, fought
berjumst	fight
best	the-horse
betr	better
betra	better
biða	abide
biðr	asked
bind	tie
bindr	tied
biskups	the-bishop
bítast	bite
bítr	bite
Bjarna	Bjarni (name), Bjarni's (name)
Bjarni	Bjarni (name)
bjó	lived
bjóða	to-invite
björg	help
blinda	the-blind
Böðvarsdal	Bodvarsdale (name)
bœta	compensation

Word List (Old Norse to English)

Old Norse	English
bœtrnur	compensation
bograt	stoop
bolinn	torso
borð	the-table
borða	the-tables
borði	the-table
Borg	Borg (place)
bræðr	brothers
bregð	move
brugðust	broke
brúnina	eyebrow
búi	estate
búit	prepared
bústú	settle
býr	prepared

D, d

Old Norse	English
dældarmaðr	gentle-man
dag	day, the-day
daga	day
dagmálum	mid-morning
dauða-dags	death-day
digr-helgi	0
dilka-höfuð	sheep-heads
dœmi	judging
dóttir	daughter, daughter-of
dóttur	daughter
draga	drag
drekk	drink
drengskap	honour
drepit	killed
dugi	spirit
durum	doorway

E, e

Old Norse	English
eðr	or
ef	if
eftir	after
eggja	encouraging
eiga	have
eigi	none, not, not-be
eigu	only
eina	one
Einars	Einar (name)
einn	alone, one
einum	one
einvigis	single-combat
einvígis	single-combat
eitt	one-thing
ek	I, I-am
ekki	not
eldhúsveggnum	fire-house-wall
elli	age
ellri	older
em	am
en	and
engan	none
engi	none, no-one, nothing
engir	none
engis	nothing, only
enn	and, as, but, still, than, then, when
er	am, are, as, at, but, is, is-it, than, that, was, what, when, where, which, who, who-are, with
erfiðinu	difficulty
erindislaust	errand-lost
ert	are
ertú	are-you
eru	are, are-you, they-are, were
erum	are

É, é

Old Norse	English
énn	but

F, f

Old Norse	English
fá	few, get, give
faðir	father, father-of
fann	found
far	go, Travel
fara	going, to-go, to-travel, travel, travelled, went

Word List (Old Norse to English)

Old Norse	English
farinn	gone
farit	going, gone
fastlegra	fixed
feðgar	father-and-son
feginn	joyful
fekk	got
félitill	fee-little
fell	fell
ferð	journey
ferr	travel, travelled
finna	find
finnim	finding
fjár	fee
fjölmenni	followers
fjölmennr	followers
fjörsins	life
flekk	stain
fóður	father
föður	father, father-of
fœra	bring, travelled
fœri	brought, went
fœrir	brought
fór	travelled, went
för	for
forlagðir	mislaid
forverk	for-work
forverka	working
fótum	feet
frá	from
frændi	kinsmen
frændum	kinsmen
framar	from-going
framfœrslumenn	paupers
frekr	eager
frekt	eagerly
fretkarla	contemptible-man
fróa	console
frýju-orð	taunting
fullgoldit	fully-golded
fylgdi	followed
fyrir	before, for
fyrnast	age

G, g

Old Norse	English
gæfa	gift
gætti	guarded
gakk	come, go
gamall	old
ganga	go, going, went
garð	fences
garðinu	meadow
gegnum	through
gekk	went
geldinga-höfuð	ram-heads
gengi	went
gengr	went
gengu	went
gera	do
gerði	did
gerðist	became
gerðú	do-you
gerir	make
gert	done
gissurar	Gissurar
gjarnan	gladly
glœp	the-wicked
góða	the-chieftain
gott	one
gráta	weeping
Guðmundar	Gudmund's (name)
Guðnýjar	Gudny (name)
Guðríðr	Gudrid (name)
Guðrún	Gudrun (name)
Guðrúnar	Gudrun (name)

H, h

Old Norse	English
hætta	conclude, concluded, risk
hafa	had, have
hafði	had
hafi	had, has, have
haft	had
hála	neck
haldkvæmara	hold-fulfil
halds	hold
Halla	Halla (name)
Hallfríðr	Hallfrid (name)
hana	her

Word List (Old Norse to English)

Old Norse	English
handsöl	pledge
hann	he, him
hans	him, his
happi	luck
harðfengi	toughness
harmar	harm
haustit	autumn
höggunum	the-blows
hefi	have
hefir	had, has, have
hefna	revenge
heill	healthy
heim	home
heima	home
heiman	home
heimskr	stupid
heimta	claim
heit	promises
heitir	named
heitum	called
heldr	rather
Helgu	Helga (name)
heljarmannsins	cursed-man-this
helt	held
helzt	rather
hendi	arms
hendinni	his-hand
hendir	happens
hendr	hand, hands
hér	here
heraðinu	the-district
herjast	fighting
hesta	horses
hesta-ats	horse-fight
hestana	horses
hestarnir	the-horses
hestastafnum	horse-staffs
hestasvein	horse-boy
hestaþingi	horse-fight
hesta-þinginu	horse-fight
hesthúsinn	horse-house
hesti	horse
hestr	horse
hestum	horses
hestunum	horses
hét	named, was-named
hey	hay
heyrðu	heard
hiífar	protection
hingat	here, there
hinir	they
hinn	the
hit	then
hitta	met
hitti	met
hittir	found
hjá	beside
hjó	struck
hjóstu	have-you-hit
hjuggust	hewed
hleypr	ran
hlífarlauss	helpless
hljóp	ran
hlut	part
hlýða	listen
hlýddi	followed
höfði	head
höfðingja	chieftains
höfðu	had
Hofi	Hof (place)
hofs	Hof, Hof (place)
höfuð	head
höfuðbeinum	head-bone
högg	a-strike, been-struck, blow, striking
höggr	struck
höggum	blows
höggva	strike
höggvið	the-blow
hól	hill
hólinn	hill
hölinn	the-hill
höllinn	the-hill
hon	her, it, she
honum	he, him, his
hræddr	scared
hrósit	praise
hreysti	valour
hrossa	horses, the-horses
hrossahúsi	horse-house
hrossahússins	horse-house

Word List (Old Norse to English)

Old Norse	English
hrossamaðr	horse-man
hrossin	horses
hug	thoughts
hugða	thought
hugði	thought
hundr	a-dog
húskarl	servant
húskarla	servants
húskarlar	servants
húss	house
hváftana	mouths
hvar	where
hvarf	disappeared
hvárn	each
hvárrtveggja	each
hvárt	whether
hvárumtveggja	each-other
hvat	what
hvatti	sharpened
hvenær	when
hvernig	how
hverr	any, each, who, why
hversu	how-many
hvert	what, which
hvi	Why
hvílir	rested

I, i

illt	ill
Ingveldr	Yngvild (name)
Ingveldra	Yngvild's (name)
inn	in, inside

Í, í

í	at, in, into, on, this, to

J, j

jafnhátt	equally
jarða	buried
jarðaðr	earthed
jarls	the-earl
Jól	Yule (name)
Jóns	Jon (name)

K, k

kalla	call
kallaðr	called
kals	taunted
kann	know
kappi	warriors
karl	old-man, the-old-man
karls	the-old-man
kaup	purchase
kemr	came, comes
kenna	be-known
kenni	know
kipti	dragged
kné	knees
Kolbeinn	Kolbein (name)
kölluðu	called
kom	came
koma	came
kominn	came, come, coming
komit	coming
komnir	coming
kona	the-woman
konan	the-woman
konu	woman
konum	women
konur	women
köstuðust	exchanged
kvað	said
kváðust	said
kvenna	women
kynlegt	surprised, wonder
kyrt	peace, still

L, l

lá	lay
lægi	laying
lætr	behaved, had, has
lagði	had

Word List (Old Norse to English)

Old Norse	English
lágði	laid
lagðist	laid
lambahöfuðin	lambs-heads
láta	had
lausir	loose
laust	struck
leggja	to-lay
leið	pass
leik	sport
leit	looked
leita	look-for, looking-for
lengi	along
lengr	along
lét	had
letja	discourage
leyfa	allow
leyna	keep-secret
líðr	passed
lifir	alive, live
liflr	live
liklegastir	likeliest
litlu	little
lítt	little
lœkjarins	stream
lofa	promise
lögsögumaðr	lawspeaker
lokhvílu	bed-closet
lostinn	struck
lýkr	ends
lýstr	struck
lýtr	stooped

M, m

Old Norse	English
má	may
maðr	a-man, man, the-man
maðrinn	the-man
mæl	say
mæla	speak
mælast	speak
mælir	speak
mælt	speaking, spoken
mælti	said, spoke
mæltu	spoke-of
mætta	may, might
Magnus	Magnus (name)
Magnúsar	Magnus (name)
Magnúss	Magnus (name)
maki	matched
makligleikum	serves-you-right
málit	a-case
man	shall, should
mánaðar-frá	a-month-from
mann	man, people
manna	men, people's
manns	man, man's
mant	shall, would
mantú	should
marga	many
margir	many
margt	many
með	between, with
meðan	as-long-as
megi	may-be
meira	more
meirr	more
men	but
menn	men, people
mér	for-me, I, me, met, myself, to-me
mesti	most
meta	meet
mik	me, meet, to-me
mikil	great
mikill	great
mikit	much
miklar	much
miklir	much
miklu	much
min	me
mín	mine
mína	mine
mínir	mine
minn	mine
minnar	my
minni	mine
mínum	mine, my
mislagðar	misplaced
missa	miss
mjök	much
móðir	mother-of

Word List (Old Norse to English)

Old Norse	English
móður	mother-of
mörgum	many
morgun	morning
morguninn	morning
móti	towards
mun	shall, should
munda	would
mundak	would
mundi	could, thought, would
mundir	would
mundu	would
mundum	would
muni	would
muntú	shall-you

N, n

nær	near
naut	a-bull, bull
né	nor
nefndr	named
nenni	bothers, care
nenta	wanted
niðr	down, downed
nökkura	some
nökkuru	somewhat
nökkurum	some
nökkut	any-at-all
nóttina	the-night
nú	now

O, o

of	of
ofan	across, down, over
ofmælt	said-too-much
oft	often
oftar	often
og	and
ok	also, and
okkr	us
oklíklegt	and-likely
orð	words
orða	words
orðit	worded, words
orðum	words
Orms	Orm (name)
oss	us, we

Ó, ó

ógæfa	misfortune
ógifta	un-gift
óhapp	mishap
óhefnt	without-revenge
ójafnaðar	un-equal-man
ómegð	without
ómjúkir	unremarkable
ór	from
ósœmd	dishonour
óvanari	not-used-to

Ö, ö

öðru	another
öðrum	other, the-other
öflugr	powerful
Ögmundar	Ogmund (name)
Ögmundr	Amundi (name)
öllu	all
öndvegi	foremost-seat
öngu	none
ör	out-of
öttu	matched
öxina	axe

Œ, œ

œptu	called-out
œsku	youth

P, p

prests	the-priest

Word List (Old Norse to English)

Old Norse	English
R, r	
ráða	decide
ragan	coward, cowardly
rann	ran
Rannveig	Rannveig (name)
reið	ride
reiðhesta	riding-horses
reis	rose
reist	carved
rekkjugðlfit	bed-closet
rekkjugólfit	bed-closet
ríkar	stronger
rikara	more-powerful
riks	noble
rísa	rose
rœða	discussing
Rúmaborg	Rome-city (place)
runnit	slipped
S, s	
sá	saw, so
sæng	bed
sæti	sat
sagði	said, said, told
sagt	told
sakir	sake
saklausa	without-cause
sama	the-same
saman	together
samheraðs	same-district
sárunum	injury
sat	sat
satt	TRUE
sátu	sat
sax	short-sword
saxi	short-sword
saxinu	short-sword
sé	is, see
seg	tell
segi	say, tell
segir	said, say, told
segja	tell, told
seint	weak
sekan	guilty
seldu	sold
sem	as, as-if, which
sendi	sent
sér	himself, themselves, to-you
síðan	afterwards, then
síðar	afterwards
siðara	last
Siðu-Hallsson	Sidu-Hallson (name)
Sighvats	Sighvat (name)
Sigríði	Sigrid (name)
sín	him, his
sína	his, theirs
sinn	his
sinnar	his
sinni	his
síns	hers, his
sínu	his
sínum	his, theirs
siti	situated
sitja	settle
sitt	yours
sjálfbjarga	self-supported
sjálfr	himself, myself
sjðnlausum	sight-less
sjónlitill	seeing-little
skal	shall
skalt	shall
skaltú	shall, shall-you
skamt	short
skap	mood
skapi	mind
Skegg-Broddi	Skegg-Broddi (name)
skelfr	shaking
skifta	exchange
skilit	divided
skip	ship
skjöldinn	shield
skjöldr	shield
skjöldu	shields
skógarmaðr	outlaw
skógarmaðrinn	outlawed
skoltinn	jaw
skörugligast	noble

Word List (Old Norse to English)

Old Norse	English
skóþvengir	shoe-thongs
skyldi	should, should-be
skyldu	should
skyrtublaði	shirt-sheet
skyrtum	shirts
slæfast	blunt
slika	such
slíka	such
slíkt	such
slikum	such
slita	wear-out
smærra	a-smaller
snarligra	speedily
snemma	early
Snorra	Snorri (name)
sofa	slept
sögur	the-sagas
sögu-þætti	the-saga-tale
sóknum	sake
son	a-son, son
sonar	son, son's
sonar-dauðinn	son-death
sonr	son
spara	spare
spurði	asked
spyrr	asked
stað	place
stakk	pushed
standa	stand
Stangarhögg	Staff-Struck (name)
Stangarhöggs	Staff-Struck (name)
stangat	gored
stórmenna	prestigious-people
sté	stepped
Steins	Stein (name)
stendr	standing
stilltr	orderly
stiltr	composed
stóð	stood
stoða	stand
stoðar	avail, support
stóðhross	stud-horses
stórt	great
stundarsakir	awhile's-sake
stundu	time
Sturlusona	the-Sturlusons (name)
sú	that
suðr	south
sumar	summer
Sunnudal	Sunnudal (place)
svá	so
svarar	answered
svefns	sleep
sverð	sword
sverðit	sword, the-sword
svíða	singe
sviðelda	bonfires
sviðit	singe
svíkja	betray
svima	dizziness
Svínfellings	Svinafellings (name)
svivirðing	worthy
svöruðu	answered
syni	son
sýnist	seems
sýta	mourn

T, t

Old Norse	English
tak	take
taka	take, takes, took
talat	talking, told
tali	talking
tals	talk
taumana	reins
tekr	takes, took
teljast	tell-you
tiðast	news
tíðast	news
tíðinda	news
til	there, to, towards, until
tíl	to
tilgert	to-do
tilræði	assault
títt	reported
togat	pulled
tók	took
tókum	taking

Word List (Old Norse to English)

Old Norse	English
troll	trolls
trú-maðr	true-man
trúr	TRUE
trútt	truth
tungu	tongue
tungunni	tongue
tuni	field
tvá	two

Þ, þ

Old Norse	English
þá	then
það	that
þaðan	from
þær	there
þagat	silence
þar	there
þarf	needs
þat	it, it, that, this
þau	then, they
Þórarinn	Thorarin (name)
Þórsteinn	Thorstein (name)
þefri	there
þegar	straightaway
þeim	their, them, those
þeir	they
þeira	their, they, those
þeiri	their, there
þenna	this
þér	to-you, you, you-two
þess	this
þessarra	this
þessu	this
þessum	this
þetta	that, this
þik	you
þín	you, yours
þína	yours
þingmönnum	assembly-men
þings	the-assembly
þinn	yours
þíns	yours
þínu	you
þínum	you, yours
þit	this
þo	though
þó	though
þoli	tolerate
Þórarinn	Thorarin (name)
Þórarins	Thorarin (name)
Þórð	Thord (name)
Þórðar	Thord (name), Thord's (name)
Þórdísar	Thordis (name)
Þórðr	Thord (name)
Þórgeirs	Thorgeir (name)
Þórgríms	Thorgrim's (name)
Þórhall	Thorhall (name)
Þórhallr	Thorhall (name)
Þórkatla	Thorkatla (name)
Þórn	Thora (name)
Þórstein	Thorstein (name)
Þórsteini	Thorstein (name), Thorstein's (name)
Þórsteinn	Thorstein (name)
Þórsteins	Thorstein (name), Thorstein's (name)
Þóru	Thora (name)
Þórvald	Thorvald (name)
Þórvaldr	Thorvald (name)
þótt	though
þótti	thought
þræla	thralls
þraut	struggle
þrautbeztr	persistent
þrek	strength
þriflst	thrives
þriggja	three
þrjá	three
þú	you
þuklaði	felt
þungt	difficulty
þurfa	need
Þuriðar	Thorid (name)
því	accordingly, because, since, therefore, which
þykki	consider, seems, think
þykkir	seem, seemed, seeming, seems, seens, think

153

Word List (Old Norse to English)

Old Norse	English
þykkja	to-think
þykkjast	consider, thought
þyrstir	thirsty

U, u

Old Norse	English
um	about
undan	away, away-from, from-under
undir	submit, under, up-to
ungum	young
unz	until
upp	got-up, up
uppá	up
uppaustrarmenn	gossipers

Ú, ú

Old Norse	English
út	out, outside
útan	out, out-travel
úti	out, outside

V, v

Old Norse	English
váðaverk	accident, an-accident
vægt	mercy
vænt	expect
væri	was, would
vaknar	awoke
vakti	awoke
valdi	will
Valería	Sutri (place)
vanheilsu	failing-health
vann	worked
vant	difficulty, want
vápn	weapon, weapons
vápna	weapons
vápnaskiftum	weapons-exchange
var	was, were
vara	would-be
varð	was
varði	expected
varðist	defended
varðveitti	looked-after
várir	our
varlega	warily
varnaði	warn
vartú	were-you
váru	were
veginn	killed
vegit	killed
veit	know
veita	to-give
veitti	granted
vekja	wake
vel	well
ver	be
vér	we, we-are
vera	be, had-been
verða	be, became, become, comes
verðr	become, worth
verit	been, have
verk	work
verks	work
verr	worse, worst
verra	worse
vetrinn	winter
við	against, in, with
víða	widely
vig	killing
Víga-Bjarna	Killer-Bjarni (name)
vigit	the-killing
vígkœnn	battle-cunning
víkingr	viking
vil	wish
vilda	will, wish
vildi	willed, would
vilit	wish
vilja	will, wish
vill	will
vilt	will, wish
vinna	win
vinsælli	popular
virðingu	honour, worthiness
virðir	valued
visar	saw
vísar	refer
vist	hospitality, provisions

Word List (Old Norse to English)

Old Norse	English
víst	certain, knew
vísu	certain
vit	with
vita	know, known
víti	penalty
vits	wits
vitum	know

Y, y

yðr	you
yður	of-you
yfir	over

Word List (English to Old Norse)

Word List (English to Old Norse)

English	*Old Norse*	*English*	*Old Norse*
		asked	bað, biðr, spurði, spyrr
		as-long-as	meðan
		a-smaller	smærra
A, a		a-son	son
a	á	assault	tilræði
abide	bíða	assembly-men	þingmönnum
about	á, um	a-strike	högg
a-bull	naut	at	á, at, er, í
a-case	málit	autumn	haustit
accident	atburð, váðaverk	avail	stoðar
accordingly	því	away	undan
across	ofan	away-from	undan
a-dog	hundr	awhile's-sake	stundarsakir
after	eftir	awoke	vaknar, vakti
afterwards	síðan, síðar	axe	öxina
against	við		
age	elli, fyrnast	**B, b**	
alive	lifir		
all	alla, allan, allr, allra, allt, allt, öllu		
all-many	allmargt	back	bak
allow	leyfa	battle-cunning	vígkœnn
alone	einn	be	ver, vera, verða
along	lengi, lengr	became	gerðist, verða
also	ok	because	því
am	em, er	become	verða, verðr
a-man	maðr	bed	sæng
a-month-from	mánaðar-frá	bed-closet	lokhvílu, rekkjugólfit, rekkjugólfit
Amundi (name)	Ögmundr		
Amundi's (name)	Ámunda	been	verit
an-accident	váðaverk	been-struck	högg
and	en, enn, og, ok	before	áðr, fyrir
and-likely	oklíklegt	behaved	lætr
another	annarr, annarri, öðru	be-known	kenna
another's	annars	bench	bekk
answered	svarar, svöruðu	beside	hjá
any	hverr	betray	svíkja
any-at-all	nökkut	better	betr, betra
are	er, ert, eru, erum	between	með
are-you	ertú, eru	bite	bítast, bítr
arms	hendi	Bjarni (name)	Bjarna, Bjarni
Arnbjorg (name)	Arnbjargar	Bjarni's (name)	Bjarna
as	enn, er, sem	blow	högg
as-if	sem	blows	höggum
ask	beiðast	blunt	slæfast

156

Word List (English to Old Norse)

English	Old Norse
Bodvarsdale (name)	Böðvarsdal
bonfires	sviðelda
Borg (place)	Borg
both	báða, bæði
bothers	nenni
bound	batt
bring	fœra
broke	brugðust
brothers	bræðr
brought	fœri, fœrir
bull	naut
buried	jarða
but	enn, énn, er, men

C, c

English	Old Norse
call	kalla
called	heitum, kallaðr, kölluðu
called-out	œptu
came	kemr, kom, koma, kominn
care	nenni
carried	bar, barizt
carved	reist
certain	víst, vísu
chieftains	höfðingja
claim	heimta
come	gakk, kominn
comes	kemr, verða
coming	kominn, komit, komnir
compensation	bœta, bœtrnur
composed	stiltr
conclude	hætta
concluded	hætta
consider	þykki, þykkjast
console	fróa
contemptible-man	fretkarla
could	mundi
coward	ragan
cowardly	ragan
cursed-man-this	heljarmannsins

D, d

English	Old Norse
daughter	dóttir, dóttur
daughter-of	dóttir
day	dag, daga
death-blow	banahögg
death-day	dauða-dags
decide	ráða
defended	varðist
did	gerði
died	andaðist
difficulty	erfiðinu, þungt, vant
disappeared	hvarf
discourage	letja
discussing	rœða
dishonour	ósœmd
divided	skilit
dizziness	svima
do	gera
done	gert
doorway	durum
down	niðr, ofan
downed	niðr
do-you	gerðú
drag	draga
dragged	kipti
drink	drekk

E, e

English	Old Norse
each	hvárn, hvárrtveggja, hverr
each-other	hvárumtveggja
eager	frekr
eagerly	frekt
early	snemma
earthed	jarðaðr
Einar (name)	Einars
encouraging	eggja
ends	lýkr
equally	jafnhátt
errand-lost	erindislaust
estate	búi
evening	aftan
events	atburði
excellent	afbragðs
exchange	skifta

Word List (English to Old Norse)

English	Old Norse
exchanged	köstuðust
expect	vænt
expected	varði
eye	augat
eyebrow	brúnina

F, f

English	Old Norse
failing-health	vanheilsu
father	faðir, fóður, föður
father-and-son	feðgar
father-of	faðir, föður
fee	fjár
fee-little	félitill
feet	fótum
fell	fell
felt	þuklaði
fences	garð
few	fá
field	tuni
fight	berjast, berjumst
fighting	berjast, herjast
find	finna
finding	finnim
fire-house-wall	eldhúsveggnum
fixed	fastlegra
followed	fylgdi, hlýddi
followers	fjölmenni, fjölmennr
for	för, fyrir
foremost-seat	öndvegi
for-me	mér
for-work	forverk
fought	berjast
found	fann, hittir
from	frá, ór, þaðan
from-going	framar
from-under	undan
fully-golded	fullgoldit

G, g

English	Old Norse
gentle-man	dældarmaðr
get	fá
gift	gæfa
Gissurar	gissurar
give	fá
gladly	gjarnan
go	far, gakk, ganga
going	fara, farit, ganga
gone	farinn, farit
gored	stangat
gossipers	uppaustrarmenn
got	fekk
got-up	upp
granted	veitti
great	mikil, mikill, stórt
guarded	gætti
Gudmund's (name)	Guðmundar
Gudny (name)	Guðnýjar
Gudrid (name)	Guðríðr
Gudrun (name)	Guðrún, Guðrúnar
guilty	sekan

H, h

English	Old Norse
had	átt, átti, áttu, hafa, hafði, hafi, haft, hefir, höfðu, lætr, lagði, láta, lét
had-been	vera
Halla (name)	Halla
Hallfrid (name)	Hallfríðr
hand	hendr
hands	hendr
happens	hendir
harm	harmar
has	hafi, hefir, lætr
have	eiga, hafa, hafi, hefi, hefir, verit
have-you-hit	hjóstu
hay	hey
he	hann, honum
head	höfði, höfuð
head-bone	höfuðbeinum
healthy	heill
heard	heyrðu
held	helt
Helga (name)	Helgu

Word List (English to Old Norse)

English	Old Norse
help	björg
helpless	hlífarlauss
her	hana, hon
here	hér, hingat
hers	síns
hewed	hjuggust
hill	hól, hólinn
him	hann, hans, honum, sín
himself	sér, sjálfr
his	hans, honum, sín, sína, sinn, sinnar, sinni, síns, sínu, sínum
his-hand	hendinni
Hof	hofs
Hof (place)	Hofi, Hofs
hold	halds
hold-fulfil	haldkvæmara
home	heim, heima, heiman
honour	drengskap, virðingu
horse	hesti, hestr
horse-boy	hestasvein
horse-fight	hesta-ats, hestaþingi, hesta-þinginu
horse-house	hesthúsinn, hrossahúsi, hrossahússins
horse-man	hrossamaðr
horses	hesta, hestana, hestum, hestunum, hrossa, hrossin
horse-staffs	hestastafnum
hospitality	vist
house	húss
how	hvernig
how-many	hversu

I, i

English	Old Norse
I	ek, mér
I-am	ek
if	ef
ill	illt
in	á, í, inn, við
injury	sárunum
inside	inn
intended	ætluðu
into	í
invited	bauð
is	er, sé
is-it	er
it	at, hon, þat, þat
it, that, to	at

J, j

English	Old Norse
jaw	skoltinn
Jon (name)	Jóns
journey	ferð
joyful	feginn
judging	dœmi

K, k

English	Old Norse
keep-secret	leyna
killed	drepit, veginn, vegit
Killer-Bjarni (name)	Víga-Bjarna
killing	vig
kinsmen	frændi, frændum
knees	kné
knew	víst
know	kann, kenni, veit, vita, vitum
known	vita
Kolbein (name)	Kolbeinn

L, l

English	Old Norse
laid	lágði, lagðist
lambs-heads	lambahöfuðin
last	siðara
lawspeaker	lögsögumaðr
lay	lá
laying	lægi
life	æfi, ævi, fjörsins
likeliest	liklegastir
listen	hlýða
little	litlu, lítt
live	lifir, liflr
lived	bjó
looked	leit

Word List (English to Old Norse)

English	Old Norse	English	Old Norse
looked-after	varðveitti	much	mikit, miklar, miklir, miklu, mjök
look-for	leita	my	minnar, mínum
looking-for	leita	myself	mér, sjálfr
loose	lausir		
luck	happi		

M, m

N, n

English	Old Norse
Magnus (name)	Magnus, Magnúsar, Magnúss
make	gerir
man	maðr, mann, manns
man's	manns
many	marga, margir, margt, mörgum
married	átti
matched	maki, öttu
may	má, mætta
may-be	megi
me	mér, mik, min
meadow	garðinu
meet	meta, mik
men	manna, menn
mercy	vægt
met	hitta, hitti, mér
mid-morning	dagmálum
might	mætta
mind	skapi
mine	mín, mína, mínir, minn, minni, mínum
miserable	armastr
misfortune	ógæfa
mishap	óhapp
mislaid	forlagðir
misplaced	mislagðar
miss	missa
mood	skap
more	meira, meirr
more-powerful	rikara
morning	morgun, morguninn
most	mesti
mother-of	móðir, móður
mourn	sýta
mouths	hváftana
move	bregð

English	Old Norse
named	heitir, hét, nefndr
near	nær
neck	hála
need	þurfa
needs	þarf
never	aldregi
news	tiðast, tíðast, tíðinda
noble	riks, skörugligast
none	eigi, engan, engi, engir, öngu
no-one	engi
nor	né
not	eigi, ekki
not-be	eigi
nothing	engi, engis
not-used-to	óvanari
now	nú

O, o

English	Old Norse
of	á, af, af, of
off	af
often	oft, oftar
of-the-other	annarrar
of-you	afþér, yður
Ogmund (name)	Ögmundar
old	gamall
older	ellri
old-man	karl
on	á, í
one	annarr, eina, einn, einum, gott
one-thing	eitt
only	eigu, engis
or	eðr
orderly	stilltr
Orm (name)	Orms

Word List (English to Old Norse)

English	*Old Norse*	*English*	*Old Norse*
other	aðrir, annarra, öðrum	Rannveig (name)	Rannveig
our	várir	rather	heldr, helzt
out	út, útan, úti	refer	vísar
outlaw	skógarmaðr	reins	taumana
outlawed	skógarmaðrinn	reported	títt
out-of	ör	rested	hvílir
outside	út, úti	revenge	hefna
outstanding-man	afbragðsmaðr	ride	reið
out-travel	útan	riding-horses	reiðhesta
over	ofan, yfir	risk	hætta
overcome	bart	Rome-city (place)	Rúmaborg
		rose	reis, rísa

P, p

S, s

English	*Old Norse*	*English*	*Old Norse*
part	hlut	said	kvað, kváðust, mælti, sagði, sagði, segir
pass	leið	said-too-much	ofmælt
passed	líðr	sake	sakir, sóknum
paupers	framfœrslumenn	same-district	samheraðs
peace	kyrt	sat	sæti, sat, sátu
penalty	víti	saw	sá, visar
people	mann, menn	say	mæl, segi, segir
people's	manna	scared	hræddr
persistent	þrautbeztr	see	sé
place	stað	seeing-little	sjónlitill
pledge	handsöl	seem	þykkir
popular	vinsælli	seemed	þykkir
powerful	öflugr	seeming	þykkir
praise	hrósit	seems	sýnist, þykki, þykkir
prepared	búit, býr	seens	þykkir
prestigious-people	stðrmenna	self-supported	sjálfbjarga
promise	lofa	sent	sendi
promises	heit	seriously	alvöru
protection	hiífar	servant	húskarl
provisions	vist	servants	húskarla, húskarlar
pulled	togat	serves-you-right	makligleikum
purchase	kaup	settle	bústú, sitja
pushed	stakk	shaking	skelfr
		shall	man, mant, mun, skal, skalt, skaltú
		shall-you	muntú, skaltú

R, r

English	*Old Norse*
ram-heads	geldinga-höfuð
ran	hleypr, hljóp, rann

sharpened	hvatti
she	hon
sheep-heads	dilka-höfuð

Word List (English to Old Norse)

English	Old Norse	English	Old Norse
shield	skjöldinn, skjöldr	standing	stendr
shields	skjöldu	Stein (name)	Steins
ship	skip	stepped	sté
shirts	skyrtum	still	enn, kyrt
shirt-sheet	skyrtublaði	stood	stóð
shoe-thongs	skóþvengir	stoop	bograt
short	skamt	stooped	lýtr
short-sword	sax, saxi, saxinu	straightaway	þegar
should	man, mantú, mun, skyldi, skyldu	stream	lœkjarins
		strength	þrek
should-be	skyldi	strike	höggva
Sidu-Hallson (name)	Siðu-Hallsson	striking	högg
sight-less	sjónlausum	stronger	ríkar
Sighvat (name)	Sighvats	struck	hjó, höggr, laust, lostinn, lýstr
Sigrid (name)	Sigríði		
silence	þagat	struggle	þraut
since	því	stud-horses	stóðhross
singe	svíða, sviðit	stupid	heimskr
single-combat	einvigis, einvígis	submit	undir
situated	siti	such	slika, slíka, slíkt, slikum
Skegg-Broddi (name)	Skegg-Broddi	summer	sumar
sleep	svefns	Sunnudal (place)	Sunnudal
slept	sofa	support	stoðar
slipped	runnit	suppose	ætla, ætlar, ætlum
Snorri (name)	Snorra	surprised	kynlegt
so	sá, svá	Sutri (place)	Valería
sold	seldu	Svinafellings (name)	Svínfellings
some	nökkura, nökkurum	sword	sverð, sverðit
somewhat	nökkuru		
son	son, sonar, sonr, syni		
son-death	sonar-dauðinn		
son's	sonar		

T, t

English	Old Norse
south	suðr
spare	spara
speak	mæla, mælast, mælir
speaking	mælt
speedily	snarligra
spirit	dugi
spoke	mælti
spoken	mælt
spoke-of	mæltu
sport	leik
Staff-Struck (name)	Stangarhögg, Stangarhöggs
stain	flekk
stand	standa, stoða

English	Old Norse
take	tak, taka
takes	taka, tekr
taking	tókum
talk	tals
talking	talat, tali
taunted	kals
taunting	frýju-orð
tell	seg, segi, segja
tell-you	teljast
than	at, enn, er
that	at, er, sú, það, þat, þetta
the	hinn
the-assembly	þings

Word List (English to Old Norse)

English	Old Norse	English	Old Norse
the-bishop	biskups	Thord's (name)	Þórðar
the-blind	blinda	Thorgeir (name)	Þórgeirs
the-blow	höggvið	Thorgrim's (name)	Þórgríms
the-blows	höggunum	Thorhall (name)	Þórhall, Þórhallr
the-chieftain	góða	Thorid (name)	Þuriðar
the-day	dag	Thorkatla (name)	Þórkatla
the-district	heraðinu	Thorstein (name)	Þŏrsteinn, Þórstein, Þórsteini, Þórsteinn, Þórsteins
the-earl	jarls		
the-hill	hölinn, höllinn		
the-horse	best	Thorstein's (name)	Þórsteini, Þórsteins
the-horses	hestarnir, hrossa	Thorvald (name)	Þórvald, Þórvaldr
their	þeim, þeira, þeiri	those	þeim, þeira
theirs	sína, sínum	though	þo, þó, þótt
the-killing	vigit	thought	hugða, hugði, mundi, þótti, þykkjast
them	þeim		
the-man	maðr, maðrinn	thoughts	hug
themselves	sér	thralls	þræla
then	enn, hit, síðan, þá, þau	three	þriggja, þrjá
the-night	nóttina	thrives	þriflst
the-old-man	karl, karls	through	gegnum
the-other	öðrum	tie	bind
the-priest	prests	tied	bindr
there	hingat, þær, þar, þefri, þeiri, til	time	stundu
		to	á, at, í, til, tíl
therefore	því	to-be	at
the-sagas	sögur	to-do	tilgert
the-saga-tale	sögu-þætti	together	saman
the-same	sama	to-give	veita
the-Sturlusons (name)	Sturlusona	to-go	fara
the-sword	sverðit	to-invite	bjóða
the-table	borð, borði	to-lay	leggja
the-tables	borða	told	sagði, sagt, segir, segja, talat
the-wicked	glœp		
the-woman	kona, konan	tolerate	þoli
they	hinir, þau, þeir, þeira	to-me	mér, mik
they-are	eru	tongue	tungu, tungunni
think	þykki, þykkir	took	taka, tekr, tók
thirsty	þyrstir	torso	bolinn
this	í, þat, þenna, þess, þessarra, þessu, þessum, þetta, þit	to-think	þykkja
		to-travel	fara
		toughness	harðfengi
Thora (name)	Þórn, Þóru	towards	móti, til
Thorarin (name)	Þŏrarinn, Þórarinn, Þórarins	to-you	sér, þér
		Travel	far, fara, ferr
Thord (name)	Þórð, Þórðar, Þórðr	travelled	fara, ferr, fœra, fór
Thordis (name)	Þórdísar	trolls	troll

Word List (English to Old Norse)

English	Old Norse
true	
true	
true-man	trú-maðr
truth	trútt
two	tvá

U, u

English	Old Norse
under	undir
un-equal-man	ójafnaðar
un-gift	ógifta
unremarkable	ómjúkir
until	til, unz
up	upp, uppá
up-to	undir
us	okkr, oss

V, v

English	Old Norse
valour	hreysti
valued	virðir
viking	víkingr

W, w

English	Old Norse
wake	vekja
want	vant
wanted	nenta
warily	varlega
warn	varnaði
warriors	kappi
was	er, væri, var, varð
was-named	hét
we	oss, vér
weak	seint
weapon	vápn
weapons	vápn, vápna
weapons-exchange	vápnaskiftum
we-are	vér
wear-out	slita
weeping	gráta
well	vel

English	Old Norse
went	fara, fœri, fór, ganga, gekk, gengi, gengr, gengu
were	eru, var, váru
were-you	vartú
what	er, hvat, hvert
when	enn, er, hvenær
where	er, hvar
whether	hvárt
which	er, hvert, sem, því
who	er, hverr
who-are	er
why	hverr, hvi
widely	víða
will	valdi, vilda, vilja, vill, vilt
willed	vildi
win	vinna
winter	vetrinn
wish	vil, vilda, vilit, vilja, vilt
with	er, með, við, vit
without	ómegð
without-cause	saklausa
without-revenge	óhefnt
wits	vits
woman	konu
women	konum, konur, kvenna
wonder	kynlegt
worded	orðit
words	orð, orða, orðit, orðum
work	verk, verks
worked	vann
working	forverka
worse	verr, verra
worst	verr
worth	verðr
worthiness	virðingu
worthy	svivirðing
would	mant, munda, mundak, mundi, mundir, mundu, mundum, muni, væri, vildi
would-be	vara

Y, y

Word List (English to Old Norse)

English	Old Norse
Yngvild (name)	Ingveldr
Yngvild's (name)	Ingveldra
you	þér, þik, þín, þínu, þínum, þú, yðr
young	ungum
yours	sitt, þín, þína, þinn, þíns, þínum
youth	œsku
you-two	þér
Yule (name)	Jól

The Tale of Thorstein Staff-Struck (*Old Icelandic*)

Old Icelandic	Literal	English
1	**1**	**1**
Maður hét Þórarinn er bjó í Sunnudal, gamall maður og sjónlítill.	A-man was-named Thorarin who lived in Sunnudal, old man and seeing-little.	There was a man named Thorarin who lived in Sunnudal, he was an old man and nearly blind.
Hann hafði verið rauðavíkingur í æsku sinni.	He had been fierce-viking in youth his.	He had been a fierce viking in his youth.
Hann var eigi dældarmaður þótt hann væri gamall.	He was not gentle-man though he was old.	He was not a gentle man even though he was old.
Son átti hann sér einn er Þorsteinn er nefndur.	A-son had he himself one who Thorstein was named.	He had a son who was named Thorstein.
Hann var mikill maður og öflugur og vel stilltur og vann svo fyrir búi föður síns að eigi mundi þriggja verk manna annarra hallkvæmara.	He was great man and powerful and well composed and worked so for estate father his that not could three work men other hold-fulfil.	He was a great and powerful man and well composed, and he worked so hard on his father's estate that three other men could not fulfil.
Þórarinn var heldur félítill maður en vel margt átti hann vopna.	Thorarin was rather fee-little man but well many had he weapons.	Thorarin was rather a poor man but he had many weapons.
Þeir áttu og stóðhross feðgar og var þeim það helst til fjár er þeir seldu undan hestana því að engir brugðust að reið né hug.	They had also stud-horses father-and-son and was their that rather to fee that they sold away horses because that none broke to ride nor spirit.	They also had some stud horses and that was their main source of wealth, for the horses they sold were not broken by riding nor broken in spirit.
Þórður er maður nefndur.	Thord was a-man named.	There was a man named Thord.
Hann var húskarl Bjarna frá Hofi.	He was servant Bjarni's from Hof.	He was a servant of Bjarni from Hof.
Hann varðveitti reiðhesta Bjarna því að hann var kallaður hrossamaður.	He looked-after riding-horses Bjarni's accordingly that he was called horse-man.	He looked after Bjarni's riding-horses and was therefore called horse-man.
Þórður var ójafnaðarmaður mikill og lét hann marga þess og kenna er hann var ríkismanns húskarl.	Thord was un-equal-man much and had he many this and be-known that he was noble-man's servant.	Thord was very much an arrogant man and he had it known that he was a nobleman's servant.

The Tale of Thorstein Staff-Struck (Old Icelandic)

Old Icelandic	Literal	English
En eigi var hann sjálfur að meira verður og eigi varð hann að vinsælli.	But not was he himself the more worth and not was he that popular.	But this did not add to his worth or his popularity.
Þeir menn voru enn á vist með Bjarna er annar hét Þórhallur en annar Þorvaldur.	They men were then in hospitality with Bjarni who one named Thorhall and another Thorvald.	There were then men staying with Bjarni, one was named Thorhall, and another Thorvald.
Þeir voru uppaustrarmenn miklir um allt það er þeir heyrðu í héraði.	They were gossipers much about all that which they heard in the-district.	They were very much gossipers about all that the heard in the district.
Þeir Þorsteinn og Þórður mæltu til hestaats ungum hestum.	They Thorstein and Thord spoke-of to horse-fight young horses.	Thorstein and Thord spoke about a horse fight for their young horses.
Og er þeir öttu þá vildi hestur Þórðar verr bítast.	And when they matched then would horse Thord's worst bite.	And when they fought, Thord's horse was bitten the worst.
Þórður lýstur nú á skoltinn hesti Þorsteins er honum þótti sinn hestur verr hafa, mikið högg.	Thord struck now to jaw horse Thorstein's when he thought his horse worse had, much been-struck.	Thord now struck the jaw of Thorstein's horse when he realised that his horse had been struck worse.
En Þorsteinn sá það og lýstur á móti hest Þórðar heldur meira högg og rann nú hesturinn Þórðar og æptu menn þá með kappi.	Then Thorstein saw that and struck to towards the-horse Thord's rather more striking and ran now horse Thord's and called-out men then with warriors.	Then Thorstein saw that and struck at Thord's horse rather more, and Thord's horse backed away, and then the warriors who were with them called out.
Þá lýstur Þórður Þorstein með hestastafnum og kom á brúnina og hljóp hún ofan fyrir augað.	Then struck Thord Thorstein with horse-staffs and came to eyebrow and ran it over before eye.	Then Thord struck Thorstein with his horse staff which came to his eyebrow and ran over his eye.
Þá risti Þorsteinn af skyrtublaði sínu og bindur upp brúnina og lætur sem ekki hafi að orðið og biður að menn leyni þessu föður hans.	Then carved Thorstein off shirt-sheet his and bound up eyebrow and behaved as-if not had which worded and asked that people keep-secret this father his.	Then Thorstein carved from his shirt and bandaged his eyebrow and behaved thus that he did not say anything about it, and he asked people to keep this a secret from his father.
Og féll þetta þar nú niður.	And fell that there now down.	And the matter fell down there.

The Tale of Thorstein Staff-Struck (Old Icelandic)

Old Icelandic	Literal	English
Þeir Þorvaldur og Þórhallur höfðu þetta fyrir kallsi og kölluðu hann Þorstein stangarhögg.	They Thorvald and Thorhall had this before taunted and called him Thorstein Staff-Struck.	Thorvald and Thorhall has thus taunted him and called him Thorstein Staff-Struck.
Litlu fyrir jól um veturinn risu konur til verks í Sunnudal.	Little before Yule about winter rose women to work in Sunnudal.	A little before Yule in winter when women got up to work in Sunnudal.
Þá stóð Þorsteinn og upp og bar inn hey og lagðist síðan niður í bekk.	Then stood Thorstein and got-up and carried in hay and laid then down on bench.	Then Thorstein got up and carried some hay inside and then lay down on a bench.
Nú kemur Þórarinn karl innar, faðir hans, og spurði hver þar lægi.	Now came Thorarin old-man in, father his, and asked why there laying.	Now Thorarin his father, an old man, came in and asked him why he was laying there.
Þorsteinn sagði til sín.	Thorstein said to him.	Thorstein told him.
"Hví ertu svo snemma á fótum sonur?"	"Why are-you so early about feet son?"	"Why are you up on your feet so early, son?",
sagði Þórarinn karl.	said Thorarin old-man.	said Thorarin the old man.
Þorsteinn svarar:	Thorstein answered:	Thorstein answered:
"Við fá þykir mér að meta það sem hér er að vinna",	"With few seems to-me to meet that which here is to win",	"With few it seems to me that might help me here",
sagði Þorsteinn.	said Thorstein.	said Thorstein.
"Er þér ekki illt í höfuðbeinunum sonur?"	"Are you not ill in head-bone son?"	"Are you not ill in the head, son?",
kvað Þórarinn karl.	said Thorarin old-man.	said the old man.
"Eigi kenni eg þess",	"Not know I this",	"Not that I have noticed",
sagði Þorsteinn.	said Thorstein.	said Thorstein.
"Hvað segir þú mér sonur af hestaþinginu því er í fyrra sumar var? Varstu ekki lostinn í svíma frændi sem hundur?"	"What say you to-me son of horse-fight which that in before summer was? Were-you not struck to dizziness kinsmen as a-dog?"	What can you tell me about the horse fight last summer? Were you not struck dizzy by your kinsmen like a dog?"
"Engi þykir mér virðing í vera",	"Nothing seems to-me worthy to be",	"It is not worthy to me",

The Tale of Thorstein Staff-Struck (Old Icelandic)

Old Icelandic	Literal	English
sagði Þorsteinn, "að kalla það heldur högg en atburð".	said Thorstein, "to call that rather striking than accident".	said Thorstein, "to call it rather a blow than an incident".
Þórarinn mælti:	Thorarin said:	Thorarin said:
"Ekki mundi mig þess vara að eg mundi ragan son eiga".	"Not thought me this would-be that I would cowardly son have".	"Not would this be to me, that I would have a coward son".
"Mæl þú það eitt um nú faðir",	"Say you that one-thing about now father",	"Tell me one thing about now, father",
sagði Þorsteinn, "er þér þykir eigi ofmælt síðar".	said Thorstein, "that you seem not or-speaking afterwards".	said Thorstein, "which you do not think is said-too-much later".
"Ekki mun eg hér svo mikið um mæla",	"Not shall I here so much about speak",	"I will not speak so much here",
sagði Þórarinn, "sem mér er að skapi".	said Thorarin, "as to-me is to mind".	said Thorarin, "of what I am in the mood to say".

2

Nú reis Þorsteinn upp og tók vopn sín og gekk síðan heiman og fór uns hann kom til hrossahúss þess er Þórður gætti hesta Bjarna í og var hann þar fyrir.	Now rose Thorstein up and took weapon his and went afterwards home and travelled until he came to horse-house this that Thord guarded horses Bjarni's in and was he there before.	Now Thorstein got up and took his weapon, and then went away from home, and went until he came to the horse-house where Thord looked after Bjarni's horses, and he was there before.
Þá hittir Þorsteinn Þórð og mælti til hans:	Then found Thorstein Thord and spoke to him:	Then Thorstein met Thord, and said to him,
"Vita vildi eg það Þórður minn hvort það varð þér voðaverk er eg fékk af þér högg í fyrra sumar á hestaþingi eða hefir það að vilja þínum orðið og hvort bæta muntu þá vilja yfir".	"Know wish I that Thord me whether that was you accident that I got of you a-strike in before summer at horse-fight or have that to wish you words and whether compensation you-should then will over".	"I wish to know, my Thord, whether it was a tragedy to you when I was beaten by you last summer at a horse meeting, or whether it has been at your will, and whether you will make amends for it".
Þórður svarar:	Thord answered:	Thord answered:

The Tale of Thorstein Staff-Struck (Old Icelandic)

Old Icelandic	Literal	English
"Ef þú átt tvo hvoftana þá bregð þú tungunni sitt sinn í hvorn og kalla í öðrum voðaverk ef þú vilt en í öðrum kalla þú alvöru.	"If you had two mouths then move you tongue yours that in each and call in the-other an-accident if you wish but in the-other call you seriously.	"If you had two mouths, then you could move your tongue into each and call it either an accident if you wish but in another call it serious.
Og eru það nú bæturnar þær er þú munt af mér fá".	And are-you that now compensation there that you shall of me get".	And now those are the benefits you'll get from me".
"Búst þú þá svo við",	"Settle you then so with",	"Settle with that as you will",
sagði Þorsteinn,	said Thorstein,	said Thorstein,
"að vera má að eg heimti eigi oftar".	"to be may that I claim not often".	"it may be that I don't make this claim often".
Síðan hleypur Þorsteinn að honum og höggur Þórð banahögg, gekk síðan til húss að Hofi og hitti úti konu eina og mælti við hana:	Then ran Thorstein at him and struck Thord death-blow, went afterwards to house at Hof and met outside woman one and spoke with her:	Then Thorstein ran at him and stuck Thord his death-blow, and went afterwards to the house at Hof and met a woman outside and spoke with her:
"Seg þú Bjarna að naut hafi stangað Þórð hestasvein hans og mun hann bíða þar til þess er hann kemur hjá hestahúsinu".	"Tell you Bjarni that bull has gored Thord horse-boy his and should he abide there to this that he comes beside". horse-house".	"Tell Bjarni that a bull has gored Thord horse-man, and he should wait there until he comes to the stable".
"Far þú heim maður",	"Travel you home man",	"Go back home, man",
sagði hún,	said she,	she said,
"en eg segi þá er mér sýnist".	"then I say then what to-me seems".	"and I will way when it seems to me to do so".
Nú fer Þorsteinn heim en konan fer til verks síns.	Now travelled Thorstein home and the-woman went to work hers.	Now Thorstein travelled home and the woman went to her work.

3

Bjarni reis upp um morguninn og er hann var undir borð kominn þá spurði Bjarni hvar Þórður væri og svöruðu menn að hann mundi til hrossa farinn.	Bjarni rose up about morning and as he was under the-table came then asked Bjarni where Thord was and answered people that he would to the-horses gone.	Bjarni got up that morning and was sitting at the table, then Bjarni asked where Thord was, and people answered that he would have travelled to the horses.

The Tale of Thorstein Staff-Struck (Old Icelandic)

Old Icelandic	Literal	English
"Heim hugði eg hann þó mundu kominn",	"Home thought I he though would come",	"I thought he would have come home",
kvað Bjarni,	said Bjarni,	said Bjarni,
"ef hann væri heill".	"if he was healthy".	"if he was well".
Þá tók kona til orða, sú er Þorsteinn hafði hitta:	Then took the-woman to words, that which Thorstein had met:	Then the woman that Thorsten had met took to words:
"Satt er það er oss er oft sagt konum að þar er lítið til vits að taka sem vér erum konur.	"True is that which we are often told women that there is little to wits to take which we are women.	"It is true what is told of us women, that there is little to wits taken as we are women.
Hér kom Þorsteinn stangarhögg í morgun, kvað naut hafa stangað Þórð svo að hann mundi eigi sjálfbjargi verða.	Here came Thorstein Staff-Struck in morning, said a-bull had gored Thord so that he would not self-supported be.	Thorstein Staff-Struck came here this morning, and said a bull had struck Thord so that he could not support himself.
En eg nennti eigi þá að vekja þig og þá hvarf mér úr hug síðan".	But I wanted not then to wake you and then disappeared to-me from thoughts afterwards".	But I didn't want to wake you, and then it disappeared from my thoughts afterwards".
Bjarni sté þá undan borði, gekk þá til hrossahússins og fann þar Þórð veginn og var hann síðan jarðaður.	Bjarni stepped then from-under the-table, went then to horse-house and found there Thord killed and was he afterwards earthed.	Bjarni stepped out from under the table, and then went to the stable and found Thord there killed, and he was buried afterwards.
Bjarni býr nú mál til og gerir Þorstein sekan um vígið.	Bjarni prepared now a-case towards and make Thorstein guilty about the-killing.	Bjarni now prepared a case to make Thorstein guilty of the killing.
En Þorsteinn sat heima í Sunnudal og vann fyrir föður sínum og lét Bjarni þó kyrrt vera.	Then Thorstein sat home in Sunnudal and worked for father his and had Bjarni though still be.	But Thorstein stayed at home in Sunnudal and worked for his father, and Bjarni had little done though.
Um haustið sátu menn við sviðuelda að Hofi en Bjarni lá úti á eldahússveggnum og hlýddi þaðan til tals manna.	About autumn sat people with bonfires at Hof when Bjarni lay out on fire-house-wall and followed from there talk people's.	About autumn the people of Hof had bonfires, and Bjarni lay outside on the fire-house-wall and followed other people's talking.
Nú taka þeir bræður til orða, Þórhallur og Þorvaldur:	Now took they brothers to words, Thorhall and Thorvald:	Now the brothers Thorhall and Thorvald took to words:

The Tale of Thorstein Staff-Struck (Old Icelandic)

Old Icelandic	Literal	English
"Eigi varði oss þess þegar vér tókum vist með Víga-Bjarna að vér mundum hér svíða dilkahöfuð en Þorsteinn skógarmaður hans skyldi svíða geldingahöfuð.	"Not expected us this when we-are taking provisions with Killer-Bjarni that we would here singe sheep-heads when Thorstein outlaw his should singe ram-heads.	"We did not expect when we came to stay with Killer-Bjarni that we would be here singing sheeps" heads when Thorstein the outlaw would be singing rams' heads.
Væri eigi verra að hafa meir vægt frændum sínum í Böðvarsdal og sæti nú eigi skógarmaðurinn jafnhátt honum í Sunnudal.	Would not-be worse than have more mercy kinsmen his in Bodvarsdale and sat now not outlawed equally him in Sunnudal.	It would not have been worse to have his merciful kinsmen in Bodvarsdale and not sat equally with the outlaw in Sunnudal.
En lagðir verða forlagðir ef fyrir sárunum verða og eigi vitum vér hvenær hann vill þenna flekk má af virðingu sinni".	But had become mislaid if before injury comes and not know we when he will this stain may of worthiness his".	But what is laid becomes mislaid when it becomes faced with injury, and we don't know when he will off this stain from his honour".
Maður einn svaraði:	Man one answered:	One man answered:
"Slíkt er verr mælt en þagað og líklegt að ykkur hafi tröll togað tungu úr höfði.	"Such is worse spoken than silence and likely that you have trolls pulled tongue out-of head.	"Such that is spoken is worse than silence, and it's likely that the trolls pulled the tongue out of your head.
Ætlum vér að hann nenni eigi að taka björg frá föður hans sjónlausum og annarri ómegð þeirri sem í Sunnudal er.	Suppose we that he bothers not to take help from father his sight-less and another without there as in Sunnudal at.	We think that he does not bother to take help from his blind father and other dependants there at Sunnudal.
En kynlegt þykir mér ef þið svíðið oft lambahöfuðin hér eða hrósið því hvað í Böðvarsdal var títt".	About surprised think I if you-two singe often lambs-heads here or praise therefore what in Bodvarsdale was reported".	But I will be surprised if you two singe many more lamb's heads here, or talk about what happened at Bodvarsdale".
Nú fara menn til borða og síðan til svefns og fann ekki á Bjarna hvað talað hafði verið.	Now travelled men to the-tables and then to sleep and found not of Bjarni what told had been.	Now the people went to the tables and then to sleep and Bjarni gave nothing away of what had been told.

4

Um morguninn vakti Bjarni þá Þórhall og Þorvald og bað þá ríða í Sunnudal og færa sér höfuð Þorsteins við bolinn skilið að dagmálum	About morning awoke Bjarni then Thorhall and Thorvald and asked then to-ride to Sunnudal and travelled themselves head Thorstein's with torso divided that mid-morning	About morning Bjarni woke Thorhall and Thorvald and asked them to ride to Sunnudal and bring Thorstein's severed head divided from its torso by mid-morning

The Tale of Thorstein Staff-Struck (Old Icelandic)

Old Icelandic	Literal	English
"og þykir mér þið", sagði hann, "líklegastir til að færa flekk af virðingu minni ef eg hefi ekki þrek til sjálfur".	"and seems to-me you", said he, "likeliest to that bring stain of worthiness mine if I have not strength to myself".	"and it seems to me that you", he said, "will bring the stain off my honour if I have not the strength to myself".
Nú þykjast þeir víst ofmælt hafa og fara þeir nú þó uns þeir koma í Sunnudal.	Now thought they knew said-too-much had and travelled they now though until they came to Sunnudal.	Now they thought that they had said too much, but they travelled until they came to Sunnudal.
Þorsteinn stóð í durum og hvatti sax.	Thorstein stood in doorway and sharpened short-sword.	Thorstein stood in the doorway and sharpened a short-sword.
Og er þeir komu þar þá spurði hann hvert þeir ætluðu	And as they came there then asked he what they intended	And as they came he asked them what their intentions were,
en þeir sögðust hrossa leita skyldu	then they said horses looking-for should	and they said that they were looking for some horses,
en Þorsteinn kvað þeirra mundu skammt að leita, "er hér eru við garð".	then Thorstein said they would short to look-for, "but here they-were with fences".	then Thorstein said that they would not have to look far "but they are here by the fence".
"Eigi er víst að við finnum hrossin ef þú vísar okkur eigi gerr til".	"Not is-it certain that with finding horses if you refer us not do to".	"It is not certain that we will find the horses if you do not refer us".
Þorsteinn gengur þá út.	Thorstein went then outside.	Then Thorstein went outside.
Og er þeir koma í garðinn ofan þá færir Þorvaldur upp öxina og hleypur að honum en Þorsteinn stakk við honum hendi sinni svo að hann féll fyrir.	And as they came to meadow across then brought Thorvald up axe and ran at him but Thorstein pushed against him arms his so that he fell before.	And as they went across the meadow, Thorvald brought up an axe and ran at him but Thorstein pushed against his arms so that he fell before him.
Þorsteinn lagði saxinu í gegnum hann.	Thorstein laid short-sword in through him.	Thorstein laid his short-sword through him.
Þá vildi Þórhallur veita honum tilræði og hafði hann slíka för sem Þorvaldur.	Then willed Thorhall to-give him assault and had he such for as Thorvald.	Then Thorhall wished to assault him, and he had the same as Thorvald.
Þá bindur Þorsteinn á bak báða þá og lætur upp taumana á háls hestinum og vísar á leið öllu saman og ganga hestarnir nú heim til Hofs.	Then tied Thorstein to back both then and had up reins to neck horses and saw to pass all together and went the-horses now home to Hof.	Then Thorstein tied both back and had the reins up to the horses necks and saw them off together, an the horses went home to Hof.

The Tale of Thorstein Staff-Struck (Old Icelandic)

Old Icelandic	Literal	English
Húskarlar voru úti að Hofi og gengu inn og sögðu Bjarna að þeir Þorvaldur voru heim komnir og sögðu þá eigi erindlaust farið hafa.	Servants were out at Hof and went in and told Bjarni that they Thorvald were home coming and told then not errand-lost gone had.	The servants were outside at Hof and went in and told Bjarni that Thorvald and Thorhall had come home, and said that their errand had not gone in vain.
Gengur nú Bjarni út og sér nú hvernig um er búið og hefir ekki orða um fleira,	Went now Bjarni out and himself now how about was prepared and have not words about more,	Now Bjarni went out himself about what had happened, and had no more words about it, and had them buried.
lætur nú jarða þá. Og er nú kyrrt allt uns jól líður.	had now buried then. And was now peace all until Yule passed.	And it was now all peaceful until Yule had passed.

5

Old Icelandic	Literal	English
Þá tekur Rannveig til orða einn aftan er þau komu í sæng sína, Bjarni og hún:	Then took Rannveig to words one evening when they came to bed theirs, Bjarni and her:	Then Rannveig spoke one evening when her and Bjarni came to their bed:
"Hvað ætlar þú að nú sé tíðast talað í héraðinu?"	"What suppose you that now is news talking in the-district?"	"What do you suppose people are talking about in the district?"
kvað hún.	said she.	she said.
"Eigi veit eg",	"Not know I",	"I do not know",
sagði Bjarni.	said Bjarni.	said Bjarni.
"Margir þykja mér ómerkir í sínum orðum", sagði hann.	"Many think me unremarkable in their words", said he.	"I think many of their words are unremarkable", he said.
"Það er nú tíðast að ræða að menn þykjast eigi vita hvað Þorsteinn stangarhögg mun þess gera að þér muni þurfa þykja að hefna.	"This is now news that discussing that people consider not known what Thorstein Staff-Struck would this do that you would need to-think to revenge.	"This is now what people are talking about, they think they don't know what Thorstein Staff-Struck would have to do for you to take revenge.
Hefir hann nú vegið húskarla þína þrjá.	Has he now killed servants yours three.	He has now killed three of your servants.
Þykir þingmönnum þínum eigi vænt til halds þar sem þú ert ef þessa er óhefnt og eru þér mjög mislagðar hendur í kné".	Think assembly-men yours not expect to hold there as you are if this is without-revenge and are your much misplaced hands on knees".	Your assembly-men do not expect to stay here as you are, if this is without revenge, and you have misplaced your hands on your knees.

The Tale of Thorstein Staff-Struck (Old Icelandic)

Old Icelandic	Literal	English
Bjarni svarar:	Bjarni answered:	Bjarni answered:
"Nú kemur hér að því sem mælt er að engi lætur sér annars víti að varnaði en hlýða mun eg þér hvað er þú mælir.	"Now comes here that since which spoken is that no-one has himself another's penalty to warn but listen should I to-you what is you speak.	"Now it comes to what is said, that no one gives himself another's misfortune as a warning, but I will obey you what you say.
Hefir Þorsteinn og fá saklausa drepið".	Has Thorstein and had without-cause killed".	Thorstein has killed few without cause".
Hætta þau þessu tali og sofa af um nóttina.	Concluded then this talking and slept of about the-night.	Then their talking concluded and they slept through the night.
Um morguninn vaknar Rannveig er Bjarni tók ofan skjöld sinn og spurði hún hvert hann skyldi.	About morning awoke Rannveig as Bjarni took down shield his and asked her where he should-be.	In the morning Rannveig woke up when Bjarni took down his shield and she asked where he was going.
Hann svarar:	He answered:	He answered:
"Nú skal skipta virðingu með okkur Þorsteini í Sunnudal",	"Now shall exchange honour between us Thorstein in Sunnudal",	"Now we shall exchange honour between us, Thorstein in Sunnudal",
segir hann.	said he.	he said.
"Hversu fjölmennur skaltu fara?"	"How-many followers shall travel?"	"How many followers shall you travel with?",
segir hún.	said she.	she said.
"Ekki mun eg draga fjölmenni að Þorsteini",	"Not shall I drag followers to Thorsteini",	"I shall not drag followers to Thorstein",
segir hann,	said he,	he said,
"og mun eg einn fara".	"and shall I alone travel".	"and I shall travel alone".
"Gerðu eigi það",	"Do-you not that",	"Do not do that",
segir hún,	said she,	she said,
"að hætta þér einn undir vopn heljarmannsins".	"to risk to-you one up-to weapons cursed-man-this".	"to risk yourself alone up against the weapons of this cursed man".

The Tale of Thorstein Staff-Struck (Old Icelandic)

Old Icelandic	Literal	English
Bjarni mælti:	Bjarni spoke:	Bjarni spoke:
"Mun þér nú eigi verða þeirra kvenna dæmi er það gráta á annarri stundu er eggja á annarri? En eg þoli oft lengi frýjuorð bæði þér og öðrum en þá stoðar og ekki að letja mig þá er eg vil fara".	"Should you now not become those women judging who-are this weeping at another time who-are encouraging in another? But I tolerate often along taunting both of-you and others but then support and not to discourage me then as I wish to-go".	"Should you not now become one-of-those women who deem to weep at one moment but encourage at another? Before I have tolerated frequently and long enough the taunts of you and others, but then support me and not discourage me as I wish to go".
Bjarni fer nú í Sunnudal og stendur Þorsteinn í durum og köstuðust þeir á nokkurum orðum.	Bjarni went now to Sunnudal and standing Thorstein in doorway and exchanged they of some words.	Bjarni now went to Sunnudal and there was Thorstein standing in the doorway, and they exchanged some words.
Bjarni mælti:	Bjarni spoke:	Bjarni spoke:
"Þú skalt til einvígis ganga við mig í dag Þorsteinn á hól þenna er hér er í túni".	"You shall to single-combat go with me to day Thorstein on hill this which here is in field".	"You shall go to single combat with me today Thorstein, on this hill which is here in the field.
"Allt er mér til þess vant",	"All is me to this difficulty",	"This is all to my difficulty",
kvað Þorsteinn,	said Thorstein,	said Thorstein,
"að berjast við þig en eg skal þegar utan er skip ganga því að eg kann drengskap þinn að þú munt fá föður mínum forverk ef eg fer frá".	"to fight with you then I shall straightaway out-travel with ship going because that I know honour yours that you would give father mine for-work if I travel from".	"to fight with you, but I shall immediately travel out with the first ship going, because I know your honour, that you would give my father labour if I leave".
"Ekki stoðar nú undan að mælast",	"Not avail now from-under that speak",	"You cannot speak to avail yourself out from under this",
segir Bjarni.	said Bjarni.	said Bjarni.
"Leyfa muntu mér þá að eg finni föður minn áður",	"Allow shall-you for-me then that I find father mine before",	"Will you allow me that I can find my father before",
sagði Þorsteinn.	said Thorstein.	said Thorstein.
"Að vísu",	"To-be certain",	"Certainly",
sagði Bjarni.	said Bjarni.	said Bjarni.

The Tale of Thorstein Staff-Struck (Old Icelandic)

Old Icelandic	Literal	English
Þorsteinn gekk inn og sagði föður sínum að Bjarni var þar kominn og bauð honum til einvígis.	Thorstein went inside and told father his that Bjarni was there coming and invited him to single-combat.	Thorstein went inside and told his father that Bjarni was here and had invited him to single-combat.
Þórarinn karl svaraði:	Thorarin old-man answered:	Thorarin, the old man, answered:
"Von má hver maður þess vita ef hann á við sér ríkara mann og sitji samhéraðs honum og hafi þó gert honum nokkura ósæmd að hann mun eigi mörgum skyrtum slíta og kann eg því ekki að sýta þig að mér þykir þú mikið til hafa gert.	"Expect may any man this know if he to against himself more-powerful man and situated same-district his and has though done him some dishonour that he should not many shirts wear-out and know I therefore not to mourn you that to-me seems you much to have done.	"Any man may know to expect this, if he has done some discredit against a more powerful man in his own district, that he will not wear out many more shirts, and I know therefore not to mourn you because it seems to me that you have done much.
Tak nú vopn þín og ver þig sem skörulegast því að þar mundi verið hafa minnar ævi að ekki mundi eg bograð hafa fyrir slíkum sem Bjarni er. Er Bjarni þó hinn mesti kappi.	Take now weapons yours and be you as noble because that there would been have my life that not would I stoop have before such as Bjarni is. Is Bjarni though the most warrior.	Now take your weapons and be noble, because in my life I would not have stooped before such a man as Bjarni is. Even though he is the best warrior.
Þykir mér og betra að missa þín en eiga ragan son".	Consider I also better to miss you than own cowardly son".	I consider it better to lose you than to have a coward for a son".

6

Nú gengur Þorsteinn út og fara þeir síðan út á hólinn og taka til að berjast með harðfengi og hjuggust mjög hlífar fyrir hvorumtveggja.	Now went Thorstein out and went they afterwards out to the-hill and took to that fighting with toughness and hewed much protection before each-other.	Now Thorstein went outside and then they went out to the hill and took to fighting with toughness and struck down much of each other's shields.
Og þá er þeir höfðu mjög lengi barist þá mælti Bjarni til Þorsteins:	And then when they had much long carried then spoke Bjarni to Thorstein:	And then when they had carried on for a long time, Bjarni spoke to Thorstein:
"Þyrstir mig nú því að eg em óvanari erfiðinu en þú".	"Thirsty me now because that I am not-used-to difficulty as you".	"I am thirsty now because I am not used to such difficulty as you".
"Gakk þú þá til lækjarins",	"Go you then to stream",	"Then go to the stream",

The Tale of Thorstein Staff-Struck (Old Icelandic)

Old Icelandic	Literal	English
sagði Þorsteinn,	said Thorstein,	said Thorstein,
"og drekk".	"and drink".	"and drink".
Bjarni gerði svo og lagði niður sverðið hjá sér.	Bjarni did so and had downed the-sword beside himself.	Bjarni did so and put his sword down beside himself.
Þorsteinn tók upp, leit á og mælti:	Thorstein took up, looked at and spoke:	Thorstein took it up, looked at it, and spoke:
"Eigi mundir þú þetta sverð hafa í Böðvarsdal".	"Not would you this sword have at Bodvarsdale".	"You would not have had this sword at Bodvarsdale".
Bjarni svaraði engu.	Bjarni answered none.	Bjarni did not answer.
Ganga þeir nú upp á hólinn og berjast um stundar sakar	Went they now up the hill and fought about awhile's sake	Now they went up the hill and fought awhile,
og þykir Bjarna maðurinn vígkænn og þykir fastlegra fyrir en hann hugði.	and seemed Bjarni the-man battle-cunning and seemed fixed before than he thought.	and Bjarni seemed convinced that Thorstein was a cunning fighter and the fight seemed more fixed than before.
"Margt hendir mig nú í dag",	"Many happens to-me now this day",	"Everything is happening to me today",
sagði Bjarni,	said Bjarni,	said Bjarni,
"laus er nú skóþvengur minn".	"loose is now shoe-thongs mine".	"my shoe-thong is loose".
"Bind þú hann þá",	"Tie you it then",	"Then tie it",
kvað Þorsteinn.	said Thorstein.	said Thorstein.
Nú lýtur Bjarni niður en Þorsteinn gekk inn og hefir út skjöldu tvo og sverð eitt, gengur nú á hólinn til Bjarna og mælti við hann:	Now stooped Bjarni down then Thorstein went inside and had out shields two and sword one, went now to the-hill to Bjarni and spoke with him:	Now Bjarni stooped down and then Thorstein went inside and brought out two shields and one sword and went to the hill to Bjarni and spoke with him:
"Hér er skjöldur og sverð er faðir minn sendi þér og mun þetta eigi sljóvgast meir í höggunum en það sem þú hefir áður.	"Here is shield and sword that father mine sent you and should this not blunt more in the-blows than this which you had before.	"Here is a shield and sword that my father has sent you, and this should not be blunt with each blow like the sword you used before.

The Tale of Thorstein Staff-Struck (Old Icelandic)

Old Icelandic	Literal	English
Nenni eg og eigi að standa hlífarlaus lengur undir höggum þínum en gjarna vildi eg nú hætta þessum leik því að eg em hræddur að meira muni mega gæfa þín en ógifta mín og er hver frekur til fjörsins	Care I also not to stand helpless longer under blows yours and gladly will I now conclude this sport because that I am scared that more shall may-be gift yours than un-gift mine and that each eager to life	Also I do not care to stand helpless any longer under your blows and I would gladly conclude this sport because I am scared that your good luck shall be greater than my bad luck, and also each of us are eager to struggle to live,
um alla þraut ef eg mætti nokkuru um ráða".	about all struggle if I may somewhat about decide".	and I would if I could decide it".
"Eigi mun nú stoða að beiðast undan",	"Not should now stand to ask away-from",	"You should not try to ask your way out of it",
sagði Bjarni,	said Bjarni,	said Bjarni,
"berjast skal enn".	"fighting shall still".	"the fight must go on".
"Eigi mundi eg frekt höggva",	"Not would I eagerly strike",	"I wouldn't want to strike the first blow",
sagði Þorsteinn.	said Thorstein.	said Thorstein.
Þá höggur Bjarni allan skjöldinn af Þorsteini en þá hjó Þorsteinn skjöldinn af Bjarna.	Then struck Bjarni all shield of Thorstein's but then struck Thorstein shield of Bjarni's.	Then Bjarni struck and destroyed Thorstein's shield, and Thorstein struck and destroyed Bjarni's shield.
"Stórt er nú höggvið",	"Great is now the-blow",	"The striking is greater now",
kvað Bjarni.	said Bjarni.	said Bjarni.
Þorsteinn svaraði:	Thorstein answered:	Thorstein answered:
"Ekki hjóstu smærra högg".	"Not have-you-hit a-smaller blow".	"Your strike was no smaller".
Bjarni mælti:	Bjarni spoke:	Bjarni spoke:
"Betur bítur þér nú hið sama vopnið er þú hefir áður í dag haft".	"Better bite you now then the-same weapon than you have before in the-day had".	"Now it bites better than the same weapon that you had before in the day".
Þorsteinn mælti:	Thorstein spoke:	Thorstein spoke:

The Tale of Thorstein Staff-Struck (Old Icelandic)

Old Icelandic	Literal	English
"Spara mundi eg við mig óhapp ef eg mætti svo gera og berst eg hræddur við þig.	"Spare would I with me mishap if I might so do and fight I-am scared against you.	"I wish to spare myself from bad luck if I might do so, and I am scared to fight with you.
Vildi eg enn allt á þínu valdi vera láta".	Wish I then all to you will be had".	I wish for you to settle all of the matter".
Þá átti Bjarni að höggva og var nú hvortveggi hlífarlaus.	Then had Bjarni to strike and was now each helpless.	Then it was Bjarni's turn to strike and now each man was helpless.
Bjarni mælti þá:	Bjarni spoke then:	Then Bjarni spoke:
"Það mun illt kaup að taka glæp við miklu happi.	"It should ill purchase that takes the-wicked with much luck.	"It would ill afford to take much wickedness with luck.
Ætla eg mér fullgoldið fyrir þrjá húskarla mína þig einn ef þú vilt mér trúr vera".	Suppose I myself fully-golded for three servants mine you alone if you will to-me true be".	I would suppose myself fully paid for my three servants if you alone will serve me faithfully".
Þorsteinn sagði:	Thorstein said:	Thorstein said:
"Orðið hafa mér svo færi í dag á þér að eg mætti svíkja þig ef ógæfa mín gengi ríkara en lukka þín og mun eg eigi svíkja þig",	"Words have me so brought to day in you that I may betray you if misfortune mine went stronger than luck yours and should I not betray you",	"I have had many words with you today where I might have betrayed you if my misfortune was stronger than your luck, and so I will not betray you",
sagði Þorsteinn.	said Thorstein.	said Thorstein.
"Sé eg að þú ert afbragðsmaður", sagði Bjarni.	"See I that you are excellent-man", said Bjarni.	"I see now that you are an excellent man", said Bjarni.
"Lofa muntu mér að eg gangi inn til föður þíns",	"Promise shall-you me that I go inside to father yours",	"You will promise me that I go inside to your father",
sagði hann,	said he,	he said,
"og segja honum slíkt sem eg vil".	"and tell him such as I wish".	"and tell him about this as I wish".
"Gakk sem þú vilt fyrir mínum sökum",	"Go as you wish for my sake",	"Go as you wish, for my sake",
kvað Þorsteinn,	said Thorstein,	said Thorstein,
"og far þó varlega".	"and go though warily".	"and go carefully".

The Tale of Thorstein Staff-Struck (Old Icelandic)

Old Icelandic	Literal	English
# 7	# 7	# 7
Þá gekk og Bjarni að lokhvílu þeirri er Þórarinn karl lá í.	Then went also Bjarni to bed-closet there where Thorarin old-man lay in.	Then Bjarni went in to the bed closet where Thorarin the old man was laying.
Þórarinn spurði þá hver þar færi en Bjarni sagði til sín.	Thorarin asked then who there went then Bjarni told to him.	Thorarin then asked who went there and Bjarni told him.
"Hvað segir þú tíðinda Bjarni minn?"	"What say you news Bjarni mine?"	"What news do you speak about, my Bjarni?",
kvað Þórarinn.	said Thorarin.	said Thorarin.
"Víg Þorsteins sonar þíns",	"Killing Thorstein son yours",	"The killing of your son",
kvað Bjarni.	said Bjarni.	said Bjarni.
"Varðist hann nokkuð?"	"Defended he any-at-all?"	"Did he defend himself at all?",
kvað Þórarinn.	said Thorarin.	said Thorarin.
"Engan mann ætla eg snarlegra verið hafa í vopnaskipti en Þorstein son þinn".	"None man suppose I speedily been have I weapons-exchange than Thorstein son yours".	"I do not think I have been in such a speedy exchange of weapons as with your son Thorstein".
"Eigi er kynlegt að því",	"Not is wonder that therefore",	"It is no wonder therefore",
kvað karl,	said the-old-man,	said the old man,
"að þungt veitti við þig í Böðvarsdal er þú barst nú af syni mínum".	"that difficulty granted with you at Bodvarsdale that you overcome now of son mine".	"that you granted such difficulty to those at Bodvarsdale, that you have now overcome my son".
Þá mælti Bjarni:	Then spoke Bjarni:	Then Bjarni spoke:
"Eg vil bjóða þér til Hofs og skaltu sitja þar í öðru öndvegi meðan þú lifir og mun eg vera þér í sonar stað".	"I wish to-invite you to Hof and shall-you settle there in another foremost-seat as-long-as you live and should I be to-you in son's place".	"I wish to invite you to Hof, and you shall settle there in one of the foremost seats as long as you live, and I shall be in your son's place".
"Svo er mér farið",	"So is to-me going",	"So it goes to me",

The Tale of Thorstein Staff-Struck (Old Icelandic)

Old Icelandic	Literal	English
kvað karl,	said the-old-man,	said the old man,
"sem þeim er ekki eiga undir sér og verður heitum heimskur maður feginn.	"which those who not only submit to-you and worth called stupid man joyful.	"that those who do not alone accept you and your promise joyfully are stupid.
En svo eru heit yður höfðingja þá er þér viljið fróa manninn eftir slíka atburði að það er mánaðarfró en þá erum vér virðir eftir það sem aðrir framfærslumenn og fyrnast við það seint vorir harmar.	But so are promises of-you chieftains then that you wish console people after such events that it is a-month-from that then they-are we valued after it as other paupers and age with it weak our harm.	But so are the promises of you chieftains whom you wish to console after such events, that a month from then they are valued as paupers and their harm does not weaken with age.
En sá maður er handsöl tekur af slíkum manni sem þú ert má þó vel una sínum hlut hvað sem að dæma er.	Still so the-man who pledge takes of such man as you are may though well content with-his lot that which was deemed of.	Still, the man who takes a pledge with such a man as you may well be deemed to be content with his lot.
Mun eg og þessi handsöl taka af þér og gakk þú nú hingað til mín í rekkjugólfið og verður þú nær að ganga því að karl skelfur nú allur á fótum fyrir elli sakar og vanheilsu en eigi trútt að mér hafi eigi í skap runnið sonardauðinn".	Should I also this pledge take of you and come you now here to me in bed-closet and become you near to going because that old-man shaking now all on feet before age sake and failing-health but none truth to me has alone in mood slipped son-death".	So I should also take this pledge with you, and now come here to me in the bed closet and come nearer because I am an old man shaking on his feet for the sake of age and ill health, but one truth alone has caused my mood to slip, the death of my son".
Bjarni gekk nú í rekkjugólfið og tók í hönd Þórarni karli.	Bjarni went now into bed-closet and took in hand Thorarin the-old-man.	Bjarni now went into the bed closet and took Thorarin the old man's hand.
Hann fann þá að hann þuklaði á saxi og vildi þá leggja að Bjarna.	He found then that he felt a short-sword and willed then to-lay at Bjarni.	He then found that he felt a short sword that he wished to lay at Bjarni.
Hann kippti hendinni og mælti:	He dragged his-hand and spoke:	He drew his hand and spoke:
"Allra fretkarla armastur",	"All contemptible-man miserable",	"You are an all contemptible and miserable man",
sagði Bjarni.	said Bjarni.	said Bjarni.
"Nú mun að makleikleika fara með okkur.	"Now will it serve-you-right going between us.	"How it will serve you right what happens between us.

The Tale of Thorstein Staff-Struck (Old Icelandic)

Old Icelandic	Literal	English
Þorsteinn sonur þinn lifir og skal hann fara heim með mér til Hofs en þér skal fá þræla til forverks og skal þér einskis vant meðan þú lifir".	Thorstein son yours alive and shall he travel home with me to Hof and you shall get thralls to working and shall you nothing want as-long-as you live".	Thorstein your son is alive and he shall travel home with me to Hof, and you shall get servants to work for you and you shall want for nothing as long as you live".
Þorsteinn fór nú heim með Bjarna til Hofs og fylgdi honum allt til dauðadags og þótti nær einskis manns maki vera að drengskap og hreysti.	Thorstein travelled now home with Bjarni to Hof and followed him all until death-day and thought near only man matched had-been in honour and valour.	Now Thorstein travelled home with Bjarni to Hof and followed him in everything until the day he died, and he was thought the only man near to matching him in honour and valour.

8

Old Icelandic	Literal	English
Bjarni hélt vel virðingu sinni og var hann því vinsælli og betur stilltur sem hann var eldri og var allra manna þrautbestur og gerðist trúmaður mikill hinn síðasta hluta ævi sinnar.	Bjarni held well worthiness his and was he therefore popular and better orderly as he was older and were all men persistent and became true-man great the last part life his.	Bjarni held his standing well and became more popular and more self-controlled as he got older, and he was of all men the most persistent, and he became a great man of true faith for the last part of his life.
Bjarni fór utan og gekk suður og andaðist í þeirri ferð.	Bjarni travelled out and went south and died on their journey.	Bjarni travelled abroad and went south and died on that journey.
Hann hvílir í Borg þeirri er Vateri heitir og er það mikil Borg, skammt hingað frá Rómaborg.	He rested in Borg there was Sutri named and was that great Borg, short there from Rome-city.	He rested at a city that was named Sutri, and that was a great city, a short distance from the city of Rome.
Bjarni varð kynsæll maður.	Bjarni became kin-blessed man.	Bjarni became a man blessed with kin.
Hans sonur var Skegg-Broddi er víða kemur við sögur og var hinn mesti afbragðsmaður um sína daga.	His son was Skegg-Broddi who widely came in the-sagas and was the most outstanding-man about his day.	His son was Beard-Broddi who appears widely in the sagas, and he was the most outstanding man of his day.
Dóttir Bjarna hét Halla, móðir Guðríðar er Kolbeinn lögsögumaður átti.	Daughter Bjarni's named Halla, mother-of Gudrid who Kolbein lawspeaker married.	Bjarni had a daughter named Halla, the mother of Gudrid, who married Kolbein the lawspeaker.

The Tale of Thorstein Staff-Struck (Old Icelandic)

Old Icelandic	Literal	English
Yngvildur var og dóttir Bjarna er Þorsteinn Síðu-Hallsson átti og var þeirra sonur Magnús, faðir Einars, föður Magnúss biskups.	Yngvild was also daughter Bjarni's was Thorstein Sidu-Hallson married and was their son Magnus, father-of Einar, father-of Magnus the-bishop.	Bjarni had another daughter named Yngvild who married Thorstein Sidu-Hallson, their son was Magnus, the father of Einar, the father of Magnus the bishop.
Ámundi var og sonur Þorsteins og Yngvildar.	Amundi was also son Thorstein's and Yngvild's.	Thorstein and Yngvild also had a son named Amundi.
Hann átti Sigríði dóttur Þorgríms blinda.	He married Sigrid daughter Thorgrim's the-blind.	He married Sigrid, the daughter of Thorgrim the blind.
Hallfríður var og dóttir Ámunda, móðir Ámunda, föður Guðmundar, föður Magnúss goða og Þóru er Þorvaldur Gissurarson átti, og annarrar Þóru, móður Orms Svínfellings.	Hallfrid was also daughter Amundi's, mother Amundi's, father Gudmund's, father-of Magnus the-chieftain and Thora was Thorvald Gizurarson married, and of-the-other Thora, mother-of Orm Svinafellings.	Amundi also had a daughter named Hallfrid, the mother of Amundi, the father of Gudmund, the father of the chieftain Magnus, and of Thora who married Thorvald Gizurarson, and the other Thora who was the mother of Orm of Svinafell.
Guðrún var og Ámundadóttir, móðir Þórdísar, móðir Helgu, móður Guðnýjar Böðvarsdóttur, móður Sturlusona, Þórðar og Sighvats og Snorra.	Gudrun was also Daughter-of-Amundi, mother-of Thordis, mother-of Helga, mother-of Gudny Daughter-of-Bodvar, mother-of The-Sturlusons, Thord and Sighvat and Snorri.	Amundi had another daughter called Gudrun, the mother of Thordis, the mother of Helga, the mother of Gudny Bodvar's daughter, the mother of the Sturlusons, Thord, Sighvat, and Snorri.
Rannveig var og Ámundadóttir, móðir Steins, föður Guðrúnar, móðir Arnfríðar er Digur-Helgi átti.	Rannveig was also Daughter-of-Amundi, mother-of Stein, father-of Gudrun, mother-of Arnfrid who-was Digur-Helgi married-to.	Amundi also had a daughter named Rannveig, the mother of Stein, the father of Gudrun, the mother of Arnfrid, who was married to Stout-Helgi.
Þorkatla var og Ámundadóttir, móðir Arnbjargar, móður Finns prests og Þorgeirs og Þuríðar.	Thorkatla was also Daughter-of-Amundi, mother-of Arnbjorg, mother-of Fin the-priest and Thorgeir and Thorid.	Thorkatla was also a daughter of Amundi, the mother of Arnbjorg, the mother of Fin the priest, and Thorgeir and Thurid.
Og hefir margt höfðingsmanna frá þeim komið.	And have many prestigious-people from them coming.	And there were many prestigious people descended from them.
Og lýkur þar að segja frá Þorsteini stangarhögg.	And ends there to say from Thorstein Staff-Struck	And there ends the saga of Thorstein Staff-Struck.

Word List (Old Icelandic to English)

Word List (Old Icelandic to English)

Old Icelandic	English	Old Icelandic	English

A, a

að	at, in, it, than, that, the, to, to-be, was, which		
aðrir	other		
af	of, of, off		
afbragðsmaður	excellent-man, outstanding-man		
aftan	evening		
alla	all		
allan	all		
allra	all, all		
allt	all, all		
allur	all		
alvöru	seriously		
andaðist	died		
annar	another, one		
annarra	other		
annarrar	of-the-other		
annarri	another		
annars	another's		
armastur	miserable		
Arnbjargar	Arnbjorg (name)		
Arnfríðar	Arnfrid (name)		
atburð	accident		
atburði	events		
augað	eye		

Á, á

á	a, about, at, in, of, on, the, to
áður	before
Ámunda	Amundi's (name), Amundi's (name)
Ámundadóttir	Daughter-of-Amundi (name)
Ámundi	Amundi (name)
átt	had
átti	had, married, married-to
áttu	had

Æ, æ

æptu	called-out
æsku	youth
ætla	suppose
ætlar	suppose
ætluðu	intended
ætlum	suppose
ævi	life

B, b

bað	asked
báða	both
bæði	both
bæta	compensation
bæturnar	compensation
bak	back
banahögg	death-blow
bar	carried
barist	carried
barst	overcome
bauð	invited
beiðast	ask
bekk	bench
berjast	fight, fighting, fought
berst	fight
betra	better
betur	better
bíða	abide
biður	asked
bind	tie
bindur	bound, tied
biskups	the-bishop
bítast	bite
bítur	bite
Bjarna	Bjarni (name), Bjarni's (name)
Bjarni	Bjarni (name)
bjó	lived
bjóða	to-invite

Word List (Old Icelandic to English)

Old Icelandic	English
björg	help
blinda	the-blind
Böðvarsdal	Bodvarsdale (name)
Böðvarsdóttur	Daughter-of-Bodvar (name)
bograð	stoop
bolinn	torso
borð	the-table
borða	the-tables
borði	the-table
Borg	Borg (place)
bræður	brothers
bregð	move
brugðust	broke
brúnina	eyebrow
búi	estate
búið	prepared
búst	settle
býr	prepared

D, d

Old Icelandic	English
dældarmaður	gentle-man
dæma	deemed
dæmi	judging
dag	day, the-day
daga	day
dagmálum	mid-morning
dauðadags	death-day
Digur-Helgi	Digur-Helgi (name)
dilkahöfuð	sheep-heads
dóttir	daughter
dóttur	daughter
draga	drag
drekk	drink
drengskap	honour
drepið	killed
durum	doorway

E, e

Old Icelandic	English
eða	or
ef	if
eftir	after
eg	I, I-am
eggja	encouraging
eiga	have, only, own
eigi	alone, none, not, not-be
eina	one
Einars	Einar (name)
einn	alone, one
einskis	nothing, only
einvígis	single-combat
eitt	one, one-thing
ekki	not
eldahússveggnum	fire-house-wall
eldri	older
elli	age
em	am
en	about, and, as, but, still, than, that, then, when
engan	none
engi	no-one, nothing
engir	none
engu	none
enn	still, then
er	are, as, at, but, is, is-it, of, than, that, was, what, when, where, which, who, who-are, who-was, with
erfiðinu	difficulty
erindlaust	errand-lost
ert	are
ertu	are-you
eru	are, are-you, they-were
erum	are, they-are

F, f

Old Icelandic	English
fá	few, get, give, had

Word List (Old Icelandic to English)

Old Icelandic	English
faðir	father, father-of
færa	bring, travelled
færi	brought, went
færir	brought
fann	found
far	go, Travel
fara	going, to-go, travel, travelled, went
farið	going, gone
farinn	gone
fastlegra	fixed
feðgar	father-and-son
feginn	joyful
fékk	got
félítill	fee-little
féll	fell
fer	travel, travelled, went
ferð	journey
finni	find
Finns	Fin (name)
finnum	finding
fjár	fee
fjölmenni	followers
fjölmennur	followers
fjörsins	life
fleira	more
flekk	stain
föður	father, father-of
fór	travelled
för	for
forlagðir	mislaid
forverk	for-work
forverks	working
fótum	feet
frá	from
frændi	kinsmen
frændum	kinsmen
framfærslumenn	paupers
frekt	eagerly
frekur	eager
fretkarla	contemptible-man
fróa	console
frýjuorð	taunting
fullgoldið	fully-golded
fylgdi	followed
fyrir	before, for
fyrnast	age
fyrra	before

G, g

Old Icelandic	English
gæfa	gift
gætti	guarded
gakk	come, go
gamall	old
ganga	go, going, went
gangi	go
garð	fences
garðinn	meadow
gegnum	through
gekk	went
geldingahöfuð	ram-heads
gengi	went
gengu	went
gengur	went
gera	do
gerði	did
gerðist	became
gerðu	do-you
gerir	make
gerr	do
gert	done
Gissurarson	Gizurarson (name)
gjarna	gladly
glæp	the-wicked
goða	the-chieftain
gráta	weeping
Guðmundar	Gudmund's (name)
Guðnýjar	Gudny (name)
Guðríðar	Gudrid (name)
Guðrún	Gudrun (name)
Guðrúnar	Gudrun (name)

H, h

Old Icelandic	English
hætta	conclude, concluded, risk

Word List (Old Icelandic to English)

Old Icelandic	English	Old Icelandic	English
hafa	had, have	*hestana*	horses
hafði	had	*hestarnir*	the-horses
hafi	had, has, have	*hestastafnum*	horse-staffs
haft	had	*hestasvein*	horse-boy
halds	hold	*hestaþingi*	horse-fight
Halla	Halla (name)	*hestaþinginu*	horse-fight
Hallfríður	Hallfrid (name)	*hesti*	horse
hallkvæmara	hold-fulfil	*hestinum*	horses
háls	neck	*hestum*	horses
hana	her	*hestur*	horse
handsöl	pledge	*hesturinn*	horse
hann	he, him, it	*hét*	named, was-named
hans	him, his	*hey*	hay
happi	luck	*heyrðu*	heard
harðfengi	toughness	*hið*	then
harmar	harm	*hingað*	here, there
haustið	autumn	*hinn*	the
hefi	have	*hitta*	met
hefir	had, has, have	*hitti*	met
hefna	revenge	*hittir*	found
heill	healthy	*hjá*	beside
heim	home	*hjó*	struck
heima	home	*hjóstu*	have-you-hit
heiman	home	*hjuggust*	hewed
heimskur	stupid	*hleypur*	ran
heimti	claim	*hlífar*	protection
heit	promises	*hlífarlaus*	helpless
heitir	named	*hljóp*	ran
heitum	called	*hlut*	lot
heldur	rather	*hluta*	part
Helgu	Helga (name)	*hlýða*	listen
heljarmannsins	cursed-man-this	*hlýddi*	followed
helst	rather	*höfði*	head
hélt	held	*höfðingja*	chieftains
hendi	arms	*höfðingsmanna*	prestigious-people
hendinni	his-hand	*höfðu*	had
hendir	happens	*Hofi*	Hof (place)
hendur	hands	*hofs*	Hof, Hof (place)
hér	here	*höfuð*	head
héraði	the-district	*höfuðbeinunum*	head-bone
héraðinu	the-district	*högg*	a-strike, been-struck, blow, striking
hest	the-horse		
hesta	horses	*höggum*	blows
hestaats	horse-fight	*höggunum*	the-blows
hestahúsinu	horse-house	*höggur*	struck
		höggva	strike

Word List (Old Icelandic to English)

Old Icelandic	English
höggvið	the-blow
hól	hill
hólinn	hill, the-hill
hönd	hand
honum	he, him, his
hræddur	scared
hreysti	valour
hrósið	praise
hrossa	horses, the-horses
hrossahúss	horse-house
hrossahússins	horse-house
hrossamaður	horse-man
hrossin	horses
hug	spirit, thoughts
hugði	thought
hún	her, it, she
hundur	a-dog
húskarl	servant
húskarla	servants
húskarlar	servants
húss	house
hvað	that, what
hvar	where
hvarf	disappeared
hvatti	sharpened
hvenær	when
hver	any, each, who, why
hvernig	how
hversu	how-many
hvert	what, where
hví	Why
hvílir	rested
hvoftana	mouths
hvorn	each
hvort	whether
hvortveggi	each
hvorumtveggja	each-other

I, i

illt	ill
inn	in, inside
innar	in

Í, í

í	at, I, in, into, on, this, to

J, j

jafnhátt	equally
jarða	buried
jarðaður	earthed
Jól	Yule (name)

K, k

kalla	call
kallaður	called
kallsi	taunted
kann	know
kappi	warrior, warriors
karl	old-man, the-old-man
karli	the-old-man
kaup	purchase
kemur	came, comes
kenna	be-known
kenni	know
kippti	dragged
kné	knees
Kolbeinn	Kolbein (name)
kölluðu	called
kom	came
koma	came
komið	coming
kominn	came, come, coming
komnir	coming
komu	came
kona	the-woman
konan	the-woman
konu	woman
konum	women
konur	women
köstuðust	exchanged

Word List (Old Icelandic to English)

Old Icelandic	English
kvað	said
kvenna	women
kynlegt	surprised, wonder
kynsæll	kin-blessed
kyrrt	peace, still

L, l

Old Icelandic	English
lá	lay
lægi	laying
lækjarins	stream
lætur	behaved, had, has
lagði	had, laid
lagðir	had
lagðist	laid
lambahöfuðin	lambs-heads
láta	had
laus	loose
leggja	to-lay
leið	pass
leik	sport
leit	looked
leita	look-for, looking-for
lengi	along, long
lengur	longer
lét	had
letja	discourage
leyfa	allow
leyni	keep-secret
líður	passed
lifir	alive, live
líklegastir	likeliest
líklegt	likely
lítið	little
litlu	little
lofa	promise
lögsögumaður	lawspeaker
lokhvílu	bed-closet
lostinn	struck
lukka	luck
lýkur	ends
lýstur	struck
lýtur	stooped

M, m

Old Icelandic	English
má	may
maður	a-man, man, the-man
maðurinn	the-man
mæl	say
mæla	speak
mælast	speak
mælir	speak
mælt	spoken
mælti	said, spoke
mæltu	spoke-of
mætti	may, might
Magnús	Magnus (name)
Magnúss	Magnus (name)
maki	matched
maklegleika	serve-you-right
mál	a-case
mánaðarfró	a-month-from
mann	man
manna	men, people's
manni	man
manninn	people
manns	man
marga	many
margir	many
margt	many
með	between, with
meðan	as-long-as
mega	may-be
meir	more
meira	more
menn	men, people
mér	for-me, I, me, myself, to-me
mesti	most
meta	meet
mig	me, to-me
mikið	much
mikil	great
mikill	great, much
miklir	much
miklu	much
mín	me, mine
mína	mine

Word List (Old Icelandic to English)

Old Icelandic	English
minn	me, mine
minnar	my
minni	mine
mínum	mine, my
mislagðar	misplaced
missa	miss
mjög	much
móðir	mother, mother-of
móður	mother-of
mörgum	many
morgun	morning
morguninn	morning
móti	towards
mun	shall, should, will, would
mundi	could, thought, would
mundir	would
mundu	would
mundum	would
muni	shall, would
munt	shall, would
muntu	shall-you, you-should

N, n

nær	near
naut	a-bull, bull
né	nor
nefndur	named
nenni	bothers, care
nennti	wanted
niður	down, downed
nokkuð	any-at-all
nokkura	some
nokkuru	somewhat
nokkurum	some
nóttina	the-night
nú	now

O, o

ofan	across, down, over

Old Icelandic	English
ofmælt	or-speaking, said-too-much
oft	often
oftar	often
og	also, and
okkur	us
orða	words
orðið	worded, words
orðum	words
Orms	Orm (name)
oss	us, we

Ó, ó

ógæfa	misfortune
ógifta	un-gift
óhapp	mishap
óhefnt	without-revenge
ójafnaðarmaður	un-equal-man
ómegð	without
ómerkir	unremarkable
ósæmd	dishonour
óvanari	not-used-to

Ö, ö

öðru	another
öðrum	others, the-other
öflugur	powerful
öllu	all
öndvegi	foremost-seat
öttu	matched
öxina	axe

P, p

prests	the-priest

R, r

ráða	decide
ræða	discussing

Word List (Old Icelandic to English)

Old Icelandic	English
ragan	cowardly
rann	ran
Rannveig	Rannveig (name)
rauðavíkingur	fierce-viking
reið	ride
reiðhesta	riding-horses
reis	rose
rekkjugólfið	bed-closet
ríða	to-ride
ríkara	more-powerful, stronger
ríkismanns	noble-man's
risti	carved
risu	rose
Rómaborg	Rome-city (place)
runnið	slipped

S, s

Old Icelandic	English
sá	saw, so
sæng	bed
sæti	sat
sagði	said, said, told, told
sagt	told
sakar	sake
saklausa	without-cause
sama	the-same
saman	together
samhéraðs	same-district
sárunum	injury
sat	sat
satt	TRUE
sátu	sat
sax	short-sword
saxi	short-sword
saxinu	short-sword
sé	is, see
seg	tell
segi	say
segir	said, say
segja	say, tell
seint	weak
sekan	guilty
seldu	sold
sem	as, as-if, which
sendi	sent
sér	himself, themselves, to-you
síðan	afterwards, then
síðar	afterwards
síðasta	last
Síðu-Hallsson	Sidu-Hallson (name)
Sighvats	Sighvat (name)
Sigríði	Sigrid (name)
sín	him, his
sína	his, theirs
sinn	his, that
sinnar	his
sinni	his
síns	hers, his
sínu	his
sínum	his, their, with-his
sitja	settle
sitji	situated
sitt	yours
sjálfbjargi	self-supported
sjálfur	himself, myself
sjónlausum	sight-less
sjónlítill	seeing-little
skal	shall
skalt	shall
skaltu	shall, shall-you
skammt	short
skap	mood
skapi	mind
Skegg-Broddi	Skegg-Broddi (name)
skelfur	shaking
skilið	divided
skip	ship
skipta	exchange
skjöld	shield
skjöldinn	shield
skjöldu	shields
skjöldur	shield
skógarmaður	outlaw
skógarmaðurinn	outlawed
skoltinn	jaw
skörulegast	noble
skóþvengur	shoe-thongs
skyldi	should, should-be
skyldu	should

Word List (Old Icelandic to English)

Old Icelandic	English
skyrtublaði	shirt-sheet
skyrtum	shirts
slíka	such
slíkt	such
slíkum	such
slíta	wear-out
sljóvgast	blunt
smærra	a-smaller
snarlegra	speedily
snemma	early
Snorra	Snorri (name)
sofa	slept
sögðu	told
sögðust	said
sögur	the-sagas
sökum	sake
son	a-son, son
sonar	son, son's
sonardauðinn	son-death
sonur	son
spara	spare
spurði	asked
stað	place
stakk	pushed
standa	stand
stangað	gored
Stangarhögg	Staff-Struck (name)
sté	stepped
Steins	Stein (name)
stendur	standing
stilltur	composed, orderly
stóð	stood
stoða	stand
stoðar	avail, support
stóðhross	stud-horses
stórt	great
stundar	awhile's
stundu	time
Sturlusona	the-Sturlusons (name)
sú	that
suður	south
sumar	summer
Sunnudal	Sunnudal (place)
svaraði	answered
svarar	answered
svefns	sleep
sverð	sword
sverðið	the-sword
svíða	singe
svíðið	singe
sviðuelda	bonfires
svíkja	betray
svíma	dizziness
Svínfellings	Svinafellings (name)
svo	so
svöruðu	answered
syni	son
sýnist	seems
sýta	mourn

T, t

Old Icelandic	English
tak	take
taka	take, takes, took
talað	talking, told
tali	talking
tals	talk
taumana	reins
tekur	takes, took
tíðast	news
tíðinda	news
til	there, to, towards, until
tilræði	assault
títt	reported
togað	pulled
tók	took
tókum	taking
tröll	trolls
trúmaður	true-man
trúr	TRUE
trútt	truth
tungu	tongue
tungunni	tongue
túni	field
tvo	two

Þ, þ

Word List (Old Icelandic to English)

Old Icelandic	English
þá	then
það	it, that, this
þaðan	from
þær	there
þagað	silence
þar	there
þau	then, they
þegar	straightaway, when
þeim	their, them, those
þeir	they
þeirra	their, they, those
þeirri	their, there
þenna	this
þér	of-you, to-you, you, your
þess	this
þessa	this
þessi	this
þessu	this
þessum	this
þetta	that, this
þið	you, you-two
þig	you
þín	you, yours
þína	yours
þingmönnum	assembly-men
þinn	yours
þíns	yours
þínu	you
þínum	you, yours
þó	though
þoli	tolerate
Þórarinn	Thorarin (name)
Þórarni	Thorarin (name)
Þórð	Thord (name)
Þórðar	Thord (name), Thord's (name)
Þórdísar	Thordis (name)
Þórður	Thord (name)
Þorgeirs	Thorgeir (name)
Þorgríms	Thorgrim's (name)
Þórhall	Thorhall (name)
Þórhallur	Thorhall (name)
Þorkatla	Thorkatla (name)
Þorstein	Thorstein (name)
Þorsteini	Thorstein (name), Thorstein's (name)
Þorsteinn	Thorstein (name)
Þorsteins	Thorstein (name), Thorstein's (name)
Þóru	Thora (name)
Þorvald	Thorvald (name)
Þorvaldur	Thorvald (name)
þótt	though
þótti	thought
þræla	thralls
þraut	struggle
þrautbestur	persistent
þrek	strength
þriggja	three
þrjá	three
þú	you
þuklaði	felt
þungt	difficulty
þurfa	need
Þuríðar	Thorid (name)
því	accordingly, because, since, therefore, which
þykir	consider, seem, seemed, seems, think
þykja	think, to-think
þykjast	consider, thought
þyrstir	thirsty

U, u

Old Icelandic	English
um	about
una	content
undan	away, away-from, from-under
undir	submit, under, up-to
ungum	young
uns	until
upp	got-up, up
uppaustrarmenn	gossipers
utan	out, out-travel

Ú, ú

Word List (Old Icelandic to English)

Old Icelandic	English	*Old Icelandic*	English
úr	from, out-of	víg	killing
út	out, outside	Víga-Bjarna	Killer-Bjarni (name)
úti	out, outside	vígið	the-killing
		vígkænn	battle-cunning

V, v

Old Icelandic	English	*Old Icelandic*	English
		vil	wish
		vildi	will, willed, wish, would
vægt	mercy	vilja	will, wish
vænt	expect	viljið	wish
væri	was, would	vill	will
vaknar	awoke	vilt	will, wish
vakti	awoke	vinna	win
valdi	will	vinsælli	popular
vanheilsu	failing-health	virðing	worthy
vann	worked	virðingu	honour, worthiness
vant	difficulty, want	virðir	valued
var	was, were	vísar	refer, saw
vara	would-be	vist	hospitality, provisions
varð	became, was	víst	certain, knew
varði	expected	vísu	certain
varðist	defended	vita	know, known
varðveitti	looked-after	víti	penalty
varlega	warily	vits	wits
varnaði	warn	vitum	know
varstu	were-you	voðaverk	accident, an-accident
Vateri	Sutri (place)	von	expect
vegið	killed	vopn	weapon, weapons
veginn	killed	vopna	weapons
veit	know	vopnaskipti	weapons-exchange
veita	to-give	vopnið	weapon
veitti	granted	vorir	our
vekja	wake	voru	were
vel	well		
ver	be		

Y, y

Old Icelandic	English
vér	we, we-are		
vera	be, had-been		
verða	be, become, comes	yður	of-you
verður	become, worth	yfir	over
verið	been	ykkur	you
verk	work	Yngvildar	Yngvild's (name)
verks	work	Yngvildur	Yngvild (name)
verr	worse, worst		
verra	worse		
veturinn	winter		
við	against, in, with		
víða	widely		

195

Word List (English to Old Icelandic)

Word List (English to Old Icelandic)

English	Old Icelandic

A, a

English	Old Icelandic
a	á
about	á, á, á
at	á, á, að, að
all	alla, allan, allra, allra, allt, allt, allur, Ámunda
Amundi's (name)	Ámunda, Ámunda
Amundi (name)	Ámundi
another	annar, annarri, annars
another's	annars
Arnbjorg (name)	Arnbjargar
Arnfrid (name)	Arnfríðar
accident	atburð, atburði
asked	bað, báða, bæði
ask	beiðast
abide	bíða
after	eftir
alone	eigi, Einars
age	elli, em
am	em
and	en, en
as	en, en, er
are	er, er, er, er
are-you	ertu, eru
autumn	haustið
arms	hendi
a-strike	högg
a-dog	hundur
any	hver
along	lengi
allow	leyfa
alive	lifir
a-man	maður
a-case	mál
a-month-from	mánaðarfró
as-long-as	meðan
a-bull	naut
any-at-all	nokkuð
across	ofan
also	og
axe	öxina
as-if	sem

English	Old Icelandic
afterwards	síðan, síðar
a-smaller	smærra
a-son	son
avail	stoðar
awhile's	stundar
answered	svaraði, svarar, sviðuelda
assembly-men	þingmönnum
accordingly	því
assault	tilræði
away	undan
away-from	undan
awoke	vaknar, vakti
against	við
an-accident	voðaverk

B, b

English	Old Icelandic
before	áður, æptu, ætluðu
both	báða, bæði
back	bak
bench	bekk
better	betra, betur
bound	bindur
bite	bítast, bítur
Bjarni (name)	Bjarna, Bjarna
Bjarni's (name)	Bjarna
Bodvarsdale (name)	Böðvarsdal
Borg (place)	Borg
brothers	bræður
broke	brugðust
but	en, er
bring	færa
brought	færi, færir
became	gerðist, gerðu
beside	hjá
been-struck	högg
blow	högg
blows	höggum
buried	jarða
be-known	kenna
behaved	lætur
bed-closet	lokhvílu, lukka

Word List (English to Old Icelandic)

English	Old Icelandic
between	með
bull	naut
bothers	nenni
bed	sæng
blunt	sljóvgast
bonfires	sviðuelda
betray	svíkja
because	því
be	ver, vera, vera
become	verða, verða
been	verið
battle-cunning	vígkænn

C, c

English	Old Icelandic
called-out	æptu
compensation	bæta, bæturnar
carried	bar, barist
contemptible-man	fretkarla
console	fróa
come	gakk, gakk
conclude	hætta
concluded	hætta
claim	heimti
called	heitum, Helgu, heljarmannsins
cursed-man-this	heljarmannsins
chieftains	höfðingja
call	kalla
came	kemur, kemur, kenna, kenni, kippti
comes	kemur, kenna
coming	komið, kominn, kominn
could	mundi
care	nenni
cowardly	ragan
carved	risti
composed	stilltur
consider	þykir, þykjast
content	una
certain	víst, víst

D, d

English	Old Icelandic
Daughter-of-Amundi (name)	Ámundadóttir
died	andaðist
death-blow	banahögg
Daughter-of-Bodvar (name)	Böðvarsdóttur
deemed	dæma
day	dag, daga
death-day	dauðadags
Digur-Helgi (name)	Digur-Helgi
daughter	dóttir, dóttur
drag	draga
drink	drekk
doorway	durum
difficulty	erfiðinu, erindlaust, ert
do	gera, gerði
did	gerði
do-you	gerðu
done	gert
disappeared	hvarf
dragged	kippti
discourage	letja
down	niður, niður
downed	niður
dishonour	ósæmd
decide	ráða
discussing	ræða
divided	skilið
dizziness	svíma
defended	varðist

E, e

English	Old Icelandic
excellent-man	afbragðsmaður
evening	aftan
events	atburði
eye	augað
eyebrow	brúnina
estate	búi
encouraging	eggja
Einar (name)	Einars
errand-lost	erindlaust
eagerly	frekt

Word List (English to Old Icelandic)

English	*Old Icelandic*
eager	frekur
each	hver, hvernig, hversu
each-other	hvorumtveggja
equally	jafnhátt
earthed	jarðaður
exchanged	köstuðust
ends	lýkur
exchange	skipta
early	snemma
expect	vænt, vaknar
expected	varði

F, f

English	*Old Icelandic*
fight	berjast, berjast
fighting	berjast
fought	berjast
fire-house-wall	eldahússveggnum
few	fá
father	faðir, faðir
father-of	faðir, færa
found	fann, far
fixed	fastlegra
father-and-son	feðgar
fee-little	félítill
fell	féll
find	finni
Fin (name)	Finns
finding	finnum
fee	fjár
followers	fjölmenni, fjölmennur
for	för, forlagðir
for-work	forverk
feet	fótum
from	frá, frændi, frændum
fully-golded	fullgoldið
followed	fylgdi, fyrir
fences	garð
for-me	mér
foremost-seat	öndvegi
fierce-viking	rauðavíkingur
felt	þuklaði
field	túni
from-under	undan
failing-health	vanheilsu

G, g

English	*Old Icelandic*
gentle-man	dældarmaður
get	fá
give	fá
go	far, fara, farið, farið
going	fara, farið, farið
gone	farið, farinn
got	fékk
gift	gæfa
guarded	gætti
Gizurarson (name)	Gissurarson
gladly	gjarna
Gudmund's (name)	Guðmundar
Gudny (name)	Guðnýjar
Gudrid (name)	Guðríðar
Gudrun (name)	Guðrún, Guðrúnar
great	mikil, mikill, mikill
guilty	sekan
gored	stangað
got-up	upp
gossipers	uppaustrarmenn
granted	veitti

H, h

English	*Old Icelandic*
had	átt, átti, átti, átti, áttu, augað, bað, báða, bæði, bæta, bæturnar, bak, banahögg, bar, barist
help	björg
honour	drengskap, drepið
have	eiga, eigi, Einars, einn, eldahússveggnum
has	hafi, hafi, haft
hold	halds
Halla (name)	Halla
Hallfrid (name)	Hallfríður
hold-fulfil	hallkvæmara
her	hana, hann
he	hann, hann

Word List (English to Old Icelandic)

English	Old Icelandic	English	Old Icelandic
him	hann, hann, hans, hans	**I, i**	
his	hans, happi, harmar, haustið, hefi, hefir, hefir, hefir, heill, heim	in	á, að, að, að, áður, æptu
harm	harmar	it	að, áður, æptu, ætluðu
healthy	heill	intended	ætluðu
home	heim, heima, heiman	invited	bauð
Helga (name)	Helgu	if	ef
held	hélt	I	eg, eg, eggja
his-hand	hendinni	I-am	eg
happens	hendir	is	er, er
hands	hendur	is-it	er
here	hér, hesta	into	í
horses	hesta, hestaats, hestahúsinu, hestana, hestastafnum, hestasvein	ill	illt
		inside	inn
		injury	sárunum
horse-fight	hestaats, hestahúsinu, hestana	**J, j**	
horse-house	hestahúsinu, hestana, hestastafnum	judging	dæmi
horse-staffs	hestastafnum	joyful	feginn
horse-boy	hestasvein	journey	ferð
horse	hesti, hestinum, hestum	jaw	skoltinn
hay	hey	**K, k**	
heard	heyrðu		
have-you-hit	hjóstu		
hewed	hjuggust		
helpless	hlífarlaus		
head	höfði, höfðingja	killed	drepið, durum, ef
Hof (place)	Hofi, hofs	kinsmen	frændi, frændum
Hof	hofs	know	kann, kemur, kemur, kenna, kenni
head-bone	höfuðbeinunum	knees	kné
hill	hól, hólinn	Kolbein (name)	Kolbeinn
hand	hönd	kin-blessed	kynsæll
horse-man	hrossamaður	keep-secret	leyni
house	húss	killing	víg
how	hvernig	Killer-Bjarni (name)	Víga-Bjarna
how-many	hversu	knew	víst
himself	sér, síðan	known	vita
hers	síns		
had-been	vera		
hospitality	vist		

Word List (English to Old Icelandic)

English	Old Icelandic
life	ævi, afbragðsmaður
lived	bjó
luck	happi, harmar
lot	hlut
listen	hlýða
lay	lá
laying	lægi
laid	lagði, lagðir
lambs-heads	lambahöfuðin
loose	laus
looked	leit
look-for	leita
looking-for	leita
long	lengi
longer	lengur
live	lifir
likeliest	líklegastir
likely	líklegt
little	lítið, litlu
lawspeaker	lögsögumaður
last	síðasta
looked-after	varðveitti

M, m

English	Old Icelandic
miserable	armastur
married	átti
married-to	átti
move	bregð
mid-morning	dagmálum
more	fleira, föður, föður
mislaid	forlagðir
meadow	garðinn
make	gerir
met	hitta, hitti
mouths	hvoftana
may	má, maður
man	maður, mætti, mætti, Magnús
might	mætti
Magnus (name)	Magnús, Magnúss
matched	maki, mál

English	Old Icelandic
men	manna, manni
many	marga, margir, margt, með
may-be	mega
me	mér, mér, mesti, meta
myself	mér, mesti
most	mesti
meet	meta
much	mikið, mikil, mikill, mikill, miklir
mine	mín, mína, minn, minn, minnar
my	minnar, minni
misplaced	mislagðar
miss	missa
mother	móðir
mother-of	móðir, móður
morning	morgun, morguninn
misfortune	ógæfa
mishap	óhapp
more-powerful	ríkara
mood	skap
mind	skapi
mourn	sýta
mercy	vægt

N, n

English	Old Icelandic
none	eigi, eigi, eigi, eina
not	eigi, eigi
not-be	eigi
nothing	einskis, einskis
no-one	engi
neck	háls
named	heitir, heldur, helst
near	nær
nor	né
now	nú
not-used-to	óvanari
noble-man's	ríkismanns
noble	skörulegast
need	þurfa
news	tíðast, tíðinda

Word List (English to Old Icelandic)

English	Old Icelandic

O, o

English	Old Icelandic
of	á, á, á, á
on	á, á
other	aðrir, æsku
off	af
outstanding-man	afbragðsmaður
one	annar, annarra, annarrar, barst
of-the-other	annarrar
overcome	barst
or	eða
only	eiga, eiga
own	eiga
one-thing	eitt
older	eldri
old	gamall
old-man	karl
others	öðrum
over	ofan, öflugur
or-speaking	ofmælt
often	oft, oftar
Orm (name)	Orms
outlaw	skógarmaður
outlawed	skógarmaðurinn
orderly	stilltur
of-you	þér, þér
out-of	úr
out	út, út, utan
outside	út, utan
out-travel	utan
our	vorir

P, p

English	Old Icelandic
prepared	búið, búst
paupers	framfærslumenn
pledge	handsöl
promises	heit
protection	hlífar
part	hluta
prestigious-people	höfðingsmanna
praise	hrósið
purchase	kaup
peace	kyrrt
pass	leið
passed	líður
promise	lofa
people's	manna
people	manninn, með
powerful	öflugur
place	stað
pushed	stakk
persistent	þrautbestur
pulled	togað
popular	vinsælli
provisions	vist
penalty	víti

R, r

English	Old Icelandic
ram-heads	geldingahöfuð
risk	hætta
revenge	hefna
rather	heldur, helst
ran	hleypur, hlífar, hljóp
rested	hvílir
Rannveig (name)	Rannveig
ride	reið
riding-horses	reiðhesta
rose	reis, ríða
Rome-city (place)	Rómaborg
reins	taumana
reported	títt
refer	vísar

S, s

English	Old Icelandic
suppose	ætla, ætlar, ætlum
seriously	alvöru
stoop	bograð
settle	búst, býr
sheep-heads	dilkahöfuð
single-combat	einvígis
still	en, en, en
stain	flekk
stupid	heimskur

Word List (English to Old Icelandic)

English	Old Icelandic	English	Old Icelandic
struck	hjó, hleypur, hlífar, hljóp	self-supported	sjálfbjargi
striking	högg	sight-less	sjónlausum
strike	höggva	seeing-little	sjónlítill
scared	hræddur	short	skammt
spirit	hug	Skegg-Broddi (name)	Skegg-Broddi
she	hún	shaking	skelfur
servant	húskarl	ship	skip
servants	húskarla, húskarlar	shield	skjöld, skjöldinn, skjöldu
sharpened	hvatti	shields	skjöldu
said	kvað, kvenna, kynlegt, kynlegt, kyrrt, kyrrt	shoe-thongs	skóþvengur
		should-be	skyldi
surprised	kynlegt	shirt-sheet	skyrtublaði
stream	lækjarins	shirts	skyrtum
sport	leik	such	slíka, slíkt, slíkum
stooped	lýtur	speedily	snarlegra
say	mæl, mæla, mælast, mælir	Snorri (name)	Snorra
		slept	sofa
speak	mæla, mælast, mælir	son	son, sonar, sonar, sonardauðinn
spoken	mælt	son's	sonar
spoke	mælti	son-death	sonardauðinn
spoke-of	mæltu	spare	spara
serve-you-right	maklegleika	stand	standa, Stangarhögg
shall	mun, mun, mun, mun, mundi, mundi	Staff-Struck (name)	Stangarhögg
		stepped	sté
should	mun, mun, mun	Stein (name)	Steins
shall-you	muntu, muntu	standing	stendur
some	nokkura, nokkuru	stood	stóð
somewhat	nokkuru	support	stoðar
said-too-much	ofmælt	stud-horses	stóðhross
stronger	ríkara	south	suður
slipped	runnið	summer	sumar
saw	sá, sá	Sunnudal (place)	Sunnudal
so	sá, sæti	sleep	svefns
sat	sæti, sagði, sagði	sword	sverð
sake	sakar, saklausa	singe	svíða, svíðið
same-district	samhéraðs	Svinafellings (name)	Svínfellings
short-sword	sax, saxi, saxinu	seems	sýnist, tak
see	sé	silence	þagað
sold	seldu	straightaway	þegar
sent	sendi	struggle	þraut
Sidu-Hallson (name)	Síðu-Hallsson	strength	þrek
Sighvat (name)	Sighvats	since	því
Sigrid (name)	Sigríði	seem	þykir
situated	sitji	seemed	þykir

Word List (English to Old Icelandic)

English	*Old Icelandic*	*English*	*Old Icelandic*
submit	undir	the-old-man	karl, karli
Sutri (place)	Vateri	the-woman	kona, konan
		to-lay	leggja

T, t

the	á, á, að	the-man	maður, maðurinn
to	á, að, að, að	to-me	mér, mig
than	að, að, að	towards	móti, mun
that	að, að, að, að, að, að, aðrir, æsku	the-night	nóttina
		the-other	öðrum
to-be	að	the-priest	prests
tie	bind	to-ride	ríða
tied	bindur	told	sagði, sagði, sagt, sakar, saklausa
the-bishop	biskups		
to-invite	bjóða	the-same	sama
the-blind	blinda	together	saman
torso	bolinn	true	
the-table	borð, borða	tell	seg, segi
the-tables	borða	themselves	sér
the-day	dag	to-you	sér, síðan
then	en, en, engan, engi, engi, engir	theirs	sína
		their	sínum, sínum, sitja, sitji
they-were	eru	the-sagas	sögur
they-are	erum	time	stundu
travelled	færa, færi, far, fara	the-Sturlusons (name)	Sturlusona
Travel	far, fara, fara		
to-go	fara	the-sword	sverðið
taunting	frýjuorð	take	tak, taka
through	gegnum	takes	taka, taka
the-wicked	glæp	took	taka, talað, talað
the-chieftain	goða	talking	talað, talað
toughness	harðfengi	talk	tals
the-district	héraði, héraðinu	they	þau, þegar, þegar
the-horse	hest	them	þeim
the-horses	hestarnir, hét	those	þeim, þeir
there	hingað, hinn, hjó, hleypur, hlífar	though	þó, þoli
		tolerate	þoli
the-blows	höggunum	Thorarin (name)	Þórarinn, Þórarni
the-blow	höggvið	Thord (name)	Þórð, Þórðar, Þórðar
the-hill	hólinn	Thord's (name)	Þórðar
thoughts	hug	Thordis (name)	Þórdísar
thought	hugði, hún, húskarl, húskarla	Thorgeir (name)	Þorgeirs
		Thorgrim's (name)	Þorgríms
this	í, í, Jól, kallsi, kappi, kappi, karl, karl, karli	Thorhall (name)	Þórhall, Þórhallur
		Thorkatla (name)	Þorkatla
taunted	kallsi	Thorstein (name)	Þorstein, Þorsteini, Þorsteini, Þorsteinn

Word List (English to Old Icelandic)

English	Old Icelandic
Thorstein's (name)	Þorsteini, Þorsteinn
Thora (name)	Þóru
Thorvald (name)	Þorvald, Þorvaldur
thralls	þræla
three	þriggja, þrjá
Thorid (name)	Þuríðar
therefore	því
think	þykir, þykja
to-think	þykja
thirsty	þyrstir
taking	tókum
trolls	tröll
true-man	trúmaður
true	
truth	trútt
tongue	tungu, tungunni
two	tvo
to-give	veita
the-killing	vígið

U, u

English	Old Icelandic
un-gift	ógifta
un-equal-man	ójafnaðarmaður
us	okkur, ómegð
unremarkable	ómerkir
until	til, títt
under	undir
up-to	undir
up	upp

V, v

English	Old Icelandic
valour	hreysti
valued	virðir

W, w

English	Old Icelandic
was	að, að, aðrir, æsku, ætla
which	að, aðrir, æsku, ætla
when	en, engan, engi, engi
what	er, er, er
where	er, er, er
who	er, er
who-are	er
who-was	er
with	er, eru, erum
went	færi, far, fara, fara, fara, fara, fer, fer
working	forverks
weeping	gráta
was-named	hét
why	hver, hvert
whether	hvort
warrior	kappi
warriors	kappi
woman	konu
women	konum, konur, kvað
wonder	kynlegt
will	mun, mun, mundi, mundi, mundir, mundu
would	mun, mundi, mundi, mundir, mundu, mundum, muni, muni, munt
wanted	nennti
without-revenge	óhefnt
without	ómegð
words	orða, orðið, orðið
worded	orðið
we	oss, óvanari
without-cause	saklausa
weak	seint
with-his	sínum
wear-out	slíta
worked	vann
want	vant
were	var, vara
would-be	vara
warily	varlega
warn	varnaði
were-you	varstu
wake	vekja
well	vel
we-are	vér
worth	verður
work	verk, verks

Word List (English to Old Icelandic)

English	Old Icelandic
worse	verr, verr
worst	verr
winter	veturinn
widely	víða
wish	vil, vildi, vildi, vildi, vildi
willed	vildi
win	vinna
worthy	virðing
worthiness	virðingu
wits	vits
weapon	vopn, vopn
weapons	vopn, vopna
weapons-exchange	vopnaskipti

Y, y

youth	æsku
Yule (name)	Jól
you-should	muntu
yours	sitt, sjálfbjargi, sjónlausum, sjónlítill, skal, skalt
you	þér, þér, þess, þessa, þessi, þessu, þessum, þetta
your	þér
you-two	þið
young	ungum
Yngvild's (name)	Yngvildar
Yngvild (name)	Yngvildur

A Word Comparison of Old Norse and Old Icelandic Words

A Word Comparison of Old Norse and Old Icelandic Words

Old Norse	Old Icelandic	English	Old Norse	Old Icelandic	English
áðr	áður	before	ek	eg	I
æfi	ævi	life	ek	eg	I-am
afbragðsmaðr	afbragðsmaður	outstanding-man	ekki	eigi	not
			eldhúsveggnum	eldahússveggnum	fire-house-wall
allr	allur	all			
annarr	annar	another	ellri	eldri	older
annarr	annar	one	engis	einskis	nothing
armastr	armastur	miserable	engis	einskis	only
at	að	at	enn	en	and
at	að	it	enn	en	as
at	að	than	enn	en	but
at	að	that	enn	en	than
at	að	to	enn	en	then
at	að	to-be	enn	en	when
at	til	to	énn	en	but
augat	augað	eye	er	em	am
barizt	barist	carried	er	ert	are
bart	barst	overcome	er	sem	as
batt	bindur	bound	er	sem	which
berjumst	berst	fight	er	þegar	when
best	hest	the-horse	erindislaust	erindlaust	errand-lost
betr	betur	better	ertú	ertu	are-you
biða	bíða	abide	eru	erum	they-are
biðr	biður	asked	farit	farið	going
bindr	bindur	tied	farit	farið	gone
bítr	bítur	bite	fekk	fékk	got
bograt	bograð	stoop	félitill	félítill	fee-little
bræðr	bræður	brothers	fell	féll	fell
búit	búið	prepared	ferr	fer	travel
bústú	búst	settle	ferr	fer	travelled
dældarmaðr	dældarmaður	gentle-man	finna	finni	find
dauða-dags	dauðadags	death-day	finnim	finnum	finding
dilka-höfuð	dilkahöfuð	sheep-heads	fjölmennr	fjölmennur	followers
dœmi	dæmi	judging	fóður	föður	father
drepit	drepið	killed	fœra	færa	bring
dugi	hug	spirit	fœra	færa	travelled
eðr	eða	or	fœri	færi	brought
eigi	ekki	not	fœri	færi	went
eigu	eiga	only	fœrir	færir	brought
einum	einn	one	fór	fer	went
einvigis	einvígis	single-combat	forverka	forverks	working

A Word Comparison of Old Norse and Old Icelandic Words

Old Norse	Old Icelandic	English	Old Norse	Old Icelandic	English
framfœrslumenn	framfærslumenn	paupers	höggr	höggur	struck
frekr	frekur	eager	hölinn	hólinn	the-hill
frýju-orð	frýjuorð	taunting	höllinn	hólinn	the-hill
fullgoldit	fullgoldið	fully-golded	hon	hún	her
ganga	gangi	go	hon	hún	it
garðinu	garðinn	meadow	hon	hún	she
geldinga-höfuð	geldingahöfuð	ram-heads	hræddr	hræddur	scared
			hrósit	hrósið	praise
gengr	gengur	went	hrossahúsi	hrossahúss	horse-house
gerðú	gerðu	do-you	hrossamaðr	hrossamaður	horse-man
gjarnan	gjarna	gladly	hugða	hugði	thought
glœp	glæp	the-wicked	hváftana	hvoftana	mouths
góða	goða	the-chieftain	hvárn	hvorn	each
gott	eitt	one	hvárrtveggja	hvortveggi	each
Guðríðr	Guðríðar	Gudrid (name)	hvárt	hvort	whether
			hvárumtveggja	hvorumtveggja	each-other
hála	háls	neck	hvat	hvað	what
haldkvæmara	hallkvæmara	hold-fulfil	hverr	hver	any
haustit	haustið	autumn	hverr	hver	each
höggunum	höggunum	the-blows	hverr	hver	who
heimskr	heimskur	stupid	hverr	hver	why
heimta	heimti	claim	hvi	hví	Why
heldr	heldur	rather	í	á	in
helt	hélt	held	Ingveldr	Yngvildur	Yngvild (name)
helzt	helst	rather			
hendr	hendur	hands	Ingveldra	Yngvildar	Yngvild's (name)
hendr	hönd	hand			
heraðinu	héraði	the-district	inn	innar	in
herjast	berjast	fighting	jarðaðr	jarðaður	earthed
hesta-ats	hestaats	horse-fight	kals	kallsi	taunted
hesthúsinn	hestahúsinu	horse-house	karls	karli	the-old-man
hestr	hestur	horse	kemr	kemur	came
hestr	hesturinn	horse	kemr	kemur	comes
hestunum	hestinum	horses	kenni	kann	know
hiífar	hlífar	protection	kipti	kippti	dragged
hingat	hingað	here	koma	komu	came
hingat	hingað	there	komit	komið	coming
hit	hið	then	kváðust	sögðust	said
hleypr	hleypur	ran	kyrt	kyrrt	peace
hlífarlauss	hlífarlaus	helpless	kyrt	kyrrt	still
hlut	hluta	part	lætr	lætur	behaved
höfuðbeinum	höfuðbeinunum	head-bone	lætr	lætur	had
			lætr	lætur	has

207

A Word Comparison of Old Norse and Old Icelandic Words

Old Norse	Old Icelandic	English
lágði	lagði	laid
lausir	laus	loose
laust	lýstur	struck
lengr	lengi	along
leyna	leyni	keep-secret
líðr	líður	passed
liflr	lifir	live
liklegastir	líklegastir	likeliest
lítt	lítið	little
lœkjarins	lækjarins	stream
lögsögumaðr	lögsögumaður	lawspeaker
lýkr	lýkur	ends
lýstr	lýstur	struck
lýtr	lýtur	stooped
maðr	maður	a-man
maðr	maður	man
maðr	maður	the-man
maðrinn	maðurinn	the-man
mælti	sagði	said
mætta	mætti	may
mætta	mætti	might
Magnus	Magnús	Magnus (name)
Magnúsar	Magnúss	Magnus (name)
málit	mál	a-case
man	mun	shall
man	mun	should
mánaðar-frá	mánaðarfró	a-month-from
mann	manninn	people
mant	munt	shall
mant	munt	would
megi	mega	may-be
meirr	meir	more
mik	mig	me
mik	mig	to-me
mikit	mikið	much
min	mín	me
mínir	minn	mine
mjök	mjög	much
munda	mundi	would
mundak	mundi	would
muni	mun	would
muntú	muntu	shall-you
nefndr	nefndur	named
nenta	nennti	wanted
niðr	niður	down
niðr	niður	downed
nökkura	nokkura	some
nökkuru	nokkuru	somewhat
nökkurum	nokkurum	some
nökkut	nokkuð	any-at-all
œptu	æptu	called-out
œsku	æsku	youth
öflugr	öflugur	powerful
Ögmundr	Ámundi	Amundi (name)
ójafnaðar	ójafnaðarmaður	un-equal-man
ok	og	also
ok	og	and
okkr	okkur	us
ómjúkir	ómerkir	unremarkable
öngu	engu	none
ór	úr	from
ör	úr	out-of
orð	orða	words
orðit	orðið	worded
orðit	orðið	words
ósœmd	ósæmd	dishonour
reist	risti	carved
rekkjugōlfit	rekkjugólfið	bed-closet
rekkjugólfit	rekkjugólfið	bed-closet
ríkar	ríkara	stronger
rikara	ríkara	more-powerful
rísa	risu	rose
rœða	ræða	discussing
Rúmaborg	Rómaborg	Rome-city (place)
runnit	runnið	slipped
sagði	kvað	said
sakir	sakar	sake
samheraðs	samhéraðs	same-district
segi	segja	tell
segir	kvað	said
segir	sagði	said

A Word Comparison of Old Norse and Old Icelandic Words

Old Norse	Old Icelandic	English
segir	sagði	told
segja	sögðu	told
siðara	síðasta	last
Siðu-Hallsson	Síðu-Hallsson	Sidu-Hallson (name)
siti	sitji	situated
sjálfr	sjálfur	himself
sjálfr	sjálfur	myself
sjönlausum	sjónlausum	sight-less
sjónlitill	sjónlítill	seeing-little
skaltú	skaltu	shall
skaltú	skaltu	shall-you
skamt	skammt	short
skelfr	skelfur	shaking
skifta	skipta	exchange
skilit	skilið	divided
skjöldinn	skjöld	shield
skjöldr	skjöldur	shield
skógarmaðr	skógarmaður	outlaw
skógarmaðrinn	skógarmaðurinn	outlawed
skörugligast	skörulegast	noble
skóþvengir	skóþvengur	shoe-thongs
slæfast	sljóvgast	blunt
slika	slíka	such
slikum	slíkum	such
slita	slíta	wear-out
snarligra	snarlegra	speedily
sóknum	sökum	sake
son	sonur	son
sonardauðinn	sonardauðinn	son-death
sonr	sonur	son
spyrr	spurði	asked
Stangarhöggs	Stangarhögg	Staff-Struck (name)
stangat	stangað	gored
störmenna	höfðingsmanna	prestigious-people
stendr	stendur	standing
stilltr	stilltur	orderly
stiltr	stilltur	composed
suðr	suður	south
svá	svo	so
svarar	svaraði	answered
sverðit	sverðið	the-sword
sviðelda	sviðuelda	bonfires
sviðit	svíðið	singe
svivirðing	virðing	worthy
talat	talað	told
tekr	tekur	took
þagat	þagað	silence
þat	það	it
þat	það	that
þat	það	this
Þðrarinn	Þórarinn	Thorarin (name)
Þörsteinn	Þorsteinn	Thorstein (name)
þefri	þeirri	there
þeira	þeirra	their
þeira	þeirra	they
þeira	þeirra	those
þeiri	þeirri	their
þeiri	þeirri	there
þér	þið	you-two
þessarra	þessa	this
þik	þig	you
þo	þó	though
Þórarins	Þórarni	Thorarin (name)
Þórðr	Þórður	Thord (name)
Þórgeirs	Þorgeirs	Thorgeir (name)
Þórgríms	Þorgríms	Thorgrim's (name)
Þórhallr	Þórhallur	Thorhall (name)
Þórkatla	Þorkatla	Thorkatla (name)
Þórn	Þóru	Thora (name)
Þórstein	Þorstein	Thorstein (name)
Þórsteini	Þorsteini	Thorstein (name)
Þórsteini	Þorsteini	Thorstein (name)
Þórsteini	Þorsteini	Thorstein's (name)
Þórsteinn	Þorsteinn	Thorstein (name)

A Word Comparison of Old Norse and Old Icelandic Words

Old Norse	Old Icelandic	English
Þórsteins	Þorsteini	Thorstein (name)
Þórsteins	Þorsteins	Thorstein (name)
Þórsteins	Þorsteins	Thorstein's (name)
Þórvald	Þorvald	Thorvald (name)
Þórvaldr	Þorvaldur	Thorvald (name)
þrautbeztr	þrautbestur	persistent
Þuriðar	Þuríðar	Thorid (name)
þykki	þykir	consider
þykki	þykir	seems
þykki	þykir	think
þykkir	þykir	seem
þykkir	þykir	seemed
þykkir	þykir	seems
þykkir	þykir	think
þykkja	þykja	to-think
þykkjast	þykjast	consider
þykkjast	þykjast	thought
tíl	til	to
togat	togað	pulled
troll	tröll	trolls
trú-maðr	trúmaður	true-man
tuni	túni	field
tvá	tvo	two
unz	uns	until
útan	utan	out
útan	utan	out-travel
váðaverk	voðaverk	accident
váðaverk	voðaverk	an-accident
Valería	Vateri	Sutri (place)
vápn	vopn	weapon
vápn	vopn	weapons
vápnaskiftum	vopnaskipti	weapons-exchange
var	varð	was
várir	vorir	our
váru	voru	were
vegit	vegið	killed
verðr	verður	become
verðr	verður	worth
verit	verið	been
vetrinn	veturinn	winter
vig	víg	killing
vigit	vígið	the-killing
vígkœnn	vígkænn	battle-cunning
vilda	vildi	will
vilda	vildi	wish
vilit	viljið	wish
visar	vísar	saw
vit	við	with
yðr	ykkur	you

www.ingramcontent.com/pod-product-compliance
Lightning Source LLC
Chambersburg PA
CBHW051404070526
44584CB00023B/3291